MONTESQUIEU'S POLITICAL ECONOMY

RECOVERING POLITICAL PHILOSOPHY

SERIES EDITORS: THOMAS L. PANGLE AND TIMOTHY BURNS

PUBLISHED BY PALGRAVE MACMILLAN:

Lucretius as Theorist of Political Life
By John Colman

Shakespeare's Political Wisdom
By Timothy Burns

Political Philosophy Cross-Examined: Perennial Challenges to the Philosophic Life
Edited by Thomas L. Pangle and J. Harvey Lomax

Eros and Socratic Political Philosophy
By David Levy

Xenophon the Socratic Prince: The Argument of the Anabasis of Cyrus
By Eric Buzzetti

Reorientation: Leo Strauss in the 1930s
Edited by Martin D. Yaffe and Richard S. Ruderman

Sexuality and Globalization: An Introduction to a Phenomenology of Sexualities
By Laurent Bibard and translated by Christopher Edwards

Modern Democracy and the Theological-Political Problem in Spinoza, Rousseau, and Jefferson
By Lee Ward

Prudential Public Leadership: Promoting Ethics in Public Policy and Administration
By John Uhr

The Companion to Raymond Aron
Edited by José Colen and Elisabeth Dutartre-Michaut

Montesquieu's Political Economy
By Andrew Scott Bibby

MONTESQUIEU'S POLITICAL ECONOMY

Andrew Scott Bibby

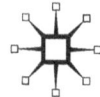

MONTESQUIEU'S POLITICAL ECONOMY
Copyright © Andrew Scott Bibby 2016
Softcover reprint of the hardcover 1st edition 2016 978-1-137-47646-3

All rights reserved. No reproduction, copy or transmission of this publication may be made without written permission. No portion of this publication may be reproduced, copied or transmitted save with written permission. In accordance with the provisions of the Copyright, Designs and Patents Act 1988, or under the terms of any licence permitting limited copying issued by the Copyright Licensing Agency, Saffron House, 6-10 Kirby Street, London EC1N 8TS.

Any person who does any unauthorized act in relation to this publication may be liable to criminal prosecution and civil claims for damages.

First published 2016 by
PALGRAVE MACMILLAN

The author has asserted their right to be identified as the author of this work in accordance with the Copyright, Designs and Patents Act 1988.

Palgrave Macmillan in the UK is an imprint of Macmillan Publishers Limited, registered in England, company number 785998, of Houndmills, Basingstoke, Hampshire, RG21 6XS.

Palgrave Macmillan in the US is a division of Nature America, Inc., One New York Plaza, Suite 4500, New York, NY 10004-1562.

Palgrave Macmillan is the global academic imprint of the above companies and has companies and representatives throughout the world.

ISBN: 978–1–349–56707–2
E-PDF ISBN: 978–1–137–47722–4
DOI: 10.1057/9781137477224

Distribution in the UK, Europe and the rest of the world is by Palgrave Macmillan®, a division of Macmillan Publishers Limited, registered in England, company number 785998, of Houndmills, Basingstoke, Hampshire RG21 6XS.

Library of Congress Cataloging-in-Publication Data

Bibby, Andrew Scott, author.
  Montesquieu's political economy / Andrew Scott Bibby.
    pages cm.—(Recovering political philosophy)
  Summary: "This book contributes to the recovery of political philosophy by analyzing Montesquieu's economic thought. Engaging, eclectic, and inventive, this fresh examination clarifies the longstanding controversy over the purpose and meaning of Montesquieu's The Spirit of the Laws"— Provided by publisher.
  Includes bibliographical references and index.
    1. Montesquieu, Charles de Secondat, baron de, 1689–1755. De l'esprit des lois. 2. Political science—Philosophy. I. Title.

JC179.M753B54 2015
320—dc23   2015021345

A catalogue record for the book is available from the British Library.

To Julie, my wife

CONTENTS

Series Editor Foreword	ix
Acknowledgments	xi
Notes on Texts	xiii
Introduction Economic Liberalism before Adam Smith	1
1. Montesquieu *Économiste*	15
2. Commerce in *The Spirit of the Laws*	33
3. Commerce, Honor, and Monarchy	55
4. The Maligned Merchant and the New History of Commerce	73
5. Commerce and the Rhetoric of Toleration	89
6. The Problem of Property in *The Spirit of the Laws*	113
Conclusion	147
Notes	153
Bibliography	207
Index	219

SERIES EDITOR FOREWORD

Palgrave's *Recovering Political Philosophy* series is committed to publishing works on important thinkers in the history of political thought—including works by philosophers, poets, artists, theologians, and scientists who may not be regarded conventionally as political theorists. The series was founded with an eye to postmodernism's challenge to the very possibility of a rational foundation for and guidance of our political lives, a challenge that has provoked a searching re-examination of the texts of past political philosophers and political thinkers. We are especially keen to find and to publish works that help to recover the classical grounding for civic reason, as well as works that clarify the strengths and weaknesses of modern philosophic rationalism. The series aims to make available outstanding scholarship in the history of political philosophy that is inspired by the rediscovery of the diverse rhetorical strategies employed by political philosophers. Our interpretive studies will be particularly attentive to historical context and language, and to the ways in which censorship and didactic concerns impelled prudent thinkers, in widely diverse cultural conditions, to employ manifold strategies of writing—strategies that allowed them to aim at different audiences with various degrees of openness to unconventional thinking. The series offers close readings of ancient, medieval, early modern and late modern works that illuminate the human condition by attempting to answer its deepest, enduring questions, and that have (in the modern periods) laid the foundations for contemporary political, social, and economic life. The editors welcome work from both established and emerging scholars that offer analyses of a single text or a thematic study of a problem or question in a number of texts.

Andrew Bibby plumbs the depths of Montesquieu's famous argument for the political importance of commerce, presenting Montesquieu's full account of the relationship of politics and economics. After examining Montesquieu's early thinking on economics, Bibby turns to books 20 and 21 of *The Spirit of the Laws*, where Montesquieu outlines the nature, causes, and effects of commerce, for good and ill, as exemplified in England. Bibby takes a close look at Montesquieu's account of the politics of free trade, public credit, trading companies, banks, and laws regulating business and commerce. This enables him to uncover Montesquieu's defense of venality—his attempt to make commerce honorable—as a means to promote upward social mobility. Bibby thereby refutes the reading of Montesquieu as an accomodationist, conservative, or defender of monarchical privilege and proprietorship. He demonstrates that Montesquieu, no less than Locke, defends private property as an extension of the person. Finally, by analyzing Montesquieu's world economic history and the revival of commerce in the modern world, Bibby shows that Montesquieu viewed the defense of commercial civilization as incomplete and in need of an account of its relation to religion. He finds Montesquieu suggesting that commerce and religion may be reconciled: with the legitimization of commerce, those religious opinions and practices that do not support liberty and commerce would eventually come to be labeled "extremist."

ACKNOWLEDGMENTS

I would like to acknowledge, first and foremost, the generous support I have received from the James Madison Program in American Ideals and Institutions at Princeton. Although I owe more than a few favors, in the course of writing this book, I owe my deepest debt of gratitude to Bradford P. Wilson, not only for his generous support for research, but for his wise counsel and good humor as this research progressed into a book.

I must acknowledge four Montesquieu scholars, in particular, for their early guidance. Steven Kautz patiently suffered through my early explorations, while graciously pointing me to more fruitful areas of investigation. William B. Allen was a touchstone, and continues to be a guiding light, in wisdom and in friendship. Paul A. Rahe was instrumental, providing inspiration with the publication of his *Montesquieu and the Logic of Liberty*, and also valuable feedback and encouragement on the first drafts.

Finally, I would like to thank Diana Schaub, of Loyola University Maryland, both for her scholarship and intellectual companionship. There may be no better defense of the value and importance of reading Montesquieu than in the preface to her *Erotic Liberalism: Women and Revolution in Montesquieu's Persian Letters*. Montesquieu, she writes, is the "only thinker whose correction of the early moderns did not take the form of a dangerous radicalization." Continuing, with a paraphrase of one of her own teachers:

> Our prospects in our third century appear to depend on the possibility that our moral resources will incline to fortify themselves at the spirited wells of modernity.

This study draws from those wells.

NOTES ON TEXTS

All references to the *Persian Letters* are by letter number, referring to the text; for example, *Persian Letters* #64. For translation and numbering, I refer to *Persian Letters: Oxford World Classics* by Margaret Mauldon and Andrew Kahn.[1] For references and translations from Montesquieu's 1734 *Considerations on the Causes of the Greatness of the Romans and Their Decline*, I refer to David Lowenthal's 1965 translation. Reference is to chapter, in capital roman numerals, and page (i.e., "IX, 93" signifies chapter nine, page 93).

References to *The Spirit of the Laws* are by capital roman numerals to indicate the book, and Arabic numerals to indicate the chapter (i.e., "XIX.29" signifies book 19, Chapter 29). For consistency, and because of the wide availability of the Cambridge version, I refer to the 1989 translation by Anne M. Cohler.[2] In circumstances where the translation is crucial to the argument, I indicate alternative translations.

INTRODUCTION

ECONOMIC LIBERALISM BEFORE ADAM SMITH

Montesquieu's Political Economy has two central aims. The first is to provide scholars and students of Montesquieu with an introductory survey of Montesquieu's economic ideas. Although a number of works have explained Montesquieu's economic ideas in isolation,[1] there are currently no book-length treatments of Montesquieu's economic philosophy as it relates to Montesquieu's political philosophy of liberalism.[2]

The second aim is to provide a fresh examination of the longstanding controversy over the meaning and purpose of Montesquieu's *The Spirit of the Laws*. A clear view of Montesquieu's political economy will not of course resolve the many attendant questions of Montesquieu's political intentions. Nor is it my aim to provide a novel or comprehensive interpretation of Montesquieu's political thought. Understanding this to be a fool's errand, I will limit myself to a narrower, and hopefully more profitable goal: to eliminate one source of the confusion that continues to cloud Montesquieu's political arguments in obscurity.

The title, *Montesquieu's Political Economy* requires some explanation. First, this study contains no claim to recover an overlooked economic system or theory. Few economic historians consider Montesquieu's economic writings to be of paramount importance for understanding the development of economic thought before Adam Smith.[3] This book is meant, more simply, as a challenge to the increasingly common view that Montesquieu's political science contains no design, no argument, in favor of one kind of government over another, or that if it does, Montesquieu's *The Spirit of the Laws* betrays a reactionary conservative's preference for the monarchy of his day.

In the following chapters, one central theme will guide the selection of evidence and commentary. In a word, commerce.[4] In book 30 of *The Spirit of the Laws*, Montesquieu provides a relevant analogy, in the context of his search for a way out of the "labrynth" of ancient feudal laws: "I find myself in a dark labyrinth full of paths and detours, I believe that I hold the end of the thread and can walk."[5] The theme of commerce is just such a thread. It is of course not the only thread to follow. And it continues to pose a number of interpretative challenges, with implications for understanding both Montesquieu's political science and the history of modern political thought.

Before outlining the plan of this book, it is necessary to acknowledge the pioneers. The classic introduction to Montesquieu's views of commerce is still Albert Hirschman's *The Passions and the Interests*. In this groundbreaking work, Hirschman connected Montesquieu's writings on commerce to the emergence of capitalism. Hirschman's scholarship on Montesquieu grew out his discontent with contemporary social science, in his words, the "incapacity" of social science "to shed light on the political consequences of economic growth."[6]

Hirschman's interest in returning to Montesquieu went beyond economics. His interest in seventeenth- and eighteenth-century political economy displayed an infectious excitement about the possibility of recovering an old field. His writing brims with a sense of adventure, and exploration, that is, in going back to an earlier age of economic expansion, where the profound divide between the "disciplines" of economics and political science did not yet exist. The return was liberating. With no interdisciplinary boundaries to cross, Hirschman pointed out, philosophers and political economists could "range freely," speculating without inhibitions on the questions of great social and political consequence. Among these questions were the possible effects of commercial expansion for peace, the social costs of rapid economic growth, and the promise of individual liberty and happiness.

In going back to Montesquieu, the "edifice" of eighteenth century social thought, Hirschman claimed to have discovered a novel interpretation of the spirit of capitalism. Previously, scholars had concentrated on the disjunction between the aristocratic ideals of he Feudal Age with the "bourgeois mentality" of the new age of commerce, and the Protestant Ethic. Hirschman challenged that view of early modern history, which presented two distinct historical processes, each with its own heroes and villains, each belonging independently to a social class. This was the Enlightenment as "pageant." The spirit of capitalism was at the vanguard, assaulting and overturning the old structures of society. Commercial civilization was inevitable, predictable, a science that could be discovered and mastered, if only it could be harnessed, like the laws of motion.

Montesquieu provided a vantage point to challenge this conception of history. According to Hirschman, Montesquieu provided an "endogenous" story of change, one in which the great thinkers, political theorists, and philosophers, were not merely swept up in social forces beyond their control, but one in which they played a significant part. They were part of a revolutionary movement, Hirschman suggested, that forever changed the trajectory of modern republicanism. But there was a catch. These champions of the spirit of capitalism were not aware, he argued, of the revolutionary potential of their own ideas. Indeed, "They would have shuddered—and revised their thinking—had they realized where their ideas would ultimately lead."

While there is no question that Hirschman's provocative thesis significantly raised the profile of Montesquieu, that is, as a proponent of capitalism "before its triumph,"[7] new problems of interpretation were raised, and old debates were revived. Did Montesquieu in fact contribute, as Hirschman claimed, to the emergence of "revolutionary commerce" in the eighteenth century? But even so, was Montesquieu conscious of his own role?

At the start of the twentieth century, the view of Montesquieu as a "liberal" revolutionary figure—conscious or not—was arguably a splinter position.[8] By the end of the twentieth century, however, it was no longer unusual or radical to suggest that Montesquieu's name should be included alongside John Locke as one of the founding fathers of modern liberalism. Indeed, similar positions had been staked out, independently of Albert Hirschman. Noteworthy contributions by Emile Faguet, Thomas Pangle, Raymond Aron, Isaiah Berlin, Judith Shklar, Pierre Manent, and Bernard Manin, provided significant weight. Montesquieu was more commonly understood now as a partisan of the "free constitution," a system in which interested rival ambitions check, but do not destroy each other, where "power" is a "check to power," warding off the ever-present possibility of despotism. Each, in their own way, recognized the political implications of Montesquieu's books on commerce. Today research continues to merge and overlap in interesting ways from Montesquieu experts across the fields of economics,[9] history,[10] political science,[11] and moral and political philosophy.

While new divisions have predictably opened up, we should not lose sight of the overlapping agreement. The most important uniting feature of the "liberal" interpretation is Montesquieu's universally acknowledged opposition to despotism. From one point of view, this is merely a banal fact. As Bertrand Binoche has put it, "for want of better government, it [despotism] is the worst."

For Montesquieu, despotism is not merely an excess of monarchy, or an object of fascination—or as one scholar has argued, a mental space to satisfy erotic perversions.[12] Rather, despotism in Montesquieu's works provides a fixed moral reference. As Céline Spector has argued, it provides a "powerful foil."[13] Or to borrow again from the liberal school, despotism "justifies in reverse" the moderate regime. However stated, despotism remains a standard, one consistently maintained throughout Montesquieu's life and throughout each work. It is manifest in his profound opposition to religious intolerance, in his absolute denunciation of slavery,[14] and in the various attempts to humanize and promote moderation through law.

More interesting are the sharp division between and among the liberal interpreters of Montesquieu's *The Spirit of the Laws*. Did Montesquieu attempt to justify a right of resistance, or did he merely identify the empirical points where resistance had been successful in the past? Was Montesquieu a friend of liberty, a partisan of liberty, a curious onlooker? Was liberty to be found in the state, in the individual, or in the experience? In which government and in what economic system is security most likely to be found and sustained?

The lack of consensus on these questions is aggravated by a persistent denial that Montesquieu's work contains a unifying plan. As Thomas Pangle states the problem: "Any commentary on *The Spirit of the Laws* must confront the almost universal scholarly opinion of two centuries that the work lacks order and a unifying plan."[15] While this may no longer be the "general view," it is still true that any attempt to discover the "plan of the author" will meet with opposition, going back at least to Voltaire, who, in his critique of Montesquieu's disorderly writing style, argued "that there is neither plan nor order and that after one has read it one doesn't know what he has read..."[16]

To accept the revolutionary-liberal interpretation, readers must further be willing to accept the testimony of d'Alembert, who distinguished between apparent and real disorder in Montesquieu's work. Indeed, d'Alembert argued that Montesquieu had in mind two kinds of readers: "vulgar" readers and those "who think," whose reason "ought to supply the voluntary and reasoned omissions."[17] The liberal reading, in other words does not necessarily require an acceptance of esotericism. The *revolutionary* liberal reading does.

At this point, it is necessary to acknowledge the significance of Thomas Pangle's *Montesquieu's Philosophy of Liberalism: A Commentary on The Spirit of the Laws*.[18] Published first in 1973, Pangle's book advanced the liberal-revolutionary reading to a high water mark. In it, Pangle argued that Montesquieu's *The Spirit of the Laws* should be a central part of the response, in his words, "to the growing crisis in the theoretical foundations" of the principles of liberal democracy. Referring to the "ferment" of the New Left, in particular, Pangle suggested that a serious political transformation was in store in the coming years; that there was a need for a "renewed awareness" of the need to understand "liberal principles" and "to be able to give a coherent defense of them."[19] The challenge, however, was not merely to show the superiority of liberal democracy to totalitarianism or tyranny, but "its merit as compared with other forms of republicanism and limited monarchic rule."

Why Montesquieu? According to Pangle, Montesquieu not only adopted the principles of his predecessors—Hobbes, Spinoza, Locke—but also, importantly, "subjected those principles to a new analysis based on a comprehensive investigation into political experience as revealed by the history of the European nations and the accounts available to him of non-European peoples." The result was a modification of those principles *and* a new presentation of them, which included a sophisticated explication of the variety of objections to liberal republicanism and the kind of society "implied in such objections."[20]

If the greatest challenge to liberal republican principles came from the old republics, characterized by direct political participation, civic virtue, and a "de-emphasis" of material prosperity, as Pangle suggested, one can immediately recognize the significance of the study of commerce in *The Spirit of the Laws*. Pangle rightly connected Montesquieu—as Hirschman would later—to the emergence of the economic-liberal tradition. He went further, arguing that Montesquieu shares with Adam Smith "the honor of being the founder of modern economics."

At the time of publication, four years before *The Passions and the Interests* came out as a book, Pangle could argue, on reasonable grounds, that Montesquieu's role in the development of liberal economic thought had been ignored. According to Pangle, this oversight was "one of the most widely ignored facts of the history of thought."[21] Why had Montesquieu's economic writings been ignored? The interpretative lapse was explainable—not as a result of ignorance on behalf of economic historians as Hirschman would suggest—but because Montesquieu "veiled" his plan in the fourth part of *The Spirit of the Laws*, concealing, consciously from his reader, the corrosive effects of commerce on traditional Christianity.

Both forms of the liberal interpretation of Montesquieu have been increasingly targeted for criticism over the decades.[22] The strongest open challenge in recent years comes from Catherine Larrère, author of *L'Invention de l'économie, Du droit naturel à la physiocratie*, and *Actualité de Montesquieu*, and a number of essays, including her 2005 "Montesquieu's Paradoxical Economics" and her 2001 "Montesquieu on Economics." The latter may still be regarded as the most succinct existing overview of Montesquieu's economic views in English.[23]

Larrère denies that there is a revolutionary "opposition" between ancient and modern, between virtue and commerce, or between the commercial humanism of England and the civic humanism of Rome. According to Larrère, Montesquieu did not only *not* adopt this conflict, but in fact was "content with reversing it."[24] If Montesquieu did not believe that there was a revolutionary tension between commerce and virtue, he would have had no reason to "conceal" his writings on commerce. If there is a "secret chain," she argues, it is only because it passes "unnoticed" by most readers "and not because it has been concealed."

Céline Spector, author of *Economie et politique dans l'oeuvre de Montesquieu*, has compiled a compelling case against Montesquieu as economic liberal.[25] Denying that Montesquieu can be read as a modern defender of "interest," Spector provides a useful overview of the weaknesses of the liberal interpretation. First, she claims, Montesquieu "as liberal" implies a retrospective reading that "runs the risk of projecting onto it the interpreters' ideological choices." Second, the liberal reading fails to take into account Montesquieu's "philosophy of liberty." According to Spector, liberty is a *subjective* perception, not an abstract standard of right.[26] Montesquieuean liberty properly understood is a psychological state (a "tranquillity of spirit"). If liberty is a feeling, not a political axiom, one cannot define *the* nature of government. A plurality of forms may equally secure this end. Finally, Spector claims that liberal interpreters have misrepresented Montesquieu's views of commerce, modern economics, and the constitution of England.

Before attempting a response, it is necessary to anticipate objections to an even more basic claim made in this book. What does it mean to speak of Montesquieu's political economy?

Montesquieu and Political Economy

First, it must be acknowledged that there is a general trend in the scholarship to separate Montesquieu the philosopher from Montesqueiu the economist. Such a separation is not without justification. Economic historians, for example, generally dismiss Montesquieu's economic writings as an historical oddity. In the few cases where economic historians do refer to Montesquieu, it is only in passing, and often taking the form of an explanation for his obscurity. Groenewegen, for example, argues that Montesquieu's economic writings were essentially rendered obsolete only a few decades after the publication of *The Spirit of the Laws* in 1748.[27] Montesquieu's insights were not unoriginal, but they were crude, bound to be surpassed.[28] According to Groenewegen, Montesquieu's economic views were surpassed by 1760, only a few years after his death.[29]

Joseph Schumpeter, in his classic work, *History of Economic Analysis* (1954), provides a more direct criticism of Montesquieu "as economist."[30]

In Schumpeter's view, Montesquieu was first and foremost a "sociologist."[31] Writing before the birth of the new science of economics, he did not possess the conceptual tools to build a coherent economic theory.[32] Schumpeter's opinion is strikingly similar to one voiced by Voltaire in 1777:

> Montesquieu had no knowledge of political principles concerning wealth, manufactories, finance and commerce. These principles had hardly been discovered yet... It would have been just as impossible for him to comment on the treatise on wealth by Smith as on the mathematical principles of Newton.[33]

While subsequent research has not validated the incredulity of Voltaire, this does raise an unavoidable question: what is meant by political economy?

At the most basic level, Montesquieu's political economy is viewed here as part of a longstanding enterprise to understand the relationship between politics and economics.[34] Montesquieu's political economy is neither systematic nor comprehensive. It does not suggest an explicit theory connecting politics to economics. Neither is it a manual for statesman on how best to manage the economic affairs of the state so as to supply wants and satisfy the desires of citizens.

The term political economy, first coined in the seventeenth century, has also acquired numerous, often contradictory meanings over its lifetime.[35] For Adam Smith and classical political economists, political economy was focused on two objectives: the production of wealth for society and the provision of the state with sufficient revenue to cover public services. This is the meaning of Smith's claim that political economy is "a branch of the science of a statesman or legislator." For Karl Marx, political economy revealed the ways in which the ownership of the means of production influenced historical processes. Marx identified the study of political economy with a search for "the anatomy of civil society."[36] For Engels, it was the "theoretical analysis of modern bourgeois society."[37]

In the following text, I will refer to political economy in the sense that it was used and understood preceding the massive reorientation of the field as a result of the great influence of later economsits like Smith and Marx. Montesquieu's political economy, first and foremost, refers to the political importance of commerce. In that sense, it grows out of—and is inseparable from—Montesquieu's political philosophy. This point is worth bearing in mind as we proceed. In the first half of the eighteenth century, political economists tended to subordinate the study of economy to political and ethical concerns, an approach that is traceable at least as far back as the Greek philosophers and medieval political philosophy. While we will see that economics begin to emerge in Montesquieu's *The Spirit of the Laws* as an autonomous force, and therefore, a subject analyzable from the calm indifference of the point of view of science, Montesquieu's political economy could not be anything else but political. This is true whether Montesquieu is considering mercantilism, the relationship between the nobility and trade, the origins and justification of private property, or the transformation of the feudal laws.

That Montesquieu's political economy is subject to *ethical* considerations is a claim that many will find harder to accept. Nonetheless, Montesquieu engaged directly with his predecessors in moral and economic philosophy. Montesquieu consciously adapted the teachings of Mandeville, for example, who had only recently reignited the ethical controversy over commercial society, the role of self-interest, luxury, and vanity, with his 1714 *Fable of the Bees*, a work that Montesquieu quoted frequently and admired (albeit in limited ways that we will explore). Hutcheson, Hume, and Adam Smith, are examples of "political economists" in this vein, following Montesquieu, who would later give the impression that modern political economy grew out of moral philosophy.[38]

It should not be surprising to find Montesquieu's political economy emerging alongside and interconnected with his political views. In the eighteenth century, economic writing flourished, as economic historians have shown, in the context of political crisis. The reunion of the *États généraux*, for example, prompted a series of protests against royal taxes, launching a public debate about the best way to manage the Kingdom's economic affairs. In 1685, near the end of Louis XIV's reign, economic publications spiked, with the revocation of the Edict of Nantes. The upsetting of the religious peace—combined with a depression—sparked another series of debates on economic questions. Political economists, in short, turned their attention to the economic consequences of intolerance and emigration, the social effects of theological debates on usury, and as will see, the role of government in finance, taxation, and public credit.

When Montesquieu published the *Persian Letters* in 1720, the list of topics in political economy had expanded beyond speculation on the effects of particular government policies. At the top of the list was war finance. Defeats at the Battle of Blenheim (1704) and Ramillies (1706) were followed by economic misery and the Great Famine in 1709. Political economists began to make daring connections to the nature of monarchy itself. Political economists began to draw the attention of the censors. Sébastien Le Prestre de Vauban, for example, who had opposed the repeal of the Edict of Nantes on economic grounds, penned a critique of the inefficiency of the French fiscal system and was condemned by the royal government. Pierre le Pesant, sieur de Boisguilbert, as another example, depicted the economic mismanagement of the regime as causing, in part, the "general ruin" of the state in his *Le détail de la France; la cause de la diminution de ses biens et la facilité du remède*. He was exiled to Auvergne.

As I will argue in the following chapter, Montesquieu's interest in political economy increased steadily throughout his life, often tracking major political developments. During the 1730s, a number of works began to appear that drew his interest, especially, treatises critical of the monarchy that drew out the lessons and implications of the John Law fiasco. These included the first edition of Melon's *Essai politique sur le commerce*, published in 1734, and Duval's *Reflexions Politiques sur le Commerce et les Finances*, published in 1738. In the late 1740s, when war spending increased again, and the regime was forced to undertake fiscal innovations, political economy in France came to the fore, and Montesquieu was at the vanguard.

In the mid-1750s, precisely at the moment of Montesquieu's passing, contemporaries began to take notice of the phenomenon gripping the intellectual atmosphere of the old regime. Voltaire attributed the dramatic increase in economic treatises to a "satiation" with moral and theological disputes. Others, less enthusiastic about the emergence of political economy, compared it to an "epidemic illness" of the French mind.[39]

It is well beyond the scope of this book to say how, or whether, Montesquieu's economic writings influenced events in the colonies of North America, if at all. One may point to the oft-repeated statistic that Montesquieu was the most quoted European political writer during the American Founding era.[40] It is commonly repeated that Montesquieu is mentioned favorably by name in the *Federalist Papers*. James Madison famously refers to Montesquieu as an "oracle" in *Federalist* No. 47. Hamilton praises Montesquieu as a "great man" in *Federalist* No. 9 (and later, "the celebrated Montesquieu," in *Federalist* No. 78).[41] But did the Founders take note of his writings on commerce and political economy?

It is clear enough that Montesquieu's views on trade, commerce, manufacturing, finance, were well known to at least two leaders of the debate on the importance of political economy in the emerging democratic republic.[42] Hamilton, for example, makes a point, in the *Federalist Papers*, of the necessity of reading the whole of Montesquieu. Hamilton makes a public challenge for readers not to make the mistake of reading Montesquieu's political writings in isolation from his careful analysis of climate, civil law, and commerce. In this, Hamilton was following Montesquieu's advice in the Preface: to not "approve or condemn the book as a whole and not some few sentences." Rightly so, Hamilton emphasized the need to compare the "sentiments" of Montesquieu in "other parts" of the work.

Of course, Hamilton was not speaking directly to the importance of the fourth part of *The Spirit of the Laws* on commerce. But his challenge—to comprehend the work as a whole, including the books on commerce—was taken up by Jefferson.[43] In 1811, Jefferson finished a major translation of Claude Destutt de Tracy's *Commentaire sur l'esprit des lois de Montesquieu* into English.[44] This was one of two of Tracy's works that impressed Jefferson. The other, *A Treatise on Political Economy* (1817) became an important work in French liberal political thought during the Napoleonic period. In the Preface to the 1817 publication, Jefferson wrote, "By diffusing sound principles of Political Economy, it will protect the public industry from the parasite institutions now consuming it"

Tracy's reading of Montesquieu will not occupy us here. It is sufficient to note that Tracy was one of the founders, in the 1790s, of the classical liberal republican group known as the Idéologues, a group that included Cabanis, Condorcet, Constant, Daunou, Say, and Madame de Staël.[45] The reason for Jefferson's admiration of Tracy's interpretation of Montesquieu is also a complicated subject. A hint of his motive is found in the preface Jefferson wrote, in 1811, for Tracy's book, explaining the purpose of his own translation. Tracy, he said, had been a friend of the Revolution, but up until a point; that is, to the point of the "tyrannies of the monster Robespierre." According to Jefferson, Montesquieu had written an "immortal work," but it contained many "inconsistencies, paradoxes, [and] whimsical combinations." Tracy's purpose, Jefferson continued, was to "correct" Montesquieu's errors: "few nations are in a situation to profit by the detection of political errors, or to shape their practice by newly developed truths."[46]

In a private letter to Tracy, Jefferson further explained his own fascination with Montesquieu:

> I cannot express to you the satisfaction which I recieved from its perusal. I had, with the world, deemed Montesquieu's a work of much merit; but saw in it, with every thinking man, so much of paradox, of false principle, & misapplied fact, as to render its value equivocal on the whole. Williams and others had nibbled only at its errors. A radical correction of them therefore was a great desideratum.[47]

A "radical" correction of Montesquieu in English was "the most precious gift the present age has received." It would become "the political rudiment of the young, and manual of our older citizens." In 1813, Jefferson wrote again to Tracy, describing his hopes for the work, and linking it directly to the political economy of the new American republic. The translated version would provide the world with a "simplified" political economy, brought within a "moderate compass."

Jefferson hoped that from there, it would "spread and become a political gospel" for the nation.[48]

The significance of Montesquieu's political economy in the American experiment can be understood, more broadly, in terms of his contribution to the difference between modern and ancient republicanism. Judith Shklar notes that Montesquieu had "set the terms" in which republicanism was to be discussed.[49] Although he was skeptical of the austere republics of antiquity, Montesquieu inspired two novel kinds of republicanism in the second half of the century.[50] One was constructed by Rousseau, a "theoretical" republicanism modeled partly on Montesquieu's portraits of the political economy of Sparta and Rome.[51] The political economy of the English system combined commerce with religion and a passion for individual liberty; this was surrounded by a constitutional machinery that was a "blueprint for self-limiting government that served the American founders at Philadelphia."[52]

During the eighteenth century, references to Montesquieu's economic thought dwindle, as do the attempts to graph Montesquieu's economic writings onto new debates about the rise of industrial capitalism, economic regulation, and distributional politics. Aside from isolated footnotes in Karl Marx's *Das Kapital*,[53] not much notice is taken of Montesquieu's economic writings until the middle of the twentieth century, when John Maynard Keynes notes, in the Preface to the French edition of *The General Theory of Employment, Interest and Money* (1975), that Montesquieu was the greatest French economist and the "French equivalent" of Adam Smith. Addressing the French reading public, Keynes makes the following (now famous) remark:

> Montesquieu was the real French equivalent of Adam Smith. The greatest of your economists, head and shoulders above the physiocrats in penetration, clear-headedness, and good sense (which are the qualities an economist should have).

Keynes does not appear to have read Montesquieu closely, and the meaning of his remark is still debated.[54] The comment is not mysterious, however, if one considers Keynes' pacifism, and his appreciation for peaceful economic cooperation between nations. In short, Keynes was merely echoing Montesquieu's insight in book 20 of *The Spirit of the Laws*:

"it is better that a man should tyrannize over his bank account than over his fellow-citizens."[55]

Overview of the Chapters

To begin to uncover the outlines and major features of Montesquieu's political economy, it is necessary to combine the desire for coherence and chronology with an appreciation of Montesquieu's methodoligical eclecticism. Chapter 1 introduces the reader to some of the less well-known episodes in Montesquieu's life, connecting his writings on economics and commerce with his emergence as a political economist. Using biographical episodes to illuminate the development of Montesquieu as an economic theorist, this chapter aims to establish the kinds of early impressions and experiences that likely influenced Montesquieu's thinking on political economy, especially as these are revealed in his early treatise on state debt, reflections on commerce and virtue in the *Persian Letters*, and Montesquie's notebooks, written during and after his voyage to England.[56]

Chapter 2 addresses the remainder of Montesquieu's writing on commerce in book 20 of *The Spirit of the Laws*. Here, Montesquieu outlines the foundational assumptions of his political economy including the "nature," the "causes" and the "effects" of commerce. The chapter has two related goals; first, to dispel of the notion that Montesquieu was a simple partisan of commercial England. Commerce was not a "grand panacea." The rest of the chapter attempts to clarify the historical and political reasons for Montesquieu's endorsement of modern commerce, and the English constitution in particular. Focusing especially on Montesquieu's analysis of the strengths and weakenesses of the republics of Holland and Marseilles, England, by comparison, emerges as an abstracted ideal. I argue in conclusion that these opening chapters of book 20[57] provide the positive goal—the bearing, so to speak—of Montesquieu's political economy.

Chapter 3 is an examination of the relationship between wealth and honor in the French monarchy.[58] A closer look at the politics of free trade, public credit, trading companies, banks, and the minutiae of specific laws regulating business and commerce, reveals a strong political subtext that culminates in Montesquieu's controversial defense of venality—a practice that Montesquieu is fully aware might lead to a radical transformation of the second estate. The end of book 20 is not, as is too often assumed, an attempt to entrench noble privileges and to perpetuate rank-honor. Instead, Montesquieu's proposal for an upward social mobility can be read as an historically grounded attempt to transform French views of honor. Specifically, it points to a strategy of making commerce honorable, and of reversing the prejudice against commerce and agriculture as ignoble professions.[59]

Chapter 4 is an extended analysis of Montesquieu's "history of commerce" in book 21. On the most basic level, Montesquieu's dramatic recreation of world economic history explains the decline, destruction, and revival of commerce in the modern world, a revolution that Montesquieu locates in the invention of the "bills of exchange," likened famously to a cure for the disease of "Machiavellianism." The cure for Machiavellianism is both bittersweet and more importantly, insufficient for restoring honor to commerce as a profession. Comparing Montesquieu's apology for commerce to earlier English attempts to refashion a sympathetic imagery of the merchant, it becomes clear that Montesquieu viewed the defense of commercial civilization in Part 4 of *The Spirit of the Laws* as radically incomplete. At least two critical factors make a comparison with his English forerunners in political economy more complicated, requiring a further study of Montesquieu's views on commerce as it relates to two major topics: religion and property, the respective themes of the final two chapters.

Chapter 5 opens by surveying three broad alternative readings of Montesquieu's views of religion. Is the endorsement of commercial values and institutions part of a strategy to transform and emasculate religion? Or is the aim less radical? Might commerce and religion ultimately share the same roots, opening up a possible reconciliation or synthesis of commercial and religious interests? Or is Montesquieu's interest in religion and economics primarily of a sociological character? In my view, the second of the three competing positions is most convincing. While Montesquieu clearly viewed commerce as the weapon of choice in the battle plan against religious extremism, it also seems implausible that Montesquieu viewed secularization as the long-term goal. Montesquieu's comparative analysis of religion indicates a different strategy: to provide modern liberalism with the conceptual tools to arbitrate, on reasonable grounds, between religious opinions and practices that support liberty and commerce, and those that do not.[60] The chapter concludes by arguing that the goal of moderating extremists is best achieved through moderation, which Montesquieu's sociological account of religious belief is meant to provide.

Finally, chapter 6 examines Montesquieu's views on property and civil law, which have so far attracted little attention of specialists. This chapter argues that critics of the liberal-revolutionary view have placed too much weight in Montesquieu's claim that property is mere convention, as opposed to his more considered view, which is that property is an extension of the person. As in the above debate on religion, Montesquieu is conventionally viewed as a conservative champion of the social stability of the old regime. A re-examination of Montesquieu's views on property aims to tip the scales in the other direction, by contesting the accomodationist, conservative, monarchical reading of Montesquieu as a defender of monarchical privilege and proprietorship.

Admittedly, no single work can pretend to account for the whole range and development of Montesquieu's views on political economy. Indeed, we will see that Montesquieu's interest in economic matters evolved over time, alongside his political thought. Yet in one of the earliest of Montesquieu's essays, entitled *De la Politique*, Montesquieu divulged one of the central reasons for his preoccupation and curiosity of economic things. "It is useless to attack politics directly by showing how much its practices are in conflict with morality and reason," Montesquieu reasoned. "This sort of discourse convinces everybody, but changes nobody...I believe it is better to follow a roundabout road and to try to convey to the great a distaste for certain political practices by showing how little they yield that is at all useful."[61]

The following chapter is an attempt to follow this roundabout road, tracing Montesquieu's footsteps from a pioneer theorist on the politics of state debt, to his emergence as a historian of commerce, and finally, to his mature views on the relationship between commerce and liberty in *The Spirit of the Laws*.

CHAPTER 1

MONTESQUIEU *ÉCONOMISTE*

Montesquieu's lifelong interest in matters of political economy can be divided into three major themes: first, the controversy over public debt, coinciding with the period of the Regency (1715–26) during which Montesquieu wrote the *Persian Letters* (1721). Second, the problem of war finance, coinciding generally with Fleury's France (1726–34), during which time Montesquieu composed and wrote *Considerations on the Causes of the Greatness of the Romans and Their Decline* (1734). Third, the emerging "science of commerce," a topic that interested Montesquieu during what Colin Jones has called the "Unsuspected Golden Years" (1743–56) in France. During this time, Montesquieu put the finishing touches on *The Spirit of the Laws* and published "In Defense" of *The Spirit of the Laws* (1750).[1]

Early Writings and the Context of Regency Finance

In 1700, Montesquieu was sent to Collège de Juilly near Paris, where he received an education in ancient and modern history. He then studied law at the University of Bordeaux. While little is known about this period in Montesquieu's life, there are clues that Montesquieu had significant intellectual and political ambitions beyond holding legal office. In 1711, Montesquieu wrote a treatise defending the "idolatry" of the pagans, which he later tore up, and then recalled many years later in his *Pensées*.[2] While in Paris, Montesquieu read widely, and was introduced to the *Journal des savants,* one of the earliest academic journals in Europe. As late as 1716, he took a particular interest in the Dutch gazettes. *The Gazette de Hollande* and *Gazette d'Amsterdam* were both sources that supplied him with detailed analyses of economic realities in Western and Eastern Europe.[3] These focused more on contemporary political and economic affairs. According to Shackleton, Montesquieu relied on these publications for the next 30 years of his life, often referring to them for news and information on political and economic affairs in England and Holland.

The death of his father in 1713 called Montesquieu back from Paris to La Château de la Brède in the southwest of France, near Bordeaux. Here Montesquieu took up his inheritance, became a feudal proprietor, and finalized his marriage with Jeanne Lartigue. While Montesquieu flirted with the prospect of a marriage to the daughter of a Bordeaux wine merchant, he signed a marriage contract with the wealthier Lartigue, in 1715. This provided the husband a dowry of 100,000 *livres*. The marriage also provided the young Baron an "efficient steward" for his estates.[4]

Montesquieu's interest in state finances began somewhere around this time. In September 1715, a gangrenous Louis XIV died after 72 years on the throne. On his deathbed, he is said to have confided to close advisors, "I have made war too much." When the King's nephew was installed as Regent, hopes were high for financial renewal, and Montesquieu himself embraced the brief tide of optimism at the start of the Regency.[5]

There were personal reasons to be optimistic. In April 1716, Montesquieu's uncle passed away, leaving him as sole possessor of his estates—and the inheritor of a new title and office. This succession improved the financial position of his estate significantly. At the start of the Regency, Montesquieu owed more than 20,000 *livres* to different friends.[6] By the end of 1720, Montesquieu had paid back this sum in its entirety.

Philippe duc Orléans, by contrast, was the unlucky inheritor of a crushing public debt that quickly subsumed the Regency in debate and controversy on the issue of public credit in the context of modern monarchy. According to one estimate, the debt level in 1715 was between two and three billion *livres*—a sum higher than in 1789 when adjusted for inflation.[7]

Montesquieu took an early interest in the debates on public credit; he clearly understood both the advantages and disadvantages of credit in a monarchy.[8] On the one hand, public credit entailed a degree of constitutional and representative government that modern monarchies lacked. Indeed, Montesquieu would later praise the English for having "secure credit" and a remarkable financial system that had become crucial to international success in war and trade.[9] As we will see, Montesquieu also viewed a state bank as both a key feature of the English economic system and also a fitting "establishment" that he did not believe to be compatible with French monarchy.[10]

In the context of traditional monarchy, however, the availability of public credit had a dangerous side: it was a source of war, he argued;

or more specifically, a cause of the continual preparation for war. In his notebooks, Montesquieu warned, for example, that "Europe is ruining itself and will ruin itself more unless by common consent it reduces the number of troops."[11] This opinion was repeated—using the first person plural—in 1748 in *The Spirit of the Laws*: "We are poor with the riches and commerce of the whole world; and soon, by thus augmenting our troops, we shall have nothing but soldiers, and we shall be like the Tartars."[12]

In October 1715, Montesquieu was presented with a unique opportunity to directly influence the regime's political and financial future. Fearing a downward spiral into financial insolvency, the Regent had composed a letter to the *intendants*, soliciting proposed solutions to the economic crisis. While Orléans had originally addressed the *intendants* only, the announcement was circulated more widely to encourage broader input. More than 330 submissions were received. Montesquieu's own submission, rarely discussed today, was entitled *Mémoire sur les dettes de L' état* [Memoir on state debts], and was sent directly to the Regent.[13]

The proposal in this little-known essay involved partial repudiation of the debt by moderate cuts to different groups of government investors, from the wages owed to venal office holders, to the salaries of pensioners and the king's employees, to interest owed on government bonds and short-term loans. The scheme was cautious, in that it avoided the alternative of bankruptcy advocated by Saint Simon.[14] It was moderate, in that it avoided any radical alterations to the tax system, outside minor revisions to the salt tax (*gabelles*) and reductions to the *capitation* (first levied in 1695) and the *dixieme*, more recently established by Louis XIV in 1710.[15] There was nothing radical about it, except, perhaps, that Montesquieu seems to have been optimistic about a total elimination of debt. But the social structure underlying the system of French finance was to be left more or less intact. No significant changes were recommended to the existing system of privilege and exemptions.[16]

One may interpret Montesquieu's cautious measures in "On State debts" as a reflection of the nobleman's class interests, an example of Montesquieu's attempt to protect the privileges of the nobility and clergy in the *ancien régime* at all costs. Indeed, the idea to reduce the principal of the loans of creditors would not have affected the privileged *corps* significantly, except as a minor financial burden. Montesquieu's insistence on "proportional" cuts was grounded in a morality of "shared sacrifice" that would soften the blow on investors, thus, in essence, maintaining the status quo of the social orders. The proposal for a 1 percent interest rate reduction, notably, did not touch on structural reform. Likewise, on the subject of taxes, Montesquieu's call to eliminate the "tenth" or *dixieme* could be interpreted as one part of a larger strategy to preserve noble exemptions from intrusions. Most importantly, nothing is said about the controversial *taille*, and there is no hint of replacing the regressive tax structure with principles of equal or progressive taxation.

If Montesquieu failed to join "advanced thinking" on modern state finance, it was not because he could not rise above his own class.[17] When Orléans came to power in 1715, there were a limited variety of financial instruments at his disposal for correcting the growing problem of state borrowing.[18] That Montesquieu did not recommend the United Provinces and England as positive examples only indicates how far ahead these nations were in terms of financial innovations. Among the institutions now hailed by economic historians as crucial to their success: maritime insurance, futures and options, mutual funds, and most importantly, modern investment banking.[19]

It is worth noting, moreover, that radical proposals for structural reform may not have had any effect, in any case. Neither England nor Holland matched up with France in terms of population or agricultural production. Contrary to exaggerated reports of the miserable state of the French economy, indicators suggest that France experienced moderate but sustained economic growth between 1726 and the eve of the Revolution. Estimates hover around 0.6 per cent a year for the agricultural sector, and 1.9 per cent a year for the industrial sector.[20] The most dynamic sector was foreign trade, which expanded fivefold in real terms during the years that Montesquieu composed, and published the *Persian Letters* (1716–20).[21]

Montesquieu's critical view of French political economy begins to emerge later, especially in the five years following the publication of *Mémoire sur les dettes de L' état*. As we will now see, Montesquieu's evaluation of the French economic and political system changed radically in the 1720s. First, Montesquieu began to study—and to diagnose—the structural and political factors in the Crown's fiscal distress. And as will be made clear, Montesquieu's early, conservative approach to political economy in the old regime was soon replaced by a bold critique. Importantly, Montesquieu's thoughts on political economy in these years contain a firm denunciation both of the old, inefficient system, and the attempts by radical liberal economists and reformers to institute a new "rational economic order,"[22] motivated by the prospect of human perfectibility.[23]

Political Economy and the Persian Letters

The venue or the occasion for Montesquieu's new ideas on economics was a popular satire, published in 1721. In contrast to his early essay "On state debts," Montesquieu, this time writing anonymously, portrayed

France under the aegis of the Regency as a period of social, financial, and economic chaos. Looking back with an ironic nostalgia, Montesquieu described the period during the reign of finance minister Colbert as (comparatively) a period of financial and social stability.[24] What happened?

At the time of the fictional Usbek's visit to France, the king is 75 years of age, and the economy is sinking. The monarch draws his riches not from agriculture or trade, but from the "vanity of his subjects which is more inexhaustible than mines."[25] Agriculture and cultivation have been neglected. Investments in agricultural technology have been largely abandoned.[26] Meanwhile, Usbek observes, the arable and high quality land has been parcelled out to the privileged orders. The monarchs, the courtiers and "a few private individuals" own all the wealth[27] while the French "dervishes" own and control "almost all the state's wealth." This "company of misers" perpetually "takes and never returns," constantly accumulating revenue in order to acquire capital that is then taken out of circulation, channeled away from investments in commerce, arts, science, and manufacturing.[28] Profits and surplus from land belonging to the peasantry is either reserved for royal taxes and church tithes, squandered, or simply disappear as the people prepare themselves for a bad harvest, plague, disease, or famine.[29]

Compounding the hardships, Montesquieu explained, were the high taxes on common laborers. Montesquieu alludes to a brief period of rural recovery, under the leadership of Colbert (chief minister 1661–83), who raised taxes on city-dwellers and reduced direct taxes on the peasantry.[30] But, after these "fortunate years," France descended into a 35 year period of financial instability and of almost continuous warfare. The Persian visitors describe the impact on economics and national wealth, with a combination of disgust and amazement.[31] Rica marvels at the king's ability to "undertake" and "support" great wars, with "no other resources than titles or honors."[32] By this "miracle of human vanity," the troops were paid, strongholds provisioned, and fleets equipped.[33]

The *Persian Letters* contain other such observations on political economy, not often explored. The Persian visitors recognize, for example, that prosperity in modern monarchy depends crucially on the non-agricultural sectors. In one of the earlier letters of correspondence, Usbek uses the example of the Ottoman empire to critique the French example. The Ottoman empire is "weak." It is a "sickly body" with a harsh government, and a religious elite who "buy their positions" and then "lay waste" to newly acquired lands. The government is dominated by an arrogant militia that leaves cities deserted, farmland despoiled, and "land cultivation and commerce completely abandoned."[34] Usbek predicts that in two centuries time, the agriculturally based Ottoman society ("incapable of commerce") will provide "some conqueror with a theater for his triumphs."

Meanwhile, writing from Venice, Rica delights in a city where his mind is "improved everyday" by exposure to new advances in medicine, natural philosophy, and astronomy. In Venice, Rica announces that he has stumbled upon "the secrets of commerce." Picking up on contemporary debates on the relationship between population size and national wealth, Rica announces his plans to write a treatise explaining how the two are "mutually favorable."[35] Monastic and "otherwordly" cultures destroy prosperity. Commerce "brings everything to life."[36] The visitors describe England in an extremely favorable terms by comparison. Indeed, no other government combines constitutional durability, political and religious liberty, with maritime might. This combination is a unique and powerful mix of "commerce with empire."[37]

Did Montesquieu avoid or gloss over the problems of commercial society in the *Persian Letters*? While Montesquieu's appreciation of the perils of commercial republicanism surely deepened, it is too often forgotten that Montesquieu had included, in the *Persian Letters*, a warning, in the form of a dialogue or debate between the younger Rhedi and the older Usbek, playing the role of tutor. Using the younger Rica as a mouthpiece, Montesquieu incorporates popular fears into his praise of the English example, including the invention of destructive military technology, the "emasculating" effects of the arts, the "idleness" and "effeminacy" that accompanies the explosion of comforts and amenities, and the rise of individualism and hedonism in the luxurious trading centers.[38] Usbek's reply to Rica will be analyzed later, in the concluding section of this book.

For now, the central problem raised in the *Persian Letters* is not the negative effects of commerce on society, but, more specifically, the peculiarities of the structural and financial system of the old regime. After three years in Paris, Rica observes, for example, that the financial system has been revolutionized four times.[39] He warns of "Great geniuses" who have been hired to form "new projects," created in back rooms "which the great cannot penetrate and the humble regard as sacred."[40]

Rica's comments on the economic revolutions in France raise two problems: the intervention and rise of the infamous John Law, and the explosive growth of an increasingly despotic bureaucracy. Before turning to the problem of John Law in Montesquieu's political economy, it is necessary only to make note of the evolution of the position of controller-general of finances, created first in 1665. This would become a position of great power, and it would grow, eventually, into a department that would expand to oversee the whole economic and financial affairs of the kingdom.⁴¹ During Colbert's era, which the Persians praise, the royal council of finances employed a handful of assistants. By the 1720s, roughly the period of the setting of the *Persian Letters*, this office would have been unrecognizable to the first members. Historians estimate a payroll of more than 350 persons,⁴² a number that does not include the network of officials, clerks, principal secretaries, and "intendants" of finances needed to staff the new departments created in response to the ever increasing demand for tax and economic data.⁴³

John Law

It is hard to exaggerate the importance of the controler-general's office in Montesquieu's critique of traditional monarchy. In May 1716, the year after Montesquieu submitted his essay on state debt, the Regent made a fateful decision to ignore pleas for moderate reforms—reforms similar to Montesquieu's; instead, he handed over the debt crisis to a foreigner, the notorious Scottish gambler who, although he had described himself once as a republican, had recently been "won over" by the merits of despotic economic power.⁴⁴ Disregarding moderate reform, Law was appointed Controller General of Finances, effectively giving him absolute control over the nation's internal and external commerce.

Law's reputation as an economic wizard had preceded him when he arrived in France. It was commonly known that Law had successfully guided the establishment of the Bank of England in 1694. His other experiments in banking and finance in Amsterdam, Genoa, and Turin, had attracted the attention of French officials, who looked to him as an *enchanteur* who might one day rescue the French state from financial ruin.

When Law arrived, he provided a diagnosis of the economic crisis, centering on two key problems. According to Law, the state was suffering both a monetary crisis (a shortage of currency) and a fiscal crisis (state debt and unmanageable interest rates).⁴⁵ To address the monetary crisis, Law gained authorization to establish a private bank. To address the debt, Law established the Mississippi Company in 1717. The two-track scheme was mutually reinforcing. The bank, serviced by public credit, would support the expansion of commerce.⁴⁶ The combination of increased commercial activity, with profits from colonial possessions in Louisiana, would promote economic growth and at the same time consolidate the debt. With little significant opposition from the Paris Parliament, "The Company" enjoyed a brief period of success, driven by intense speculation that enriched many speculators. In 1719, leaflets and advertisements beckoned investors with enticing descriptions: the wild mountains of

Louisana, apparently full of gold, silver, copper, and quicksilver; a climate that supported two annual harvests of rice and tobacco; "fine wool" that "leapt off the backs of the native sheep"; and friendly natives, open to volunteering their sexual services "joyfully to all comers."[47]

Nearly three decades later, Montesquieu would devote major parts of *The Spirit of the Laws* to the Law episode, arguing, famously, that Law was "one of the great promoters of despotism that had until then been seen in Europe."[48] Law, Montesquieu would later argue, was "ignorant" not of economics, but of the larger relation between economics and politics. Law assumed (wrongly, according to Montesquieu) that commerce would flourish equally in "all countries," whether in republics or monarchies.[49] Moreover, Law's plan ignored the different purposes and dynamics of republican and monarchical constitutions. His project naively assumed a fundamental restructuring of the intermediate ranks. It required "abolishing" the political bodies that provided a necessary check on absolute power. By contrast, the more prudent Montesquieu remained committed to what we could call economic contingency, the principle, as he would later conclude, that commerce was "related to the constitution."[50]

In the 1740s, as Montesquieu developed his economic theory in line with his typology of governments, Montesquieu would distinguish further between the "commerce of luxury" and the "commerce of economy." This distinction, as we will see later, would become the cornerstone of his most important response to Law. Montesquieu's foundational thesis, that commerce is related to the constitution, would provide the analytical basis for his ultimate rejection of the establishment of a bank in a centralized monarchy that depended on a commerce of luxury.[51]

In the *Persian Letters*, Montesquieu's approach is less systematic, but his criticisms are prescient, combining sociological analysis with bruising satire. "Fragments from an Ancient Greek Mythologist"[52] tells the story of the birth of a child, on an island in the Orkneys. This child is Baby Law, the product of Aelous, "god of winds." His mother is a nymph. As an infant, the young Law was blessed with a powerful gift, a rare ability to distinguish gold from other metals, like brass. As he grew up, his father taught him the secret of "imprisoning the winds" in a goatskin bottle, which he could then sell to travellers. Wind, unfortunately, was not in great demand in Scotland, so Mr. Law made his way to France.

Law's attempt to sell wind is, in part, a metaphor, for "the System," much analyzed by economic historians. To simplify, Law's economic system was a disaster: it wiped out a sizeable portion of individual fortunes, and in the process virtually emptied the state's coffers.[53] Montesquieu, in his fable, made one of the first attempts to account for the impact on national economic well being. He estimated the amount at "three-quarters" of the country's wealth.[54] David Hume, a fellow Scot, following Montesquieu's lead, later quipped that Law had caused a sick French economy "to die of the doctor."[55]

Montesquieu's analysis of Law is significant not only because it helps to place his conservative views in "On state debts" in perspective.[56] More importantly, the Law episode brings to light for the modern reader the profound difficulty or paradox of economic reform in a political system that was not prepared for transformation. The failure of Law's policies pointed to the larger question of whether it was possible to accelerate commerce and economic activity in a regime where financial stewardship was inseparable from considerations of social rank, hierarchy, and privilege.[57]

In the late 1720s, Montesquieu composed a mysterious fragment entitled "PUBLIC BANKS AND TRADING COMPANIES." The fragment, now found under the heading of *Pensées* #1690, did not make it into *The Spirit of the Laws*. Dark, humorous, and undoubtedly subversive, this tale describes the fortunes of an Algerian tyrant who finds himself positioned happily as sole ruler, but woefully lacking in one vital respect: ready access to money and capital for the ships to build his colonial trading empire. The story begins where the Law episode left off, and can be thought of loosely as a sequel. In this state, public trust is at a nadir. Like the French public in the post-Law period, the Algerian merchants are facing currency devaluation, financial instability, and possible bankruptcy. The tract describes a generation on the lookout for the next financial "wizard" promising great riches.

Taking a cue from Machiavelli, the Algerian monarch appoints a vizier, who puts into motion a cynical scheme to get around the problem of public distrust, and to overcome the state's previous failures in setting up a banking institution. In its evil simplicity, the plan illustrates the danger of economic despotism. The monarch's vizier will simply abduct the merchants, wrap them in chains, and torture them until they have "given over all their money" to the public treasury. In return for their patriotic service (however unwilling), the hapless creditors will receive an official piece of "paper" signed by six senior military officers. The revenues thus established, the king will launch his glorious "Company of the Indies." This act will set off a chain reaction among European monarchs, who, purveying the Algerian example, realize that it will be in their own best interest to bring their own "insolent" merchant class to heel. In turn, the vizier predicts a "violent setback" to the European banking system, as merchants withdraw their mobile wealth, thus propelling the Algerian state ahead of the competition for "overseas glory."

The above fragment also helps to illustrate a critically important development in Montesquieu's thinking on political economy. By the time he had finished the *Persian Letters,* Montesquieu had gone far beyond his initial forays into the French system of state finance. In satirizing Law, Montesquieu clearly placed himself at the vanguard of eighteenth-century critiques of mercantilism. But in Montesquieu's critique of Law, we also see an early criticism of the emerging "liberal" economists, who, while recognizing Law's failure, nevertheless continued to argue in favor of a "modernized" system of centralized economic administration that would operate under legal and enlightened despotism.[58] In short, Montesquieu's economic thought had evolved in two ways by the 1730s. First, he had begun to develop what we have called economic contingency, the principle that economics is dependent on and related to the constitution. Second, we see Montesquieu developing a deep interest not only in the problematic relation between public credit and commerce, but also the relationship between commerce, finances and war.

Montesquieu's expanding view of political economy had much to do with the people around him. It is safe to assume, for example, that Montesquieu would have had a chance to float his ideas on political economy during his first few years in the Academy of Bordeaux, which provided a valuable experience, and a rich setting, to explore the relation between economics and politics with some of the most important economists in France. Montesquieu would have had a chance, for example, to meet with the young Jean-François Melon. If there was anyone in these circles who could provide Montesquieu with the dialogue on matters of political economy that he surely craved, it was Melon, author of the famous 1734 *Essai politique sur le commerce,* and soon to become secretary to John Law.

While Melon enjoyed only brief fame in the spotlight as a leading French economist, his possible influence on Montesquieu should not be dismissed. Voltaire, for example, later identified Melon as the first to discuss commerce as a political phenomenon.[59] In this sense, Melon's influence is worth exploring, and we will have a chance to do so in another context.[60] But neither is it out of the realm of possibility—given the dating of Montesquieu's *Mémoire sur les dettes de l' état*—that Melon may have learned something about political economy from the young Montesquieu (Melon was born in 1675, Montesquieu 14 years later in 1689).

Montesquieu's connections in the Academy of Bordeaux also helped to inspire in him a curiosity with England, and a fascination with travel. Indeed, Montesquieu's travel notebooks provide intriguing glimpses into his writings on commerce, developed later in *The Spirit of the Laws.* Montesquieu read Chardin and Tavernier, and he used these authors as sources for his material on despotism, his knowledge of foreign religions, cultures, geography and the history of ancient civilizations. These works also provided Montesquieu with the material he needed to work out a kind of incipient comparative economics.

After the publication of the *Persian Letters*, Montesquieu made frequent visits to Paris between 1721 and 1728. But he was also a landowner. As Cohler has noted, he was preoccupied with commerce in a more banal sense, that is, in "the market for his goods." In these years, Montesquieu took a personal interest in the international trade in wine, an experience which seems to have contributed to his later argument for the benefits of *doux commerce* in *The Spirit of the Laws*.[61] Consider, for example, the following confession made in 1742. If the war continues, Montesquieu said, "I shall be forced to go and plant cabbages at La Brede."[62] Consider, as another example, one of Montesquieu's letters to a female friend in Paris. There, Montesquieu confesses that he feels comfortable, even suited, to the world inhabited by his fellow merchants and traders. This despite his noble background, and his growing reputation as a man of letters. "I hear people talk of nothing but grapevines, hard times, and lawsuits," he writes. "... fortunately enough I am fool enough to enjoy all that, that is, to be interested in it."[63]

Montesquieu's life as a merchant informs his views on the compatibility between economic growth, commercialization, modernization, and traditional monarchy. According to Michael Sonenscher, in *Before the Deluge: Public Debt, Inequality, and the Intellectual Origins of the French Revolution*, Montesquieu is, to this day, the writer who "best registered" the dilemmas of the political economy of modern monarchy. Sonenscher's argument is worth summarizing briefly before proceeding. According to Sonenscher, Montesquieu's *Persian Letters* is not merely a satiric novel, but rather, an attempt to articulate the contradiction between virtue and economic greatness. This contradiction is manifest especially in the published version of the *History of the Troglodytes*, in letters 11 to 14. As many others have noted, Montesquieu did not publish the sequel to the story of the Troglodytes. But the sequel sketched in his notebooks contains a crucially important clue as to Montesquieu's intentions. In short, Montesquieu speculated on the possibility of a modern political community that combined great wealth with virtue. In contrast to his public position in the *Persian Letters*, where virtue and wealth appear incompatible, Montesquieu appears more optimistic, in his notebook, that wealth, and virtue may go together. Yet, as Montesquieu pointed out, the compatibility between commerce and virtue requires an unsatisfying resolution: it depends on great leadership, on the good example, the extraordinary leadership, of the king. More problematically still, it depends on a severe system of state control of the economy, combined with censorship, designed to ensure that every subject produces "an honest subsistence." Sonenscher explains the problem as follows: "Once trade was established, for Montesquieu, then the survival of virtue as a ground for distinction would depend on the combined effects of moral example and a rigorous system of censorship." The emergence of harmful distinctions based on wealth would have to be counterbalanced, in Sonenscher's words, by a draconian fiscal system.[64]

According to Sonenscher, Montesquieu developed his argument in two ways, between the publication of the *Persian Letters* in 1721 and *The Spirit of the Laws* in 1748.[65] First, and most broadly, Montesquieu continued to explore and reconsider the compatibility between wealth and virtue. Second, Montesquieu began to be more persuaded of the pacific effects of international trade and mutual exchange. In Sonenscher's view, the warning in the unpublished Troglodyte series was made redundant as a result of these two developments. The system of government exemplified in the English constitution embodied both aspects of thinking on political economy. On the one hand, England showed that it could accommodate distinctions based on wealth, at least, that it could do so within limits, and far more successfully than could imperial Rome. Wealth and virtue might be in tension, but this did not spell ruin for the monarchy, nor would it require a draconian "virtuous" commerce. England also demonstrated that wealth was the basis of power and peace in modern times.

Few scholars disagree with Sonenscher's general outline, but increasingly, they disagree on whether Montesquieu changed his mind a third time. Did Montesquieu settle, with Voltaire, on England, as a superior model, which rendered the conflict between wealth and virtue obsolete?[66] Could the example of England offer a solution to the age-old dichotomy between conquest and commerce?

In the next few chapters, we will see that Montesquieu did indeed make important corrections in his political economy. Montesquieu's reservations in regard to commercial England are not dismissed or ignored. It will be argued, however, that these corrections do not constitute a significant "change of course" as others have suggested. As his reservations deepened, so too did his appreciation of the virtues of the English economic and political system.

"Monsieur Montesquieu" Abroad: 1728–31

Montesquieu found La Brède to be suitable for holidays and reflection, and it was also the place where Montesquieu worked on increasing his income in his vines, fields and pastures. A baron but also a landowner, Montesquieu took pleasure in agriculture, and in applying discoveries from English and Dutch agronomy. In 1726, citing financial difficulties, but also seeking more independence from the court, he sold his office. Depending on the biographer, Montesquieu took almost too much pride in his independence and in his commercial aspirations. To some he seemed obsessed with saving and making money. His devotion to commerce instead of law or politics raised the eyebrows of others, who questioned whether the "philosopher was a miser."[67]

The sale of his charge provided Montesquieu with freedom to travel, and to devote himself to philosophy—an opportunity he took advantage of from 1728 to 1731, in a three-year voyage, which took Montesquieu to Austria, Hungary, Italy, Germany, the United Provinces, and to England, where he would stay for 18 months.

Scholars have suggested that Montesquieu's voyage changed his opinion on the relative advantages of monarchies and republics.[68] According to Cecil Courtney, for example, Montesquieu had republican leanings in the 1720s; one reason why he satirized both the French monarchy and English society in the *Persian Letters*. Over the course of his tour, however, Montesquieu's enthusiasm for classical republics seemed to have waned, replaced by an equally open enthusiasm for the British constitution, which Montesquieu now thought of in a more sophisticated way, as a monarchy with republican features.

Montesquieu stopped first in Vienna, where he met with Prince Eugene of Savoy and his circle of libertine friends and free thinkers.[69] In Venice, Montesquieu sought out Antonio Conti, a popularizer of Newton, and who was influential in introducing Montesquieu to the prince and other leading scientists. In Hungary, Montesquieu recorded his visits to the Hungarian mines, which gave him a chance to return to his earlier interest in geology.[70]

As he traveled, Montesquieu took extensive notes on the relationship between society, politics, and economics in the countries he visited. These would form the basis for his observations later about the essential differences between the political economy of modern states. The Venetian political economy, for example, was unique in a few ways. It depended on "modesty and simplicity" in the manners of the nobles, who were required to "blend with the people, dress like them, and share all their pleasures with them," in order that the people "forget their own weaknesses."[71] To avoid hatreds and jealousies, one of the principle "sources of disorder" in aristocratic states, laws were designed to preserve the appearance of equality. For instance, Montesquieu noted, nobles should not exempt themselves from imposts or levy taxes.[72] Primogeniture, entail, and all the "means invented to perpetuate the greatness of families in monarchical states" were inappropriate in aristocracies. But if shows of great wealth were not compatible with the political system, how would the nobles spend their money? Montesquieu takes note of the circulation of money from nobleman through the brothels, an expedient not exactly recommended by Montesquieu, but in line with the principle that wealth should be dissipated carefully to avoid the appearance of inequality.

When Montesquieu arrived in Rome, it was not primarily the history, or the architecture ancient ruins that were of interest to him, but rather the notable contacts. In Italy, he met Vernet, who would later supervise the publication of *The Spirit of the Laws* at Geneva. He met Athias, a Jewish intellectual who discussed with Montesquieu the connection between Portuguese commerce, trade and the Inquisition. And he met an exile of notoriety, one John Law, nearing the end of his days. What conversations Montesquieu had with the aging and disgraced French Minister of Finance can only be imagined. Montesquieu saved his harsh criticism for the Scottish economist for 20 or more years after his death.[73] Interestingly, Law seems to have taken an interest in Montesquieu. They had a mutual connection in Melon, his secretary, who was around this time only in the draft stages of his *Essai politique sur le commerce*. Of special interest, Law handed over to Montesquieu a manuscript work on French commerce. The contents of that manuscript, and Montesquieu's opinion of it, may never be revealed; the manuscript was destroyed in the Second World War.

In Italy, Montesquieu also met Scipione Maffei, of Verona, a polymath, who, although close with the Jesuits, would later write influential works on usury—arguments that revived the debates and provoked criticism, and likely informed Montesquieu's famous discussion of lending at interest in book 21 of *The Spirit of the Laws*. Returning to Sonenscher's compelling thesis, Montesquieu's travels allowed him to reflect on the great problem he had begun to explore in the *Persian Letters*: was commercial society in fact compatible with virtue in a modern republic?

Viewed from the perspective of Venetian commerce in everyday life, Montesquieu may have realized that his narrative of the Troglodytes, in which commerce and virtue were opposed, was too simplistic. While he apparently found little virtue in the aristocracy,[74] it was also in Italy that he seems to have begun formulating his thoughts on the importance of the connection between poverty and vice. In regions where the people were oppressed by taxes, and where trade was stifled, he observed, there was more crime. The relative poor in more prosperous and commercial regions, by contrast, had more incentive to be honest in their transactions. Such observations were the seeds of the philosophy of commerce, which Montesquieu developed and then condensed into maxims in book 20 of *The Spirit of the Laws*. Commerce corrupts pure mores, but it "polishes and softens barbarous" mores, as is seen every day.[75]

The "World as it Goes"[76]: Montesquieu in England

As we have seen, Montesquieu's interest in England is apparent early in his intellectual career. There are multiple occasions, in the 1720s, in which the baron proposes the thesis that the British nation was the only people who had successfully united empire and commerce.[77] This view was first espoused in the *Persian Letters* Rica, writing to Usbek, describes a library of "modern history." While Rica does not endorse the interpretation of English history in these books, he does seem to be persuaded by the English historians who argue that English liberty has "repeatedly survived" the "flames of discord" because of the people's "impatient" character. He adds that England is also "queen of the seas," a society "unheard of until then," in its ability to combine "commerce with empire."[78]

According to Montesquieu's biographers, he was well read in the English authors well before his travels. But we should not forget that Montesquieu had already developed connections with English intellectuals in France, including Walpole, a member of the Entresol, Waldegrave, and Bolingbroke. How often Montesquieu exchanged notes, jokes, and ideas, with Britain wine merchants in Bordeaux, and the education he received from those encounters, is perhaps interesting to speculate on.

Montesquieu's arrival in London is both the most formative period of his life, and, unfortunately, one of the least well known periods of his intellectual development. In part, this is because there are major sections missing from his England journal. Montesquieu's grandson later burned them in England.[79] Of the papers still in existence, there are 15 pages of *Notes sur l'Angleterre*, first published 1818, and five letters written by Montesquieu while in England, from November 1729 to 1731.[80]

While the "Notes on England" contain fascinating, sometimes cruelly derisive comments on the English people, Montesquieu chose, on his return from his voyages, to emphasize the British constitution as a model for legislators. In his *Considerations*, for example, Montesquieu did not back away from the claim, made earlier, that the English political system is "one of the wisest" in Europe.[81] He did, however, cut back on his obvious enthusiasm. Illustrating the degree to which Montesquieu was subject to pressure from censorship, Montesquieu made a minor but telling change to this passage in *The Spirit of the Laws*. While his Dutch publisher was printing the above copy, Montesquieu arranged for a "cancel" in the copies sold in France, altering the passage to read, "The government of England is wiser" than various ancient and modern republics. Montesquieu of course was not the only, or the first, Frenchman to praise the English regime. Voltaire had traveled to England three years before Montesquieu, in 1726. Voltaire's journey was the basis of his famous portrait of English society in his *Lettres philosophiques* (1734). In contrast to Montesquieu, who suppressed his controversial comparisons to the French system, Voltaire openly celebrated the England subjects not only as more free, and more powerful, but, significantly, more "happy" than their counterparts in the French monarchy. Paul Rahe, in his 2009 *Montesquieu & the Logic of Liberty*, has summarized the importance of this episode in detail.[82] For his efforts, and for his obvious Anglophilia, Voltaire was arrested, his books burned, and the philosopher forced to flee. In turn, Montesquieu pulled his *Reflections on Universal Monarchy in Europe*, the planned "sequel" to *Considerations on the Causes of the Greatness of the Romans and Their Decline* (1734). The third part of the sequel, which would include his reflections on the English political and economic system, did not appear until 1748, in two of the most famous sections of *The Spirit of the Laws*, book 11, Chapter 6, and book 19, Chapter 27.

But it was not just the example of Voltaire that convinced Montesquieu of the necessity to tame his own enthusiasm for the English system. While in England, years before the Voltaire episode, Montesquieu noted that the English—which he much admired for the relative freedom of the press, noting that the king's solution was to levy a tax on slanderous speech, thus paying himself every time he was insulted—were not at all free from censorship. Bolingbroke, he noted, and other authors of *The Craftsman*, had "at least three lawyers" checking each issue of the paper to make sure that it did not contain anything "that would fall afoul of the law."[83]

Montesquieu's voyage to England also necessarily affected his views of England later in *The Spirit of Laws*. We know that Montesquieu had familiarized himself with the writing of Hobbes before his voyage.[84] He was familiar with the writings of Locke, in part, through his contact with the industrious Huguenot refugee, Pierre Coste, who had known Pierre Bayle and John Locke personally. Coste had assisted in the translation of several important Lockean works into French. Both Montesquieu and Voltaire possessed Coste's translation of *Essay concerning Human Understanding*. While Montesquieu's exposure to Locke's *second treatise* is harder to track, Montesquieu had read Mazzel's translation of the *Second Treatise*, even if he did not (in that version) have access to the "Preface" or the *First Treatise*.[85] Even missing the *First Treatise*, there is little reason to doubt that he knew Locke's account of the state of nature, and property—a subject that will occupy us at length in chapter 4. In brief, Montesquieu's interest in England was not solely confined to court politics, as is often assumed.[86] Courtney, for example, rightly states that Montesquieu's interest extended well beyond English political history, the separation of powers, and constitutional engineering.[87] While in England, Montesquieu also appears to have gone through a personal re-evaluation of Machiavelli, whose reputation as an apostle of political evil may have influenced Montesquieu's earlier attempts at drafting a new *Prince*. As a result of conversations with other readers of Machiavelli, during this voyage, however, Montesquieu makes an intriguing note, to the effect that he had learned not to be deceived of this simplistic view.

Perhaps equally or more important for our purposes, Montesquieu came to know *The Craftsman*, copying extensively from passages in 1730 and 1731, as well as *Cato's Letters*. Both of these sources gave Montesquieu a deeper appreciation of, and insight, in to radical English political thought. These and other experiences are evident in the incomplete "Notes on England."

Montesquieu's experience in England also had a significant impact on his development of a philosophy of liberty. Famously, Montesquieu will distinguish in *The Spirit of the Laws* between liberty of the constitution and "liberty of the citizen," the latter a result of a combination of civil laws, arranged correctly, which produce a "tranquility of mind, arising from the opinion each person has of his safety." The germ of this idea can be located in his "Notes on England." Here Montesquieu compared the freedom of the Londoner with the freedom of the Venetian city-dweller. True, English manners he found lacking: "They do not even like themselves. How could they invite us to dinner? They do not invite each other to dinner." But it was precisely this mistrustful aspect of the English character, paired with a commercial spirit, operating in the context of a dynamic, diverse, and free political system, which provided Montesquieu a clue as to the solution of modern politics and the predictable devolution of modern states into despotism.

Montesquieu's ambivalence in regards to English society has—for good reason—led many to suspect that Montesquieu despised English commercialism, and therefore, the British example. The English passion for acquisition is particularly problematic. If left unchecked, Montesquieu warned, the English would become corrupt and lose their freedom. Indeed, he hinted that this process was already underway: "The English no longer deserve their freedom. They sell it to the king; and if the king gave it back to them, they would sell it again." Neither does Montesquieu assume that the English enjoy their liberty in the fuller sense, of being content, or satisfied. In fact, Montesquieu famously argues that they are permanently unsatisfied. "The English are rich, they are free, but they are tormented by their minds. They are weary or disdainful of everything."

Many commentators have made use of this fragility of English happiness to suggest that the "extreme freedom" of English republicanism was ultimately not preferable to the French regime, the survival of which depended on the maintenance of distinctions, manners, and honor. In the following chapter, it will be argued that Montesquieu's ambivalent, often pessimistic, analysis of English freedom was offset in profound ways by his continuing study of political economy. The study of commerce—its nature, its causes, and its consequences—only increased Montesquieu's admiration for the English constitution, as he came to see the full significance of the relationship between commerce, religion, and liberty.

CHAPTER 2

COMMERCE IN *THE SPIRIT OF THE LAWS*

The Promise of Commerce

Book 20 of Montesquieu's *The Spirit of the Laws* opens with two of the most famous, and compelling, arguments in defense of commerce.[1] In the first chapter of book 20, Montesquieu highlights the "good things" that have resulted from the spread of commerce and trade in the realm of mores:

> Commerce cures destructive prejudices, and it is an almost general rule that everywhere there are gentle mores, there is commerce and that everywhere there is commerce, there are gentle mores.
> Therefore, one should not be surprised if our mores are less fierce than they were formerly. Commerce has spread knowledge of the mores of all nations everywhere; they have been compared to each other, and good things have resulted from this.[2]

In the second chapter ("On the Spirit of Commerce"), Montesquieu highlights the most significant effect of commerce in the realm of international relations:

> The natural effect of commerce is to lead to peace. Two nations that trade with each other become reciprocally dependent; if one has an interest in buying, the other has an interest in selling, and all unions are founded on mutual needs.

For many scholars, these arguments are considered not only the most famous of Montesquieu's claims in the fourth part of *The Spirit of the Laws* but also among the most influential arguments of the French Enlightenment. Albert Hirschman, in his *Passions and the Interests*, for example, has argued that Montesquieu was the most powerful advocate of the idea that commerce "softens" or "polishes" mores. Montesquieu, more than any writer of the era, he suggested, gave life to the expression *doux commerce*.³

According to Hirschman, Montesquieu's claims were significant not because they were new, but because they became a byword of the Enlightenment worldview that nations were divided between "advanced" and "backward," "developed and underdeveloped," "polished and barbarous."⁴ The novelty of Montesquieu's contribution to liberal thought was not, on this reading, to be found in the third part of *The Spirit of the Laws*, where Montesquieu outlines his justly celebrated theory of separation of powers. Montesquieu's breakthrough is found, rather, in the fourth part of *The Spirit of the Laws*, in which he first establishes the core connections between commerce and civilization. This, for Hirschman, was the true basis of Enlightenment optimism; that through economic expansion, and the spread of market morality, the world might be rescued from tyranny and barbarism.

Montesquieu's doctrine of *doux commerce* had a powerful hold on readers for a second reason. If the great promise, in the first case, was that commerce could civilize human beings on an individual level, commerce might also lead to more peaceful relations between nations. Here scholars grant Montesquieu his rightful place as the forefather of this powerful idea. Eric Gartzke, for example, has argued that Montesquieu is chiefly responsible for inspiring one of the two major intellectual traditions, one of "two paths," leading up to what we now know as the "liberal peace hypothesis." One tradition, starting with Rousseau, emphasizes the pacifying constraints of democracy and republican institutions. This tradition was extended and developed by Abbé de Saint-Pierre, Bentham, and Kant. The other tradition, beginning with Montesquieu, focuses on economic freedom and market interdependence as the most solid foundation for a liberal peace. This argument was developed and popularized by Adam Smith and Thomas Paine, who agreed, essentially, on the primary mechanism: markets would "abominate" war and, in Paine's words, "diminish the spirit, both of patriotism and military defense."⁵

Hirschman and Gartzke are no doubt right to emphasize Montesquieu's twofold influence, both in popularizing the dichotomy between civilization and barbarism, and in making intelligible for the first time the connection between trade and international peace. Yet, many readers of *The Spirit of the Laws* remain unconvinced, especially of the idea that Montesquieu should be read as an unwavering defender of the commercial liberalism represented by England in book 19 of *The Spirit of the Laws*.⁶ For some, these claims in these opening chapters are suspiciously simple.⁷ For others less sympathetic, they betray an innocent optimism.⁸

According to Pierre Manent, the first argument (that commerce softens mores) has a conventional, even "prosaic" quality to it.[9] More importantly, Montesquieu himself seems to suggest that this softening of mores comes at a steep price to society, in "manners," in the moral fabric of society, and in the high arts and "taste." Montesquieu seems to gloss over these tradeoffs, and this continues to bother scholars who are rightly sensitive to them.

The second argument, linked however fairly to the liberal peace hypothesis, has just the opposite difficulty. It is unnecessary to invoke the horrors of twentieth-century warfare, or the continuing debates on capitalist interdependence. The argument seems over-bold, even utopian.[10]

But what did Montesquieu mean in claiming that commerce cures destructive prejudice? And, is it technically correct to attribute to Montesquieu the innocent view that commerce would render war obsolete?[11]

Despite a renewed interest in Montesquieu's political thought, there is a surprising lack of analytical scrutiny of the fourth part of *The Spirit of the Laws*.[12] In relation to book 20, likely the most widely read, most commentators continue to treat book 20 in a highly selective manner.[13] Humanities scholars generally do not linger on the narrow economic issues, for reasons that will be explored below.[14] Economic historians have not ignored Montesquieu, but the politics of book 20 is often avoided. And so, when book 20 is discussed, it is generally assumed, as in one scholar's estimate, that book 20 is of interest only because it contains a "long analysis of the basic advantages of free trade."[15]

The following two chapters will analyze book 20 of *The Spirit of the Laws* with a view to the political consequences and implications of commerce. The first section reviews Montesquieu's description of the effects of commerce. The second section revisits the causes of commerce. The third section provides a response to the argument, best articulated by Pierre Manent, that commercial activity is "unnatural." The concluding section summarizes the "English formula," which provides the political and moral bearing of Montesquieu's political economy.

The Effects of Commerce

From the beginning, it is clear that Montesquieu had no intention of claiming, as Cobden once argued, that commerce is a "grand panacea." The first signal of his skepticism is seen in the disclaimer with which he opens the book:

> The following would require more extensive treatment, but the nature of this work does not permit it.

The disclaimer is a warning that the maxims of book 20 are not to be treated as philosophic dogma, much less scientific proofs. Montesquieu underscores the difficulty of capturing the economic subject matter of book 20 in a scientific theory by comparing it to a torrential river:[16] "I should like to glide on a tranquil river, I am dragged along by a torrent."

With these two caveats, Montesquieu distances himself from the revolutionary or utopian hope that commerce would transport humankind serenely out of barbarism into a civilized utopia.[17] Montesquieu's language also indicates caution. First, he notes that it is "an *almost* general rule" (*c'est presque une règle générale*) that commerce and gentle mores go together. Second, and more importantly, Montesquieu notes that commerce wields its most powerful effect on "mores" (*moeurs*). Mores are deeper than manners, as he explained earlier in book 19: "The difference between mores and manners is that the first are more concerned with internal, and the latter external, conduct."[18] Commerce, in other words, works to make the *internal conduct* or inner morality of a people less cruel. This leaves open the possibility that commerce will have no effect, or even a pernicious effect, on "manners."[19] More importantly still, this conditional hypothesis leaves open the possibility that commerce will *not* transform nations that are not in fact influenced by a unified or homogeneous set of "mores."[20] The claim that commerce works in a targeted fashion, on mores, is significant. It means, first and foremost, that the effects of commerce may not be universalized without a serious consideration of the makeup of a particular "spirit" of a nation. Some nations, like Sparta and Rome, for example, were dominated particularly by mores.[21] Others, like China and Japan, were dominated by manners and laws. Still other nations were dominated by nature and climate (Montesquieu calls these "savage" nations). If commerce is to be truly effective as a "cure" for what Montesquieu calls "destructive prejudices," it is only in those nations where mores are in fact dominant—indeed, severe.[22]

But then the opposite holds as well. If commerce works particularly well on the "internal conduct" of the citizens, the effects of commerce will not be as noticeable, or curative, in nations where the spirit is dominated by manners, laws, or, somewhat paradoxically, where the spirit of commerce is not checked by other factors. Céline Spector has correctly summarized Montesquieu's point: "Because states cannot renounce all intentions of domination, the commercial harmony of self-interests is considered by Montesquieu only as the desirable *horizon* of modernity and a *factor* for pacification."[23]

That commerce is a "factor" of pacification is a subtlety that was prepared in book 19:

> Many things govern men: climate, religion, laws, the maxims of the government, examples of past things, mores, and manners; a general spirit is formed as a result.
> To the extent that, in each nation, one of these causes acts more forcefully, the others yield to it. Nature and climate almost alone dominate savages; manners govern the Chinese; laws tyrannize Japan; in former times mores set the tone in Lacedaemonia; in Rome it was set by the maxims of government and the ancient mores.

Commerce then is not a cure-all; rather, it is offered as a curative, which may arise spontaneously, but may also be "engineered" for specific cultural circumstances. In the opening chapter of book 20, Montesquieu indicates, albeit in ambiguous terms, that commerce is most effective as an agent of transformation where morality is deeply entrenched, as for example in the classical republics devoted to virtue, or to societies organized by severe forms of religion and superstition.[24]

Montesquieu's view of the relationship between commerce and religion will be explored in chapter 5. Here it is only noted in passing that commerce, in Montesquieu's political economy, is a targeted cure. Moreover, Montesquieu does not deny the possibility of frequent revivals of religious fervor, in the face of the encroachment of secular commercial values. Recall for example the description of the English in book 19. The English are an example of a people who have managed to be "freed from destructive prejudices."[25] The English, he goes on to say, present only one alternative course.

> With regard to religion, as in this state each citizen would have his own will and would consequently be led by his own enlightenment or his fantasies, what would happen is either that everyone would be very indifferent to all sorts of religion of whatever kind, in which case everyone would tend to embrace the dominant religion, or that one would be zealous for religion in general, in which case sects would multiply.[26]

One can see in the above a bifurcated prediction, between a secular or indifferent majority, living under an established religion, and a zealous and competitive minority, living under conditions of a presumed disestablishment. One implication, for Montesquieu's view of political economy, is that the "natural" effects of commerce are not universal laws which can be confidently applied to human affairs with cast-iron certainty. The effects of commerce are variable, not only across "mores" but between different systems of political religion.

If commerce is targeted, especially in the context of "pure mores," does this mean it will have no effect in a society where religion and virtue are not primary in the order of its various laws? The answer points to Montesquieu's sobering judgment, not often discussed. In book 19, in a chapter entitled "Explanation of a paradox about the Chinese," Montesquieu argues that commerce is not likely to penetrate, let alone produce "good things." Commerce, he suggested, has a paradoxical effect. Commerce neither softens *nor* "polishes"; rather, market society exacerbates what Montesquieu calls an "unthinkable avidity for gain."

Readers have suggested that Montesquieu's criticism of Chinese materialism is evidence of an unenlightened Orientalism—or going further, a desire to project on the Orient the Occident's "desire for hegemony." His point is simpler: the good effects of commerce may be canceled out in a regime where religious and economic liberty are not primary.[27] On this reading, Montesquieu's example of China here is reflective of European monarchy; China is merely an example, an illustration of the various combinations of the "spirit" of the laws that can lead to despotism. In this case, the laws and climate work together in a unique combination to produce a hard, precarious existence for the people. Commerce, he seems to suggest, must accompany political and social reform. Without an attention to the civil and political laws, in other words, commerce will not "inspire" what Montesquieu calls, "the good faith natural to it."[28]

The first two chapters thus give rise to what appear to be two contradictory conclusions. On the bright side, commerce may soften barbarous mores and cure destructive prejudices in cultures where religion is repressive. On the other hand, the idea that simple reforms in market relations will humanize the globe and usher in an era of peaceful international relations is exceedingly unrealistic.[29] The example of China is significant as a qualification of the emerging discourse on economic liberalization. The spread of liberal principles may require much more than commercial enlightenment, much more than the spread of the instinctive love of peaceful gain; in short, much more than commerce alone can deliver.[30]

The Causes of Commerce (XX.4–7)

It would be a mistake, nonetheless, to conclude that such caveats indicate Montesquieu's preference for the status quo. Despite the above complexities, it is not true that underneath Montesquieu's liberal exterior, and behind his faith in commercial progress, Montesquieu is anti-modern or reactionary. His cautious relativism, in other words, should not be taken for proof that Montesquieu doubted the merits and perhaps even the superiority of commercial liberalism as expressed in the idealized model of the British constitution. The argument builds more slowly and requires some care to untangle.

Chapter 4 is the beginning of this deeper examination of the causes of commerce. The title of the chapter, "On commerce in the various governments," indicates a second major dimension of Montesquieu's political economy. Put simply, there are different kinds of commerce. We will see that not all kinds of commerce are compatible, more importantly, with the variety of governments and political constitutions. As Montesquieu writes:

> In government by one alone, it [commerce] is ordinarily founded on luxury, and though it is also founded on real needs, its principal object is to procure for the nation engaging in it all that serves its arrogance, its delights, and its fancies. In government by many, it is more often founded on economy.[31]

Here Montesquieu introduces a well known, much analyzed, distinction, between "commerce of luxury" and what he calls "commerce of economy."[32]

Commerce of economy is described as the "practice of gaining little and even of gaining less than any other nation and of being compensated only by gaining continually." The commerce of luxury, on the other hand, while not excluding real needs, is based on different aims and means: the "principal view with which it is carried on is to procure everything that can contribute to the pride, the pleasure, and the capricious whims of the nation."[33]

The extent to which Montesquieu's distinction serves a political purpose is often neglected in the literature, as Catherine Larrère has noted:

> What is remarkable is that the distinction between the two forms of commerce is not really an economic one. In both forms, "everything is exchanged," as [Montesquieu] remarked in one of his *Pensées*. The difference relates to the ends sought in the two forms of commerce. For nations engaged in economical commerce ... commerce itself is the object, and the success of such commerce depends on the ceaseless repetition of the same commercial operations, for it is "founded on the practice of gaining little" in each exchange (XX.4). The commerce of luxury, however, is a means to other ends.[34]

As Larrère observes, the distinction is not significant taken on its own. Of interest is the political question underlying the contest between the two types of commerce. First and foremost, it is not kinds of goods being traded that is most significant; rather, it is the analytical distinction between the two distinct ends or purposes. One is commerce itself (one might say, moderate economic growth). The other is the glory, delight, and vanity of the rulers (luxury and opulence).

Viewed in this light, the difficult question suddenly arises as to which economic ends are more or less appropriate for modern governments—in particular, the modern *moderate* state. The question of which form— republic or monarchy—is more conducive to modern liberty is now highly significant, as part of Montesquieu's political philosophy. Are republics in fact superior to monarchies in securing liberty, given this new tension, this new choice, between the commerce of economy, which relies on frugality, and a modified "commercial morality," for the sake of solid economic growth?

Here, it is sufficient to note that this contest—between republics and monarchies—will play out in the background of the rest of chapter 20. Politics and human psychology will resonate in every topic, from the appropriate limits on tariffs and duties in popular governments (XX.7), to the desirability of banks and trading companies in monarchies (XX.10), all the way down to questions of contract law, arising from "ordinary civil contracts" and the appropriate kinds of penalties for civil debts in different political situations (XX.8–XX.15).

Montesquieu elaborates on three conditions for a successful "commerce of economy." First, the people must be able to practice what is now popularly called "delayed gratification." In Montesquieu's words, economic growth is a result of "gaining little and even of gaining less than any other nation." But this implies self-restraint, moderation, and in turn, a social climate where work is valued, where frugality is a virtue, and where moderate spending is self-imposed.

Second, a strong commerce of economy requires a particular type of "daring," or ambition, which Montesquieu says is "not to be found in monarchies." A commerce of economy is not without great risk.[35] Because the individual trader must be willing to risk his own money, time, and effort, this person of "commercial daring"[36] must be relatively free, or unobstructed in his hopes to improve his "position," to move up in the world.[37] Implicit in this condition are two important social and political factors: a government that protects property; and a significant degree of social mobility. We will return to these two topics in chapters 4 and 6.

Third, trust. A successful commerce of economy requires a high degree of confidence in the laws, institutions, and even fellow citizens and leaders. It is "one's belief that one's prosperity is more certain in these states [that] makes one undertake everything, and because one believes that what one has acquired is secure," writes Montesquieu. He continues: "One dares to expose it in order to acquire more; only the means for acquisition are at risk; now, men expect much of their fortune." In which government is civic trust more likely to be found? From book 8, it is apparent that Montesquieu finds this quality, of mutual trust and stable expectations, in popular states. For Montesquieu, it is a good bet that this trust will diminish in proportion to the size and extent of the state.[38]

If the psychological conditions of the commerce of economy are themselves dependent on the political situation, and if it is true that the qualities of moderation, risk-taking, and mutual trust and confidence are qualities that only flourish in popular states, we can suggest the following principle, relating to Montesquiue's larger political economy. Republics are superior to monarchies because only they can generate the kind of citizens who will create long-term, stable, predictable economic growth.

At least three objections are anticipated. First, it is not clear *why* the old-fashioned commerce of economy is desirable in itself—why the *end* of commerce itself is more desirable than luxury and national glory. That waits to be seen. Second, it is not clear from Montesquieu's presentation whether the distinction between the commerce of economy and a luxurious commerce is, practically speaking, significant. As scholars often point out, "one commerce leads to another."[39] Is the distinction meaningless if, as Montesquieu himself suggests, it is bound to break down? And does this not imply, on Montesquieu's own grounds, that all commerce is reducible to one type of commerce, one end, to which all others eventually lead—toward luxury and economic inequality?

A third problem arises, in connection to these quandaries. If the commerce of economy tends to luxurious commerce, and if human beings naturally drift in the direction of luxury and pleasure, to what extent are the character traits desirable (let alone achievable) in themselves? So far, Montesquieu has only suggested that moderation, a work ethic, ambition, and trust, are necessary.

To what extent are these traits natural to human beings?

Commerce and Human Nature

Any attempt to clarify the political economy of Montesquieu must at least come to grips with the complexities of Montesquieu's view of human nature. Not surprisingly, there is disagreement in the literature on this very question. A few scholars believe that there is enough evidence in *The Spirit of the Laws* to answer Yes, that Montesquieu did in fact believe that commerce in the sense of "the commerce of economy" was "natural" to man, rooted in the soul, and that Montesquieu set out to defend the idea that commerce was the "most adequate response to the needs of human nature."[40]

From book 1, Montesquieu appears to defend an "earthly" and acquisitive understanding of human nature. While it is true that Montesquieu explicitly rejects Hobbes' assertion that man's first desire is the domination and subjugation of other men, it is also the case that Montesquieu, like Locke, emphasizes commercial or material pleasures, or to state his starting point more succinctly, comfortable self-preservation.

In contrast to Locke's presentation in the *Second Treatise*, however, humans have at least two unselfish natural bonds—compassion, or "humanity," and a capacious sexual drive, which "unites men and tends to bring peace and security."[41] These two aspects, for Montesquieu's liberal interpreters, are sufficient to show that the germ of economic man is there, from the start. While it is true that Montesquieu feels the need to "adorn" the books on commerce with a kind of poetry (since there is something ugly about commerce in comparison to Greek culture) this does not mean that Montesquieu doubted that commerce was *worth* adorning, and for this very reason: material acquisition is rooted in the soul and is a natural drive, a point further underscoring Montesquieu's preference for limited, liberal government.[42]

Pierre Manent has explored this question, but arrives at a different conclusion in his *La cité de l'homme*.[43] In Manent's view, Montesquieu neither provides evidence for, nor believes himself, that man is commercial "by nature."[44] It is true that commerce is "the only thing that softens mores as a general rule"[45] but there is no evidence, at least according to Manent, that the activity of human beings and the formation of commercial cities have their origins in a positive choice, made "either by the individual or the group."[46]

The difference of interpretation is not unimportant, not least, for an accurate view of Montesquieu's economic philosophy. In contrast to Thomas Pangle, author of *Montesquieu's Philosophy of Liberalism: A Commentary on the Spirit of the Laws*, and more recently, *The Theological Basis of Liberal Modernity in Montesquieu's Spirit of the Laws*, Manent focuses on the philosophical question of choice and free will. If the commercial society is one "not chosen," and if the non-human things (climate, nature, history) force what Manent calls "economic man" into being, there would be little or no value in the attempt to justify modern commercial republicanism, by connecting it back to human nature. Manent finds it futile to "seek in the human soul the positive mainspring of this activity."[47] True, as Manent concedes, Montesquieu's *The Spirit of the Laws* does provide a "favorable account" of the natural *effects* of commerce. But this does not demonstrate that commerce is any more natural, than, say, the classical republic devoted to virtue. The idea that commerce is merely a *reaction* to non-human forces is illustrated well by an example from book 20. Manent points to Montesquieu's well-known description of the commercial republicanism of Marseilles, a people said to live in a "necessary retreat" in the "midst of a stormy sea." The people of Marseilles, Manent points out, did not have any other choice *but* to live by the commerce of economy. Forced to live on the islands and shoals, by necessity, they worked hard, encouraged thrift, and rewarded moderation. Does such an example illustrate commerce as a natural "feature" of human nature? For Manent, this proves nothing but to make a virtue of necessity, as we would say today. In Manent's words, the people of Marseilles prove that commerce is only a necessary means, that is, "to a necessary end, a necessary escape."

Manent's analysis of this question is profound and illuminating, but I would like to focus on the way he poses the problem.[48] Manent is undoubtedly right in at least one important respect. Montesquieu does not show *precisely* how the origins of commercial civilization are connected to the fundamental, unchanging nature of man. Montesquieu does indeed emphasize the violence, the hunger, and severity of nature at the very genesis of commercial civilization. Chapter 5, especially, seems to betray Montesquieu's own conviction that commerce is merely a reaction. And yet, Manent's argument is incomplete, and there are a number of important passages which are overlooked.

First, the analysis does not account for the *progression* of the chapters in book 20, from harsh origins in Chapter 5, to less harsh, and more fully human types of commercial civilization in Chapters 6 and 7. We will see that these three chapters are a trio. They present three accounts, not one, of the origins of commercial society. These accounts are also an ascent. The commerce of economy begins as a mere response to the barrenness of nature in places like Marseilles (chapter 5). But it then evolves, transforms, and is elevated, as a respectable substitute for human ambition among the Dutch gamblers and whale hunters (chapter 6). Finally, it becomes tempered and integrated with political and religious liberty in a rationalized account of England (chapter 7).

Looking at these chapters more closely will show that Montesquieu did not abandon the question of the naturalness of commerce entirely. Montesquieu does not, as the "peak" of Enlightenment thought, embody a "forfeiture" of nature or reason as norm, as Manent suggested.[49] The following trio of chapters provide small, but vital, clues as to why commerce may be defended as more than a necessary escape from violence, harassment, severity, and the general discomfort of being alive.

The Spirit of Commerce in Marseilles, Holland, and England

We begin by noticing, first, that these chapters are connected to Montesquieu's mysterious comment, made in book 5, Chapter 6, in which he claims that the "spirit of commerce" brings with it *"en train"* the spirit of "frugality, economy, moderation, work, wisdom, tranquility, order, and rule." Montesquieu's description of the people of Marseilles, in Chapter 5 of book 20 are perhaps the embodiment of that claim. But they are also, importantly, the very prototype and essence of a people who engage in the "commerce of economy":

> Marseilles, a necessary retreat in the midst of a stormy sea, Marseilles, where all the winds, the shoals, and the coastline order ships to put in, was frequented by sea-faring people. The barrenness of its territory made its citizens decide on economic commerce.

At first glance, the opening of this chapter looks and *sounds* like a kind of paean to a commercial people.[50] Could this be Montesquieu's way of indicating the similarity, perhaps even the ultimate superiority, of modern Marseilles over its ancient analogue? The poetic quality to the passage does indeed remind us of Athens, as others have suggested.[51] But it betrays—I would argue emphasizes—a particular *mood* that is, in itself, an indication of the *problem* of Marseilles as a model of a commercial republic.

Marseilles is gritty and barren, and the description is dark, even somber. Here is a people "forced" to choose a way of life because of the "barrenness" of the land, and the violence of the seas. In the next paragraph, Montesquieu repeats the same lyrical pattern of the opening paragraph. The style of the passage complements the utterly bleak imagery:

> It has been seen everywhere that violence and harassment have brought forth economic commerce among men who are constrained to hide in marshes, on islands, on the shoals, and even among dangerous reefs.

The question being raised here implicates the revolutionary-liberal reading of Montesquieu: why should such bleakness be deserving of such poetry?

To answer this, it is necessary to review Montesquieu's other descriptions of Marseilles in *The Spirit of the Laws*. Marseilles is first mentioned in book 7, ironically perhaps, a book that focuses on luxury (the full title is "Consequences of the different principles of the three governments in relation to sumptuary laws, luxury, and the condition of women"). Marseilles, he says, was the "wisest of the republics of her time."[52] Montesquieu means to say that Marseilles was wise in an narrowly economic sense: "dowries could not exceed one hundred ecus in silver and five in clothing."[53] Later in book 8 it becomes clearer why Montesquieu considers Marseilles worthy of great admiration. In this passage, Montesquieu emphasizes its peaceful nature, praising Marseilles for its political neutrality in foreign policy: "The republic of Marseilles never underwent great shifts from lowliness to greatness; thus, it always governed itself with wisdom; thus, it preserved its principles."[54]

The next important passage appears in book 11, where Montesquieu highlights a unique and in some ways, alarming, aspect of Marseilles' constitution. In the fifth chapter, we discover that the *object* of Marseilles' government is not glory, like Athens, or liberty, like England, but commerce itself.[55] From this sketch of these three passages, we can conclude that Montesquieu admires three important aspects of this model of a commercial republic: frugality, prudent neutrality or independence in foreign policy, and a focus on steady economic growth through trade rather than conquest or accumulation of gold and silver.

To make this point more clear it is necessary to sift out more clearly that which is worthy of the poetry in chapter five, and the cold facts. Later in *The Spirit of the Laws*, for example, Montesquieu indicates that Marseilles was something of an accident. Its "glory," he notes, consists not in any great achievement, but because it merely *avoided* being conquered by Rome.[56] Thereafter, when Montesquieu raises the topic of Marseilles for the last time, he gives this people a rather frugal burial—nothing like the epitaph he will give to England in chapter 7. True, Marseilles was never wholly conquered from outside forces. It died a more subtle death, and was forgotten by history when it was ruined by civil wars that had an arbitrary character, in which "one had blindly to choose a party."

Marseilles, one could say, is a portrait of commerce that should be hung in a gallery next to the other commercial republics. Its obvious flaw, it should be apparent, is that Marseilles is not a republic at all. Marseilles was a city, a trading center, and a port. So it should not be a surprise that the commercial people of Marseilles are not described as free.[57] Lacking political independence, they pursue commerce as their object.[58]

To end here begs a number of questions or assumptions. The first is that Marseilles is the *peak* example of a commercial people, as opposed to the starting point of a longer argument. Recall, moreover, that Montesquieu had not only emphasized the distinction between economic commerce and the commerce of luxury; after having made that distinction, Montesquieu gave six historical examples of commercial republics, some ancient, some modern: Tyre, Carthage, Marseilles, Florence, Venice, and

Holland. Later this total is reduced from the original six to four: Tyre, Venice, Holland, and Marseilles.[59]

Such observations are of course only suggestive, but they do show, at the least, that Marseilles cannot be the pinnacle. What then can we say about the other two commercial peoples he describes, in Venice and Holland?

In book 11, Montesquieu makes it clear that Venice[60] is a commercial dinosaur, much less relevant than it once was. Today, he says, "France, England, and Holland" carry on "nearly all the navigation and commerce of Europe."[61] Holland, then, *not* Marseilles, is the more politically relevant, historically stable, financially strong, and theoretically important model of all the original six republics. In short, Manent's (1998) assumption that Marseilles is a benchmark, Montesquieu's final word, is not ultimately supportable.[62]

Montesquieu's description of Holland marks the beginning of a refinement on the example of Marseilles. It is important to note in advance, however, that it has much in common with the gloomy Marseilles. Like Marseilles, Holland has its origins in bare necessity. The people are commercial not primarily because of an original choice, but because of an odd coincidence of geography. Montesquieu refers to the harsh, relatively unfertile lowlands, where defensive options are numerous and navigation (of waterways and canals) naturally conducive to commerce. Like Marseilles, Holland is populated by hardy, industrious individuals, who have been *forced* to work the land and cultivate the virtues necessary for survival through trade. The land has been "made inhabitable by the industry of men," Montesquieu notes in book.[63] Again, necessity plays a vital role. The land could not be "abandoned to indifference or caprice." This is the proposed origin of the stereotype as a commercial people—a fact that Montesquieu also, importantly, relates to moderate government, that is, to the existence of the "legitimate power of a monarch."

So we see that Holland shares this same theoretical difficulty: as in Marseilles, the people are *compelled* to their industriousness, which only further begs the question of whether human beings, in most normal conditions, would choose to live as they do. Physical causes, not moral causes, appear to dominate the Dutch no less than they dominated the people of Marseilles.[64]

Unlike Marseilles, however, the continued attachment of the Dutch to commerce, as a way of life, is much harder to pin down on physical causes alone. Significantly, Montesquieu's analysis of Dutch trade makes it much more difficult to disentangle the origins of Dutch commerce from the origins of Dutch liberty. That is to say, Dutch commercialism is co-extensive with a strong and deeply rooted attachment to political and religious liberty. While they are infused no less than Marseilles by the "spirit of commerce,"[65] they also symbolize a spirit of liberty and political independence that was missing from the example of Marseilles. Like the English in book 19 (and unlike Marseilles in book 20) the Dutch are fiercely independent, proud, and willing to fight to protect both their commerce *and* their liberty.[66] This character of the Hollanders is best illustrated in book 8, where Montesquieu singles out the Dutch towns for having been the first nation to successfully thwart Spanish despotism in the Low Countries. In book 28 Montesquieu makes a similar argument. There, he ascribes to the Dutch an "indomitable humor" and a "rebellious spirit" that he says can be located even further back in the historical struggle of the early Saxons against the spreading empire of the Franks.[67]

Montesquieu had explored this aspect of the Dutch "spirit" many years before, in a memorable passage in the *Persian Letters*. Holland, he argued, managed to *combine* the spirit of commerce with the spirit of liberty. In one scene, Usbek marvels at the soaring birth rates in the Low Countries. For Usbek, the willingness of the Dutch people to propagate is proof that they have both liberty *and* affluence. According to Usbek, this is the greatest attraction of commercial republics: "Nothing is more attractive to foreigners," he writes, "than liberty and affluence, freedom's invariable companion; the first is sought for its own sake, while deprivation draws people to those countries where affluence reigns."[68]

Holland, then, might be thought of as a sort of "bridge" between Marseilles and England. Like Marseilles, it is dominated by a spirit of commerce that arises out of "deprivation" and a harsh original condition. But like England, it has a spirit of liberty[69] that is sought, in Usbek's words, "for its own sake." The one feature is explainable by necessity; the other feature is attributable to human choice and reason. Both of these strands are intertwined—they seem to coil back into a distant and obscure Saxon past, making it impossible to decipher exactly which came first.

There is a hint, however, that the political institutions which contribute to Dutch liberty have evolved alongside and in pace with their commercial culture. In brief, their political institutions are much superior to Marseilles. We find out in books 9 and 10, for example, that Holland has a confederal arrangement, representation, and an empire built on an extension of commerce rather than on territorial conquest. It is true that these institutions do not breed virtuous citizens. Their commercial morality is not as strict as it is in Marseilles. One is likely to find more gamblers and whalers than honest merchants. The representatives are certainly less than virtuous.[70] But Holland, unlike Marseilles, or any other previous commercial people for that matter, has secured a tangible liberty which complements and undergirds its commercial success. Through its defensive, confederal arrangement, it is able to avoid the imperial blunders which Montesquieu says ruined the offensive minded imperialism of the old commercial empires, like Carthage. It is less democratic than the city of Marseilles, but nonetheless representative. This popular element, though crude and unsophisticated from the standard of the British unwritten constitution, increases its odds of survival by increasing the chances it will avoid the factionalism and internal corruption. This fact reminds us of the turmoil that reduced the city-port of Marseilles to insignificance.[71]

It would be misleading to suggest, however, that the Dutch represent a new ideal form of government. Its confederal arrangement is primitive, and not without flaws.[72] Still, Holland is an advance on Marseilles in other important ways, as can be seen in chapter 6, which is entitled "Some effects of a great navigation."[73] Here Montesquieu raises two intriguing puzzles. First, why do the merchants here seem happy to engage in economic trade when the profit margins appear to be so small? Second, why is it that investors in commercial societies like this are willing to participate in unprofitable ventures (whale hunting), which almost "never returns what it costs?"

These two puzzles may not appear weighty, in the scheme of things. But in answering them, Montesquieu addresses two essential features of the Dutch that further distinguishes and provides clarity to his particular view of the importance of political economy in the modern world.

The solution to the first mystery is easily explained. The merchants in Holland are in fact quite happy to make small sacrifices, and to "gain very little," in the short run, because they do not expect—as the people of Marseilles *must*—to be practicing economic commerce all their lives. The merchants in Holland are lured into the discipline of economic trade because they know that there is a promise of much bigger rewards in the future.[74] Montesquieu notes that a Dutch wine merchant, for example, will be satisfied to gain nothing by importing expensive French wine—if he can make a killing on resale further to the north.[75]

As a second example, Montesquieu describes the seeming paradox of a Dutch captain who will be quite willing to import loads of marble, or timber, at little or no additional extra charge in the domestic market. Why? The captain does this because he needed ballast for his ship, which, the reader can assume, is loaded with other goods by virtue of which he expects to make a handsome profit. From this, we see that the Dutch practice the "economy of commerce" because it is to their advantage in most cases. But they are no way *constrained* to practicing the commerce of economy, in a strict sense. Unlike the commerce of economy in the port city of Marseilles, which is merely a "retreat" from hardship and suffering, and is laced with fear, Hollanders base their trade on adventure, on the expansion of human possibilities, on the universal human hope of getting filthy rich.

The second mystery is harder to explain. What may account for the enormous risk, and the great investment, which is required of the whaling captains, who go to sea with the knowledge that they will likely come out at a loss? Montesquieu's answer is worth quoting in full, for it reveals the other face—the most charming feature—of the commerce of economy, otherwise obscured in chapter 5 on Marseilles:

> Those who have been employed in the ship, those who have provided the rigging, the gear, and the provisions, are also those who take the principal interest in the hunt. Even if they[76] lose on the hunt, they have come out ahead on the equipage. This commerce is a kind of lottery, and each one is seduced by the hope of a lucky number. Everyone loves to play, and the most sober people willingly enter the play when it does not have the appearance of gambling, with all its irregularities, its violence, its dissipation, the loss of time, and even of life. (XX.6)

This passage may not inspire the faithful, or capture the imaginations of ambitious individuals. But it captures the very human spirit of industry which pervades Dutch society. We see that commerce in Holland is close to gambling, although of a more "sober" form. Holland is a place where Locke's "rational and industrious" man would be happy to call home, because there is no upper limit, so to speak, on gain.

It is now possible to explain the important difference between Marseilles and Holland, and therefore, an important qualification of Manent's (1998) critique. On the one hand, the Dutch look corrupt—even by the standards of a commercial people of Marseilles who display all the virtues listed in book 5. By comparison to these seafaring merchants, the people of Marseilles look stern and austere. And yet, it would be an error to conclude that Montesquieu viewed this corruption in the literal sense—of a corruption of what it means to be human or a corruption of human nature.[77] On the contrary, Montesquieu implies here that this more energetic form of commerce taps in to a deep and universal desire to better one's condition and to pursue commercial ambition.[78] Holland is a place where ambition is not limited, as it was in the old republics, to a "single desire."[79] In Holland, humans gamble soberly. They take adventurous but not insane risks, and are united by "whale hunting." In Holland, "Everyone loves to play." Commerce is a seduction, and

Montesquieu notes that it can be ruinous in many ways—not unlike the lottery. But Montesquieu does not equate commercial ambition with the lottery simply. Commercial risk only has the appearance of gambling.[80] Holland, to summarize, is an advance in two ways. It has an "errant" or adventuring aspect, which taps into human ambition, and also a romantic, seductive appeal, which is connected in Montesquieu's philosophy of human nature to *eros*.[81] Commerce is natural insofar as it provides an outlet for these universal desires. In solving these two trade puzzles, Montesquieu also highlights what is lacking in his presentation of the origins of commercial civilization in Marseilles. Overlooked was the romance, and the adventure; a subtle foreshadowing of the epic which Montesquieu will pen for commerce in the next book. We might even go further, and suggest that the "lottery" of commerce in its later stages is Montesquieu's way of describing a kind of natural compensation for the bleakness of its origins, for the desolation, misery, and hardship which forced human beings to trade, and to work so hard to "replace what nature refused them."[82]

The English Formula

Like Marseilles, though, Holland is imperfect, even as an abstraction. Charles-Edouard Levillain has explored these difficulties in very fine historical detail. In his "Glory without Power? Montesquieu's trip to Holland in 1729 and his vision of the Dutch fiscal-military state," Levillain finds it impossible to match the historical Holland with Montesquieu's version in *The Spirit of the Laws*. As Levillain explains, this mismatch is not owing to Montesquieu's lack of knowledge of the Dutch republic, but rather, to the fluctuating nature of Dutch political events between 1729 and 1748. In his words, "the Dutch model remained somewhat elusive in Montesquieu's broader understanding of the paradigm of republican regimes."

It is apparent, in any case, that Montesquieu had serious reservations about Holland as a *theoretical* model. There are many direct comparisons between Holland and England, for example, which serve the purpose sufficiently, and which help to explain why the English nation represents an advance on the Dutch commercial towns.

The earliest direct comparison between England and Holland appears in the *Persian Letters* (131), where Holland is described as "that *other* queen of the seas." In this passage, Rica is touring a European library, and is reporting on what is ostensibly a grand survey of world history. The library tour is a literary device. It allows Montesquieu to explore some of the historical themes that will become the basis of some of his more developed observations about the origins of modern republics in *The Spirit of the Laws*. It thus gives us an opportunity to see how Montesquieu might have viewed the Dutch republic in the "paradigm of republican regimes." When Rica comes to the section of books on the history of Holland, his "learned friend" and tour guide singles out one singular aspect. The tour guide points out that the Dutch have a remarkable talent in extending their commercial reach (he notes, for example, that the Dutch merchants not only command respect in Europe, but are so "formidable" overseas that Asian kings bow down before Dutch merchants). What is revealing about this gloss on Dutch commercial imperialism is that he is silent about Dutch politics and culture. The English histories, on the other hand, are "close by" on the same shelf and these books praise England on two dimensions. Unlike Holland, whose glory rests solely on its commercial exploits, England's glory rests on its ability to secure liberty (the tour guide says it is being praised by "the historians of England" for the way in which liberty "repeatedly survives the flames of discord"). Here we see why England and Holland deserve to be on the same shelf. Both are entitled to be called "queen of the seas." Yet the tour guide subtly points out that history has already reserved a loftier perch for England. In England, commerce is not more valued than security, to the individual liberty of the English citizen. In this little scene, we see a hint of Montesquieu's early view that England will be remembered by future historians more for its modern constitution than for its commercial or economic achievements.[83]

This passage in letter 131 was written at least seven years before Montesquieu visited England in 1729. It is therefore interesting for a second reason, as follows. The passage allows us to see that Montesquieu did not change his mind when he visited Holland, on his way to England. Here is an illuminating passage from Montesquieu's "Notes sur l'Angleterre" written during that voyage:

> In London, liberty and equality. London liberty is a liberty of respectable people, in which it differs from Venice, which is a liberty to live obscurely and with [prostitutes] and to marry them. London equality too is an equality of the respectable people, in which it differs from the liberty of Holland, which is a liberty of the rabble.[84]

In this passage, Montesquieu is shown working through the range of potential kinds, or combinations, of liberty and equality that might give different hues, in different social contexts, to commercial life. While there are other passages in which Montesquieu is highly critical of the

English as a people, here, it is enough to note that he thought that a respectable liberty was compatible with a respectable equality.[85]

Returning to chapter 7, in *The Spirit of the Laws* we see further confirmation that England is meant to symbolize a theoretical achievement, a standard by which to judge other commercial peoples. The chapter is entitled "The spirit of England concerning commerce," and it contains what may be the essential formulation of England as an ideal.

> Other nations have made commercial interests give way to political interests: England has always made its political interests give way to the interests of its commerce.
>
> This is the people in the world who have best known how to take advantage of these three great things at the same time: religion, commerce, and liberty.

Buried in the middle of Montesquieu's first book on commerce, this passage points to the model of England, not as a best regime, but as a model of political economy. Marseilles and Holland are false summits.

Commerce, liberty, and religion: these three "great things" hold England together in a balance.[86] Compare, for interest, Montesquieu's parallel formula for Roman greatness in book 8. Rome, he argued, was a "vessel held by two anchors: religion and mores."[87] The difference between these two formulars are worth consideration. In England, mores are relaxed and commercialized, religion is privatized and moderated, institutions take over for virtue; the end result is liberty.

Yet this formula for English liberty appears in an awkward position, in the middle of chapter 7, in what seems to be a dry intellectual series of speculations on trade policies. Montesquieu could have placed this important formula elsewhere (for example, in XIX.27, the chapter dedicated to the topic). Why here in the context of political economy?

From Montesquieu's private writings, it is clear that Montesquieu had severe misgivings about England, particularly, as an historical reality. Montesquieu was well aware, for example, of the extent of corruption in England. He was openly critical of the extent to which "money is sovereignly esteemed." In his "Notes sur l'Angleterre" Montesquieu notes that "the English people are no longer proud of their liberty. They sell it to their king; and if the king gave it back, they would sell it to him again."[88] Scholars often point to Montesquieu's letter to Domville to demonstrate Montesquieu's admiration for the English. Responding to Domville's anxiety regarding the future of English liberty, Montesquieu writes, "in Europe the last sigh of liberty will be given by an Englishman...your liberty is linked to your commerce and your commerce is linked in some fashion to your existence."[89] But Montesquieu is less than enthusiastic about English commercialism in a draft of that same letter, noting, "your riches are causing your corruption".[90] In *The Spirit of the Laws*, Montesquieu plainly expresses his reservations: "It is not for me to examine whether at present the English enjoy this liberty or not. It suffices for me to say that it is established by their laws, and I seek no further."[91]

The strength of its constitution, on the other hand, allows it to survive what Montesquieu calls the "furthest point of liberty." Although England has an "extreme *political* liberty"[92] it manages to avoid the spirit of extreme liberty that can destroy most republics.[93] Importantly, Montesquieu notes that England allows its political interests to give way to the "interests of its commerce." This is distinct from the model of Holland which he argues is "affected *only* by the spirit of commerce." England preserves a place for religion, even an established religion, although it does not give way to religious zealotry.[94] Also significant is the administration of justice, and its sophisticated criminal laws, which includes a vigorous respect for property and for individual security; and the right to believe in one's own god—or none at all.[95]

Conclusion

This chapter has shown that, first, commerce is no "grand panacea," and that Montesquieu intended for his reader to see why its effects are both targeted and variable, dependent on mores and on political religion. Second, Montesquieu's distinction between economic and luxury commerce is not simply descriptive, as scholars have often assumed. Montesquieu's political economy clearly favors the "commerce of economy," while being mindful of the ways in which it naturally drifts to the opposite.

Finally, we considered a profound challenge to the "liberal" interpretation of Montesquieu's political economy. Are the character traits associated with a commercial society natural, or good, and are they rooted in the human soul? In partial agreement with Pierre Manent, we paused to consider this central question. By contrast to Manent's critique of Montesquieu, we emphasized the literary "ascent" from Marseilles as a primitive model of a commercial port, to Holland, where commerce is a mix, of choice and necessity. It was suggested, in conclusion, that Holland represents a bridge to England, where the tension between harsh natural origins and promising new ends is blurred or forgotten.

The chapter on England is something of an early climax, however. While the memorable formulation shows conclusively that Montesquieu praised the English system in the abstract, the precise reason for this success is not entirely explained in book 20. In the following chapter, we turn to a different set of questions. If the British constitution "prevails" over, and is successful, as Montesquieu suggests, in balancing, and containing, the powerful forces of commerce, religion, and liberty, to what extent does it do so *as* a commercial republic? Thus far, a core interpretive difficulty of Montesquieu's political economy has not yet been addressed. England is a republic that "hides" under the form of monarchy. As is well known, honor is the dominant passion of monarchies, for Montesquieu. More to the point, honor, on Montesquieu's own grounds, is disdainful of material acquisition. Rewarded by preferences, sustained by distinctions, honor would seem to be incompatible with commercial society, let alone, a commercial republic.[96] If honor and commerce are to go together, either the meaning of honor must be radically challenged, or commerce must be made honorable.

In chapter 3, it will be argued that Montesquieu's new political economy contains both strategies. To see how, we will now turn to examine Montesquieu's controversial ban on a commercial nobility in the context of the French monarchy, the subject of the remaining chapters of book 20.

CHAPTER 3

COMMERCE, HONOR, AND MONARCHY

The Politics of Free Trade

Scholars generally do not invite students and readers to look at the second half of book 20 closely. The neglect of this section of Book 20 leaves the political dimension of Montesquieu's argument for free trade in modern monarchy not only incomplete; it has also tended to add to the confusion surrounding Montesquieu's larger political goal in *The Spirit of the Laws*. In the second half of book 20, Montesquieu mounts an important challenge to the tradition of honor, while preparing for a much longer discussion, in book 21, of the ways in which commerce as a profession can be made honorable.

The major reasons for the neglect of book 20 are worth repeating. According to Joseph Schumpeter, Montesquieu's economic philosophy in this part of *The Spirit of the Laws* is unimportant; he made no breakthroughs, Schumpeter argued, because he, Montesquieu, was primarily a sociologist, and therefore lacking the conceptual tools of the "economists."[1] Likewise, Montesquieu scholars view his analysis of trade as piecemeal, or simply a rehearsal of common criticisms of mercantilist theory. Economic historians point out that Montesquieu's economic writings were overshadowed within just a few years of their publication by more sophisticated and superior works of political economy.[2]

The assumptions underlying the disregard of Montesquieu's writings on trade in book 20 are not shared by those who have studied the political dimension of Montesquieu's economic philosophy. Henry C. Clark's *Compass of Society* (2007) is just one such exception. According to Clark, Montesquieu's discussion of trade in book 20 is inseparable from his view of monarchical politics, in particular, the controversy over the idea of "corporate privilege" in the old regime:

> The relationship between trade and corporate privilege was...a crucial element of Montesquieu's *The Spirit of the Laws*, published at the end of the Austrian war in 1748. The President's discussion of commerce and related issues had more effect on the relevant public discourse than any other single work during this period, a fact that is coming to be better appreciated by recent scholarship.[3]

In Clarks' analysis, book 20 is not simply an inchoate economic theory of free trade. It contains, rather, a subversive analysis of the tensions between commerce, nobles, princes, and society.[4]

Skeptics of Clark's view often repeat a longstanding criticism, in brief, that Montesquieu was a conservative monarchist who never abandoned the political economy of the old regime. According to the simplest form of this argument, Montesquieu's trade policies are simply reflections of common mercantile assumptions and theories.[5] A more sophisticated version of this argument treats Montesquieu's discussion of the politics of trade as revealing his preference for the political "status quo." The second half of Book 20 is an attempt to "defend the monarchy from republican attacks."[6] Still others, especially those suspicious of a "liberal" or revolutionary reading, contend that it is misguided to view Montesquieu as a forerunner of the project to "import" or extend the English model of commerce to France. This project, associated with the group of Gournay in the 1750s, not only militated in favor of the recognition of the importance of commerce. Gournay and his followers would push to foster its development "by all means possible" including—if necessary—the involvement of the nobility in commerce and trade.[7]

To sort out Montesquieu's position on a mercantile nobility, it is useful to review Montesquieu's basic case for monarchy from an economic point of view. Monarchies have distinct economic advantages over pure republics in many aspects of commercial policy.[8] By contrast to popular governments, monarchies enjoy efficiency in the "execution of public business" (V.10). Virtue is "less needed" in a monarchy (III.3). The principle of honor—itself a form of selfishness—acts as a stimulus for industry (III.7; V.19). Moreover, monarchies are uniquely resilient to the corrupting effects of luxury, traditionally conceived as the ruin of republics, which depend on the love of equality and the cultivation of public spiritedness (VII.4).[9]

To these advantages—efficiency, self-interested honor, and stability—Montesquieu added one more: sexual freedom. In a society where sexual mores are less pure, Montesquieu argued, there thrives a "commerce" between men and women that stimulates consumption. On the one hand, the heightened intensity of sexual commerce stimulates male *vanity*. While vanity, in Montesquieu's view, is both the well-spring of "innumerable goods" *and* "infinite evils" (XX.8), its causes cannot be controlled; they must be channeled correctly, specifically, in the direction of *work* (if channeled incorrectly, Montesquieu noted, vanity leads to arrogance, an important cause of the aristocratic disdain for labor).[10]

The liberation of sexual mores also stimulates female vanity, in the form of ornamentation and fashion. Viewing fashion as an economic good, Montesquieu argues that it provides the nation with two benefits: first, it provides an antidote, so to speak, to the numbing effects of bourgeois attitudes toward wealth and work. More importantly, it increases "the branches of commerce" (XIX.8). Social and sexual freedom intertwine, providing a "sociable humor" where strict mores have been "spoiled" by an all-encompassing "taste for the world" (XX.6).

The disadvantages of monarchy, as a condition of successful commerce, are much more revealing of Montesquieu's final judgment. Paul Rahe has explored these disadvantages in depth in *Montesquieu and the Logic of Liberty*.[11] In a significant chapter on "Monarchy's Plight" Rahe has conclusively demonstrated the flaws of the "traditionalist" interpretation of Montesquieu's political economy. Commerce, he shows, is radically subversive, both to the nature (structure) and the principle (dominant passion) of the monarchical state. In this illustrative passage, Rahe contends that Montesquieu was well aware of the destructive capacity of commerce, and indeed, actively promoted it:

> To the extent that the spirit of commerce permeates a monarchical society and propagates within it the norms and expectations of the marketplace, it will subvert its principle. When Montesquieu remarks that "commerce cures destructive prejudices," he has more in mind than he is willing on this occasion to say (4.20.1). One is left wondering whether he is not intimating that, within what would later come to be called the *ancient régime*, commerce is not, in fact, a Trojan Horse.[12]

The metaphor of commerce as a Trojan Horse is useful in a few ways. As we will see shortly, Chapters 8–18 of book 20 can be thought of as a series of "trade paradoxes" that push this interpretation further; specifically, these chapters demonstrate the clear incompatibility of traditional monarchy with the imperatives of commerce. In following the politics of trade in *The Spirit of the Laws* more closely, Montesquieu's subversive intent becomes increasingly clear. Traditional monarchy is not only socially and psychologically vulnerable to destructive commercial forces, but institutionally incapable of maintaining the kind of sustained economic growth that is necessary for liberty in a world of competing commercial powers.[13]

Montesquieu and the Jealousy of Trade

The first and most general defect of traditional monarchy is encapsulated in the phrase, "jealousy of trade" (XX.8).[14] Echoing what would later become one of the standard critiques of mercantilism, Montesquieu begins by observing that traditional monarchies are necessarily jealous of the commercial success of neighboring rivals. But the trading states are often popular, or republican, and thus, they present a dual threat to the idea of monarchy. They present a challenge both to the political ideals of monarchy and, increasingly, to its economic advantage.

Commercial jealousy "hampers" commerce through the erection of barriers, aimed at "[lowering] the states that engage in economic commerce." Barriers to trade should be the exception, not the rule, in any nation. "The true maxim," Montesquieu writes, "is to exclude no nation from one's commerce without great reasons." Two examples are provided: either when the home country is devastatingly poor, like Poland, which has "abandoned the expectation of becoming rich," or deceived, like the rulers of Japan, who believe that their exclusive trade with the Chinese and the Dutch is one of the causes of their economic self-sufficiency (e.g., XX.23; XX.9).

Many of the observations on monarchy's flaws in the following chapters flow from this defect. The first and most important consequence is a general confusion between political and economic interests. Because princes see themselves as both the "rulers and clerks" of the universe, they naturally tend to confuse great projects (of the state) with small ones (of commerce) (XX.4). This confusion is itself the cause of a number of evils, from the absence of simple contract enforcement, to the temptation to protect monopolies, to the exploitation of the people by courtiers and nobles, who tend to be "more avid and more unjust" than even the most selfish prince. Referring to the historical example of Law's fated experiment, Montesquieu also makes careful note of the loss of public trust in the "justice" of the state. The disjunction between the opulence of the court and deprivation and poverty in the provinces is difficult to hide from the people. This is not primarily a moral argument. Montesquieu's description of mass poverty is directed inward, at those readers that would recognize the connection between economic ruin in the people and the collapse of the financial base of the court royalty itself.[15]

Public Credit, Trading Companies, and Free Ports

Was Montesquieu's criticism of monarchy an endorsement of liberal commercialism? Indeed, critics of the liberal view are likely to point out that Montesquieu opposed "liberal" institutions and practices, such as the expansion of public credit, the support of large commercial companies, and most importantly, a mercantile nobility.[16] In other words, Montesquieu criticized monarchy, but opposed economically liberal institutions in order to "ease the tide" of the commercial spirit in France.

But where does the evidence come from for Montesquieu's opposition to these institutions? The objection to banks and commercial companies are based, according to critics, on Montesquieu's experience with the Law episode, and his principled objection to these two key components of the Law system (banks and trading companies).[17] The objection to a mercantile nobility is evidenced by multiple and overlapping statements on the instability of the English system (II.4), the "extreme" liberty of English society lacking intermediate powers (XIX.27), and the twice-mentioned "ban" on noble participation in trade (V.6; see also XX.21). True, Montesquieu spied an economic advantage in these institutions, but, skeptics say, the English example was to be avoided for political reasons.[18]

Let us begin by looking closer at Montesquieu's description of the dangers of banks and trading companies in a monarchy.[19] First, Montesquieu would have been aware of the argument on both sides. The topic had been openly debated in England.[20] In France, Samuel Bernard and Desmaretz had argued, two decades before Montesquieu, that there was no foundation for a banking establishment "in a country in which everything depends on the wishes of the king."[21]

The question for Montesquieu, however, was not whether the concentration of money and financial assets might expose the state to predatory (individual) power. The question was whether a modern monarchy—in the absence of such institutions—could expect to survive without them. Here, for reference, is Montesquieu's explanation of the dangers of banking establishments in monarchy:

> It would be wrong to introduce [banks] into states that carry on a commerce of luxury. To put them into countries governed by one alone is to assume silver on one side and power on the other: that is, on the one side, the faculty of having everything without power, and, on the other, power with the faculty of having nothing at all. In such a government, there has never been anyone but the prince who has obtained or has been able to

obtain a treasury, and wherever there is a treasury, as soon as it is excessive, it immediately becomes the princes'.[22]

Montesquieu's objection to banks here is too vague to draw the conclusion that banks were to be excluded. More to the point, this passage can be read as an argument in favor of a more diffuse or decentralized system of public credit, not, as critics suggest, the exclusion of innovatory financial instruments to promote credit and trade. More importantly, the (real) political dangers of a centralized banking system had to be weighed, in balance, against the risks of the Crown's continued reliance on "financial clans," and financiers.[23] In 1748, Montesquieu's opinion on this alternative vision of public credit had not changed: the financiers and the farming of customs, he argued, "destroys commerce by its injustices and harassments... but independently of that, it also destroys it further by the difficulties to which it gives rise and the formalities it requires."[24]

Let us look closer now at Montesquieu's supposed hostility toward trading companies. Montesquieu seems to have objected to trading companies for the same reason as to banks: the presence of these institutions provides to individuals the "force of public wealth."[25] Moreover, trading companies smack of privilege and monopoly. But did Montesquieu mean to suggest that large trading companies were to be excluded? The chapter on Holland and its "great navigation" provides necessary context. In it, Montesquieu expresses his fascination with the dynamism, and the risk-taking, of the Dutch whale hunting business:

> I have heard that in Holland whale hunting generally speaking almost never returns what it costs; but those who have been employed in building the ship, those who have provided the rigging, the gear, and the provisions, are also those who take the principal interest in the hunt. Even if they lose on the hunt, they have come out ahead on the equipage. This commerce is a kind of lottery, and each one is seduced by the hope of a lucky number.

This passage illustrates the potential for misreading Montesquieu's objection to large companies. Those who take the "principal" interest in the hunt are individual laborers, manufacturers, and suppliers. Certainly, the Dutch corporation here is a far shot from the chartered and *privileged* trading companies associated with mercantilism and Colbert. But in taking notice of such distinctions, Montesquieu's larger goal becomes apparent: his objection throughout book 20 is to *privileged* trading companies, or monopolies in particular. This is a subject that becomes central to understanding Montesquieu's critique of a trading nobility in chapter 18.[26]

Commerce and Courtiers: the Puzzle of the Prohibition

For skeptics of a "retrospective" reading of Montesquieu's economic liberalism, the last chapters of book 20 provide further proof against the liberal reading: here we find Montesquieu's third, and major, objection to accelerating commerce in France on the English model,[27] namely, Montesquieu's famous ban on a commercial nobility.

Montesquieu appears to be on the side of the defenders of the status quo, worried that a commercialization of social relations would undermine the "nature" of monarchy, while also corroding the principle of honor, which defines the "principle" of monarchy itself. According to critics of the revolutionary-liberal view, the challenge for Montesquieu in these passages was to preserve the advantages of commerce while preventing social destabilization. His solution, in short, was to put a barrier between the trading and non-trading sectors, allowing merchants to become nobles, but prohibiting nobles from engaging in commerce.[28]

This compromise was not novel to Montesquieu. In the seventeenth century, Pierre Nicole, the marquis de la Rochefoucauld, and Pierre Bayle, had developed variant theories, in which the animating desire for "honor" could be manipulated, by channeling economic ambition to serve the public good, and compelling individuals to behave virtuously, despite the desire not to. The awarding of "honors" would therefore serve two complementary functions: it would prevent the destruction of the nobility, while taming the "antisocial" passions associated with commerce and trade. Montesquieu's *The Spirit of the Laws* simply gave this debate new currency.[29]

Before providing a contrasting interpretation, it is worth considering the range of historical reactions to Montesquieu's "prohibition." For Montesquieu's liberal critics, his attempt to separate the nobility from the damaging effects of trade was further evidence of his reactionary politics. The most notable criticism of this kind came from Abbé Coyer, who published a response aimed directly at Montesquieu, in 1756.

Coyer's *Noblesse commerçante* took up directly the theme of chapter 20.[30] Targeting Montesquieu specifically, the pamphlet criticized Montesquieu's failure to grasp the imperatives of trade and the benefits of a mercantile nobility. From Coyer's perspective, Montesquieu's prohibition appeared like nothing more than an attempt to resurrect the second estate on the lines of the ancient constitution. Barring the nobles from trade would have the further (pernicious) effect of muting questions about the status of the third estate, while evoking increasingly outdated ideas of an "honorable nobility" and "feudal liberty."

A few years later, another colorful figure entered the stage, this time apparently taking Montesquieu's side on the issue of the mercantile nobility. The counter-attack was issued by a defender of noble merit, Chevalier d'Arc, who claimed Montesquieu as an authority. Under Montesquieu's scheme, he argued, the nobility would be immunized from commerce, and therefore reinvigorated as an "honorable nobility."

The title of Chevalier d'Arc's tract, *Noblesse militaire*,[31] indicates the author's difference with the liberal Coyer. It also reveals the trap into which Coyer and his followers had been snared. In taking Montesquieu's prohibition at face value, both sides failed to take into account the complexity of Montesquieu's rationale for the prohibition. Coyer, for his part, severely underestimated the liberal implications of Montesquieu's solution. In particular, he failed to appreciate Montesquieu's radical contestation of the source of "merit."[32]

Chevalier d'Arc went farther astray. Most importantly, d'Arc completely overlooked, or ignored, the complex *reasons* for the prohibition, which on inspection, turn out to be much less flattering of—and much less defensive of—the nobility as a social class. Indeed, so taken was the knight with the baron's prohibition on commerce that he was led to describe Montesquieu as a "visionary" in helping to restore the military glory of the knighthood.[33]

The difficulty of interpreting Montesquieu's political economy of honor is not easily dismissed. Still, was Coyer right in exposing Montesquieu's "aristocratic liberalism"—despite all the indications, above, that Montesquieu's France would be better off in the long run by imitating England (including their "usage" that permitted the commerce to the nobility)? Likewise, how should the Chevalier d'Arc's reading of book 20 be understood? Did he have a point in arguing that Montesquieu was at the vanguard of a new argument for the *restoration* of the old feudal order?

Montesquieu does appear ambivalent.[34] There is a noticeable discrepancy, for example, in the tone which Montesquieu uses to open book 20, and that which closes it. The first is unabashedly liberal. This is the "enthused" defender of commerce in the prelude, who calls out with quasi-prophetical fervor to the muses for support in announcing his new discovery of the tool by which mankind might be redeemed. The second Montesquieu is exceedingly cautious, like the *chevalier,* a generic partisan of the second estate. This is the author of Chapter 21: vigilant, circumspect in his choice of words, wary of change. The closing of book 20 gives us the coy aristocrat who so annoyed Helvetius. He quibbles, and he flatters the nobility. In one critic's damning words, Montesquieu's political economy compromised too much with prejudice.[35]

The scholarship today is also divided, although there is an increasing awareness of the possibility of a synthesis. I want to highlight two examples of the debate—one from a "feudal reactionary" school, and one from an "aristocratic liberal" reading—to show how scholars outside the classical liberal perspective have tried to solve Montesquieu's prohibition on the mercantile nobility. In the conclusion, a unique solution from the liberal perspective is presented, with some thoughts on how book 20 points forward to some of the main themes of book 21.

The most direct approach is offered by scholars who focus primarily on Montesquieu as a defender of class interests.[36] At least since the 1930s, a number of scholars have followed Mathiez' lead[37] in suggesting that Montesquieu's critique of monarchy arose primarily out of a concern for the fate of his own noble class. According to this view, Montesquieu detested absolute monarchy not only because Louis XIV had successfully created a centralized national administration, but because he had—in the process—put the nobles to the curb, undercutting their historic privileges. Montesquieu's defense of the nobility at the end of book 20 can be explained as an instinctive defense of his own class against the absolutist kings and centralizing bureaucrats. Like the *chevalier* after him, it would be easy to conclude, as Mathiez does, that Montesquieu's comments were heavily laden with "class propaganda."[38]

A brilliant, although flawed, extension of Mathiez' approach is provided by Althusser's 1972 *Politics and History: Montesquieu, Rousseau, Marx.* Althusser attacked the apolitical reading of Montesquieu, detailing the ways in which a "too soothing tradition" has misled readers into believing that Montesquieu was an empirical sociologist, interested merely in scientific *discovery* of undiscovered truths about the world. Seeking "the historical Montesquieu," Althusser discovers an aristocrat caught up in the "struggles of his age," a man who never overcame his own attachments to his prejudice, his *parti pris.*

Innovating on the interpretation of the Chevalier d'Arc, Althusser goes further, in claiming to uncover a great historical irony. That is, in making the argument against despotism, Montesquieu inadvertently opened the door to the revolutionary future. In the very act of pleading for the cause of an "outdated order," Montesquieu unwittingly set himself up as a hero of the revolution. In Althusser's words, Montesquieu had made himself an unwitting opponent of a political order "which others were to make outdated."

If true—that Montesquieu was a straightforward aristocrat but an unconscious revolutionary—this would constitute a significant challenge to the liberal reading of Montesquieu. The revolutionary posterity of

Montesquieu, in Althusser's words, was a historical misunderstanding of Montesquieu's political project:

> What does it matter where the blows came from so long as they strike at the same point? And if it is true that this 'revolutionary' posterity of Montesquieu's is a misunderstanding, that misunderstanding must nonetheless be given its due: it was merely the *truth* of an earlier misunderstanding: the misunderstanding that had projected Montesquieu into right-wing opposition at a time when it no longer had any meaning.[39]

It will be necessary to return to Althusser's solution shortly. For now, we survey a much different approach, suggested by Catherine Larrère,[40] one of the few scholars to have interrogated this question in much depth.

For Larrère, Montesquieu's position is intelligible in terms of his interest in political liberty. This does not mean, however, that Montesquieu was engaged in a project to transform the social order, either liberal or conservative (as Althusser himself suggests, the revival of a feudal nobility had "lost any meaning"). Aimed therefore at maintaining the fragile status quo, Montesquieu's separation of the nobility from ordinary trade was a function of the desire to mitigate the damage a merchant aristocracy might wreak, either on freedom of trade, or to the delicate balance between the king and the nobility.

Larrère's reading has a number of obvious advantages. It helps to explain aspects of Montesquieu's anti-noblism.[41] It accounts for Montesquieu's first prohibition, in book 5, in which the Venetian ban on a mercantile nobility is praised for helping to preserve the balance of liberty. Importantly, it takes into account the rhetorical sophistication of Montesquieu's writing.

Taking the sum of arguments, and the overall structure of book 20 into account suggests a third alternative, that is, an attempt to combine short-term protections against commercial despotism with a long-term (revolutionary) reconceptualization of the source and nature of merit. Far from slowing down the spread of economic morality, Montesquieu's redefinition of merit in fact points to a conscious transfiguration of the nobility—soon to be, in Tocqueville's formulation "open to all" (2008, 32).[42]

It is necessary, first, to look more closely at Chapters 21 and 22 together (entitled "A particular reflection").

The core of Montesquieu's argument is found in Chapter 21:

> It is against the spirit of commerce for the nobility to engage in it in a monarchy. "That would be pernicious for the towns," say the emperors

Honorius and Theodosius, "and would take away the ease with which merchants and plebeians buy and sell." It is against the spirit of monarchy for the nobility to engage in commerce. The usage that permitted commerce to the nobility in England is one of the things that most contributed to weakening monarchical government there.

Begin by noting that Montesquieu gives *two* reasons for the initial prohibition. The first, quoting Honorius and Theodosius, presents an argument that privileges the point of view of the "towns." Contrast Philippe Auguste de Saint-Foix, Chevalier d'Arc. As above, Saint-Foix would later base his critique on a mercantile nobility on the fear that they would become "infected" with "a spirit of calculation."[43] This is a markedly different justification than Montesquieu, whose first line of reasoning appears to defend the "merchants" and the "plebeians" of the towns.

Scholars have tended to give more weight, however, to the second justification above: a mercantile nobility "is against the spirit of monarchy." By focusing on the latter explanation, however, Montesquieu's argument is highly simplified, reduced to an unequivocal *warning* against following the example of England. Commercialization of the upper strata contributed significantly to the weakening of the monarchy itself.

In a chapter entitled "A particular reflection," Montesquieu provides a number of significant qualifications that are not often considered.[44] First, he retains his emphasis on a dual concern for stability *and* commerce: "People who are struck by what is practiced in some states think there should be laws in France engaging the nobles to carry on commerce. This would be the way to destroy the nobility, without being of any utility to commerce."

In the next chapter, two further dimensions of the argument are introduced. Montesquieu argues that it is a "very wise" practice to allow successful merchants to become nobles ("They can have the expectation of becoming noble without the drawback of being nobles"). The wisdom in this practice consists in its application to "prosperity" and a re-evaluation of merit. Only the most "successful" merchants will be able to move up: "a profession will be better pursued when those who have excelled in it can expect to attain another. When nobility can be acquired with silver, it greatly encourages traders to put themselves in a position to attain it."

Anticipating criticism, Montesquieu denies that his defense of the sale of offices is political: "I am not examining whether it is good thus to give the prize of virtue to wealth; there are governments in which this can be quite useful."

Ironically, Montesquieu's protestations of neutrality, above, would touch off a "firestorm" that erupted in the 1750s. In defending the open sale of noble careers "open to talent," Montesquieu inserted himself awkwardly into an old controversy over venality, that is, selling offices for money, a popular resort for European states that depended on tapping wealthy subjects in exchange for annual interest, revenues from posts, fiscal and commercial privileges, and the most highly prized reward of all, ennoblement.[45]

Montesquieu's recommended prohibition on noble trade was not unusual or surprising given his commitment to a decentralized system of finance.[46] The endorsement of venality, however, was unusual, and it remains something of a puzzle for interpreters of Montesquieu's political economy.[47] The sale of posts was easily justified from the perspective of the monarchy and finance. In the French case, the sale of offices goes as far back as the Capetians in the fourteenth century. The royal treasury sold higher appointments, trading *provisions* or *finances*.[48]

In the 1730s,[49] when it became clear that Law's scheme had done little to solve the debt, the government became increasingly dependent on the creation and sales of government offices, which brought in substantial revenues for the state. As public perception of the tax-farming system became hostile, the sale of offices promised to satiate the increasing demand for new forms of state credit.[50]

If the widespread sale of "honor" made financial sense for the monarchy, however, it cut at the heart of the "great" nobility. In book 20, Montesquieu distinguished the "warlike nobility" from the nobles of the robe, arguing that the nobility of the sword was incompatible with "new money" acquired through trade and commerce. Linking virtue and prosperity with the robe, Montesquieu tied the warring function of the high nobility to honor: disdainful of wealth, the high nobles expected "only honor" as a reward.[51]

Montesquieu's strict division of estates may have been tenable in the 1740s. By the 1750s, this categorical distinction had become a fiction. It rested on the assumption that nobles were more likely to be public spirited if they had been born into a family of noble lineage, with ancestors to emulate, and an education that imparted a strong personal sense of honor.[52] Scholars have estimated that by 1789, only a minority of the Second Estate owed its origins to noble lineage; a majority came from families that had purchased a title in the last two hundred years.[53]

Conservatives like Fénelon, Saint-Simon and Boulainvilliers[54] voiced objections on the grounds that venality would cheapen noble titles and endanger noble privileges.[55] These titles had been earned in battle or passed down through the generations. In a few generations, they predicted, the great nobility would have merchants and financiers for ancestors. Nobility should be won through merit and personal superiority, not awarded through titles that could be bought and sold.[56]

Liberals and reformers opposed venality on the grounds that it would result in a further entrenchment of noble rights. While it opened up a degree of social mobility, venal offices were increasingly bought and transferred as an hereditary right. Franklin Ford's *Robe & Sword: the Regrouping of the French Aristocracy after Louis XIV*[57] demonstrates that in the 1700s, there emerged an "aristocracy of wealth and office," which then "merged" with the higher nobility, thus fortifying their prerogatives. Democratization of honor came at a high cost. Marquis d'Argenson, one of the earliest *philosophes* to oppose venality, highlighted that cost, arguing that it was, in effect, more pernicious to the fortunes of the third estate than the original usurpation of fiefs.[58] Far from strengthening the third estate, venality, for d'Argenson, was a major obstacle in the way of the "happy progress of democracy."[59] The King's prerogative to choose his own officers was drastically curtailed (d'Argenson calls this the "fairest of the prerogatives" of the executive power). More significant, for democratic liberals, venality had made it more difficult, not less, to influence public servants. Thus he concluded that venality had "destroyed in France all idea of popular government."

Montesquieu was in a unique position to influence debate. Yet for later generations of political economists and *philosophes*, Montesquieu betrayed the cause. As William Doyle has argued in *Venality: the sale of offices in eighteenth-century France*, "the only major philosophe to defend venality was Montesquieu: the most any of the others would concede was that it was a necessary evil." According to Doyle, Montesquieu's position was so unpopular that "nobody else came to its public defence again until the political crisis of 1771."[60]

To understand Montesquieu's open endorsement of venality—not only as a necessary evil, but as good in itself—requires a closer look at the complex rationale provided in different sections of *The Spirit of the Laws*.

The initial justification of venality appears in book 5:

> Venality is good in monarchical states, because it provides for performing as a family vocation what one would not want to undertake for virtue, and because it destines each to his duty and renders the orders of the state more permanent. Suidas aptly says that Anastasius had made a kind of aristocracy of the empire by selling all the magistracies. (V.19)

This is, as Ehrard has noted, a defense of venality as a factor of social mobility.[61] But the full passage can be taken out of context.

Previous to the quoted passage, Montesquieu defends venality as an essential check on absolute power, since, under despotism, the prince must be free not only to place but also "displace" his officers at will. On this point, Montesquieu was joined by duc de Saint-Simon, also suspicious of absolutism, and in favor of the entrenchment of the legal caste (the Robe). Second, the justification of the sale of posts here is derived from an indirect criticism of republican morality, which places (in Montesquieu's view) an unreasonable standard for serving in public office. In an earlier paragraph, Montesquieu contrasts modern monarchy with the republican Plato, who rejected any connection between wealth and virtue:

> Plato cannot endure such venality. "It is," he says, "as if, on a ship, one made someone a pilot or a sailor for his silver..." But Plato is speaking of a republic founded on virtue, and we are speaking of monarchy. (V.19)

Montesquieu then adds three further considerations. The *open* selling of posts (by "public regulation") is *less harmful* than the selling of posts in secret: "the courtiers' indigence and avidity would sell them all the same." Second, in anticipation of the objection that the reward for virtue will be given to arbitrary wealth, he notes that "chance" often produce better subjects than the choice of the prince.

It is at this point that Montesquieu arrives at the argument for stimulation of industry:

> Finally, advancing oneself by way of wealth inspires and maintains industry, a thing badly needed in this kind of government.[62] (V.19)

The argument for industry is expanded on in book 20:

> The laws ordering each man to stay in his profession and to pass it down to his children are and can be useful only in despotic states, where none can or should be rivals. Let it not be said that each man will follow his profession better when he cannot leave it for another. I say that a profession will be better pursued when those who have excelled in it can expect to attain another. When nobility can be acquired with silver, it greatly encourages traders to put themselves in a position to attain it.[63]

To summarize, Montesquieu's defense of venality drew on a variety of arguments from conflicting social and political imperatives. For liberal political economists in the years after Montesquieu's death, the costs of venality seemed increasingly to out weight its benefits; as the price of offices went up, it became more common to view the sale of hereditary posts as an evolution of feudalism rather than a break from it.

Condorcet singled out Montesquieu's defense of venality as evidence that he was a guilty party in the process. Montesquieu was "despite all a representative of the old order."[64] Similarly, Voltaire, who thought of venality as "France's shame," could barely bring himself to forgive Montesquieu for taking part in this "monstrous" and "shocking abuse": "Pity Montesquieu for dishonouring his work with such paradox. But forgive him. His uncle had bought an office of the president... and left it to him. Human nature is everywhere. None of us is without weakness."[65] Later in the 1780s, the academy of Bordeaux solicited *elogies*. Two participants drew attention to Montesquieu's defense of venality as the baron's one serious misjudgment.[66]

The most vocal critics of Montesquieu on the subject of venality may have overshot the mark, however. In the first place, it is well known that Montesquieu did not support the sale of posts indiscriminately.[67] Further, Montesquieu was well aware of both the implications and the full range of objections, as is plain from a comment in his notebooks, where Montesquieu admits that he occupies a distinctly minority position: "there is scarcely a sensible man in France who does not rail against the venality of offices, and who is not scandalized by it."[68]

Montesquieu was not scandalized, but not for reasons of aristocratic self-interest. Rather, critics of venality, in his view, underestimated the economic advantage, in monarchy, of managing the desire for honor. The purpose was not, as many interpreters claim, to entrench privileges, but as Montesquieu clearly argues, to promote industry.[69] In the same passage in his *Pensées*, he notes that the purpose of venality is to "encourage in citizens the desire to make a fortune." Nothing contributes more to industry, he concluded, than "making them see that wealth opens the path to honors."[70]

Montesquieu's focus on honor—to encourage commerce and agriculture—has not been ignored by the scholarship. But neither is it given the analytical or historical weight it deserves.[71] As John Shovlin has argued, the underlying logic of energizing commerce and agriculture by making it "honorable" was a staple of French political economy in the 30 years after the publication of *The Spirit of the Laws*.[72] The emerging dialogue required only a slight modification of Montesquieu's proposal. Instead of the controversial direct sale of public offices, an increasing number of proposals were made in which the state would instead "confer" honors on successful merchant families. Proponents of this strategy had different motives, and they emphasized different advantages, but their justifications were all compatible with Montesquieu's own reasons. In particular, they pointed to increase in social esteem for the profession of merchants, maximization of the nation's economic potential, and an "ennobling" of the commercial sector.[73]

If Montesquieu had lived to see the evolution of the debates on venality, honor, and commerce, he would not have been surprised to see his own arguments being taken up by liberal political economists. Of special interest is a chapter in *The Spirit of the Laws* entitled "A good custom in China." Drawing on Father [Jean Baptiste] du Halde, *Description de l'Empire de la Chine*, Montesquieu provided a highly nuanced form of the argument for managing honor, one that predates the more sophisticated discourse on the ennobling of trade in the 1760s and 1770s. In a series of chapters devoted to counteracting the enervating "vices" of climate, Montesquieu surveys various obstacles to human industry, physical and political. Among these: systems of metaphysics that encourage idleness (XIV.5), laws that take away from individuals the "spirit of ownership" (XVI.6), and laziness generated by "arrogant" cultures where people are "well impressed by the point of honor" (XIV.9). Pointing to China for critical comparison, Montesquieu lauded a ceremony in which the emperor celebrated the "opening" of the cultivation of the fields, an event that "rouses the peoples to their plowing." At the end of each year, the emperor is informed of the plowman who has "most distinguished himself in his profession"; this individual is made "a mandarin of the eighth order."[74]

While the extension of honors to *agriculture* and to farmers met with skepticism—given that farmers were not sophisticated enough to desire such honors—Montesquieu's prescription for improving agriculture by channeling honor soon became commonplace. A Breton noble, in 1756, for example, suggested the creation of a "prize" to be awarded in each parish for the farmer who "brings the most wasteland into cultivation."[75] Among political economists, it became common, even cliché, to argue that the chief obstacle to improving French agriculture was the stigma attached to cultivation of land. Why should enterprising individuals stay in a profession loaded with such contempt?[76] Of note, the Academie Royale des Belles-Lettres of Caen held an essay competition on the subject of advancing agriculture. One writer copied the argument nearly verbatim, including the detail in which the most industrious farmer becomes a mandarin.[77] The physiocrats, Quesnay in particular, picked up Montesquieu's suggestion, extending it one step further, suggesting that the emperor himself should plow the fields.[78] Indeed, the argument for honoring agriculture was recognized at the very highest levels. A famous print of the future Louis XVI ("Louis as Dauphin") printed circa

1750, shows the future king plowing a peasant's field in imitation of the Chinese emperor, attended by a group of prim aristocrats looking on, mildly interested.

Conclusion

The conclusion of book 20 is not, as is too often assumed, a straightforward entrenchment of rank-honor. Although it is not explicitly anti-noble, either, it is significant that Montesquieu's proposals for manipulating honor were engineered specifically for the aim not only of encouraging commerce and agriculture, but honoring those professions too.[79]

The problem with Montesquieu's proposal, in addition to its apparently reactionary ban on noble commerce, was that it presumed an essential compatibility between honor and commerce—an assumption that certainly could not be taken for granted in 1748. The conception of the merchant "as hero" was at least as old as Voltaire's *Philisophical Letters* (1733–4). But it was by no means a commanding argument in French high culture, as evidenced by the more notable attempts later by Joncourt, D'Alembert, and Diderot, in the *Encyclopedie* to raise the status of the merchant.[80]

The greater obstacle to Montesquieu's promotion of an honorable commerce was public opinion, especially, the stigma attached to the merchant's profession. Montesquieu's book 21 is an attempt to reverse this stigma, by way of a novel re-interpretation of commerce in world history.

CHAPTER 4

THE MALIGNED MERCHANT AND THE NEW HISTORY OF COMMERCE

In the previous chapter, we saw that Montesquieu presented a modified case for a mobile aristocracy. Rejecting a mercantile nobility in favor of an ennobled status of the merchant class, Montesquieu offered a model of growth for French commerce that might incorporate the existing structure of honor within the larger imperative of economic growth. Traders were not nobles, but "they can have the expectation of becoming noble without the drawback of being nobles."[1] In principle, this solution offered two explicit advantages and one understated benefit. First, it would avoid class-based monopolies. Second, traders could compete as true rivals in the economic sphere, stimulating industry (a thing "badly needed" in monarchy). If it might also weaken the warrior nobility, while entrenching existing privileges for the robe, Montesquieu seems not to mind, or at least, to offer no opinion.

In the previous chapters, we also saw that it is easy to exaggerate the implicit class-bias of Montesquieu's proposal in book 20. To appreciate the true extent, and indeed, the revolutionary potential of Montesquieu's political economic philosophy, it is necessary to turn now to the problem of integrating merchants into the honor-based incentive structure of monarchy. This inevitably raises questions of Montesquieu's attitude toward the "bourgeoisie."[2] Among the professions associated with the bourgeoisie—lawyers, doctors, office-holders, and increasingly, craftsmen and artisans—it was the merchant who was most suspect.[3] Montesquieu therefore turns his attention in book 21 to a recovery of the merits, and in some ways, the honor, associated with this much maligned profession.[4]

It was not clear in the middle of the eighteenth century whether the merchant class was what we would now call "bourgeoise" or something else. Tocqueville described a 1764 report, which defined the "true bourgeois," the real men at the "heart" of the middle class, "whose birth and wealth allow them to live comfortably without the need to work for money." It was clear, at least in the case of men that belonged to trade guilds or industrial companies that they did not fit this description. They were uneducated and lived "undistinguished" lives. Merchants, however, fell along a broader spectrum and were more difficult to categorize. Some were shopkeepers, of a "low background" with little business experience. Others were wholesalers, with leisure. In the latter class, one can put Risteau, a Bordeaux merchant who was highly educated, wealthy, possessing sufficient leisure to write a commentary on the economics of *The Spirit of the Laws*.[5]

From the aristocratic perspective, the wholesalers were tainted by the spirit of commerce and gain. While Condorcet noted that "the noble is beginning to regard a banker or a merchant almost as his equal," he added the caveat, "provided he is extremely rich."[6] In the 1780s a sharp distinction could still be drawn between the bourgeois capable of "living nobly" from inherited wealth or investments, and the wealthy international wholesale merchants. Montesquieu, as we will now see, devoted himself to an upending of this ranking of the idle *rentier* over the *négociant*. Turning to ancient history, Montesquieu borrowed the luster of the early adventuring traders to effectively erase the distinction between the bourgeois capable of "living nobly" and the successful trader, whose virtue was tainted by self-interest and profit.[7]

The following chapter will proceed in three parts. The first section examines the context of Montesquieu's economic history, comparing it with similar works by Paul Huet and Jean-François Melon. The second section provides an introduction and summary of the major themes and narrative structure of book 21. The concluding section re-examines Montesquieu's primary aims in book 21. Montesquieu's incorporation of economic factors with the historical analysis of governments and society paved the way for a new way of thinking not only about the merchant as "true" bourgeois but in addition, the significance of economics in modern political life.

Re-inventing the Merchant: Economic History in the Eighteenth Century

Aside from fragments in scattered treatises, Montesquieu had few forerunners. Two writers of note, before Montesquieu, had attempted a world history of commerce in a single work. In 1716, the French Bishop Paul Huet composed *Histoire du commerce et de la navigation des anciens*. Montesquieu read Huet thoroughly, preparing notes on this essay, taking particular interest (and objecting to) the bishop's interpretation of Rome as a model for modern mercantilist expansion, whose greatness, or power, was built on a combination of conquest and commerce.

In 1734, the French economist Jean-François Melon[8] composed *L'Essai politique sur le Commerce* (1734; expanded 2nd ed., 1736). Melon's goal was not only to explain the origins, evolution, and implications of trade. He provided what is likely the first political treatment of the history of commerce. As the late István Hont[9] has shown, Melon's history came complete with a set of policies to help France emulate England, and eventually replace it as a dominant commercial power.[10] Also of note was Melon's insight into the political dimension of commerce, specifically, the political dimension of the *public knowledge* of economic matters.[11] In opposition to Huet's antiquarianism,[12] and objecting to the vision of political economy as a state "secret," Melon argued that public discussion and economic literacy were key to avoiding major fiscal errors: "It is from different writings, often contradicting one another, that the truth will come to enlighten the Legislator."[13]

Montesquieu's history of commerce was meant, in part, to promote public discussion, and to encourage economic literacy. At the beginning of Book 21, Montesquieu begins cautiously, arguing that commerce and trade are sometimes beyond the legislator's control.

Physical obstacles, for example, have historically provided a limit on the legislator's regulation of trade. Terrain and climate has "fixed its nature forever," dictating both the kind and measure of the flow of goods from East to West. Montesquieu's point, considered generally, is that commerce is "embedded" in political and cultural history. Climate, religion, police, manners, and mores are the sources of people's needs and desires. A longstanding "equilibrium" has maintained a "balance" between the nations of the South, who have more natural comforts and therefore less artificial needs; and the nations of the North, who have fewer natural comforts and therefore a greater variety of needs.[14]

From time to time, however, "the world meets with situations that change commerce."[15] The commerce of the "ancients" for example is no longer comparable to the commerce of today. Ancient trade routes connected Mediterranean ports, East and West. Modern trade is much more extensive, flowing North and South, partially a result of climatic differentiation but also because of social and political upheavals.[16]

The history of commerce is not understandable, in short, except from a consideration of these different causes. The most important human cause, he argues, are moral causes, and in particular, the *opinion* of trade across political cultures. Signaling a shift away from materialist explanations, Montesquieu turns in chapter 5 from discursive analysis to a poetic account of a personified "commerce," fleeing across the globe, struggling to survive against its tormentors. The full passage, perhaps one of the most significant and arresting passages of book 21 is worth repeating here in full:

> Commerce, sometimes destroyed by conquerors, sometimes hampered by monarchs, wanders across the earth, flees from where it is oppressed, and remains where it is left to breathe: it reigns today where one used to see only deserted places, seas, and rocks; there where it used to reign are now only deserted places.

This passage provides a first glimpse of Montesquieu's project in book 21 to reverse the pernicious effects of anti-commercialism. The passage is not, however, original to Montesquieu.[17]

In February 1721, John Trenchard, a Whig republican wrote an essay entitled "Trade and Naval Power the Offspring of Civil Liberty Only, and Cannot Subsist without It." The essay is one of *Cato's Letters*.[18] Here, for comparison, is the original text from Trenchard:

> Nothing is more certain then that trade cannot be forced; she is a coy and humorous dame, who must be won by flattery and allurements, and always flies force and power; she is not confined to nations, sects, or climates, but travels and wanders about the earth till she fixes her residence where she finds the best welcome and kindest reception; her contexture is so nice and delicate, that she cannot breathe in a tyrannical air; will and pleasure are so opposite to her nature, that but touch her with the sword, and she dies; But if you give her gentle and kind entertainment, she is a grateful and beneficent mistress; she will turn deserts into fruitful fields, villages into great cities, cottages into palaces, beggars into princes, convert cowards into heroes, blockheads into philosophers.[19]

While Montesquieu ultimately retains the most important core insight of Trenchard's essay (namely, that commerce requires the "aire" of liberty to breathe) he nonetheless departs from Trenchard in the following two ways.

First, Montesquieu's commerce, in book 21, is devoid of sexuality or gender. While Trenchard describes commerce in the original (1721) portrait as a "coy and humorous dame" who must be "won by flattery and allurements," in Montesquieu's revision, she has become a refugee, a persecuted castaway, and a restless and oppressed wanderer. Stripping commerce of her natural erotic charms, Montesquieu changes one stereotype for another, adopting the perspective of the persecuted merchant.

No longer the universal object of man's desire, commerce is a victim—of war, conquest, and prejudice.

Montesquieu will return to the world-historic consequences of this contempt for commerce, in subsequent chapters. But for now, a second major change to Trenchard's passage must be accounted for. Montesquieu also corrects for Trenchard's *idealism* by changing or altering the *effects* that commerce will have in the world. The author of *Cato's Letters* depicts dame commerce as "nice and delicate," deserving of "gentle and kind entertainment." After being wooed by the rules of medieval courtship, the reward is prosperity *and* high civilization: she will blossom into a "grateful and beneficent mistress" capable of "[turning] deserts into fruitful fields... cottages into palaces... blockheads into philosophers."

Montesquieu's vision of the revolutionary potential for commerce is clearly more reserved. Global trade has both creative and destructive power. He allows, for example, that commerce may turn deserts into "fruitful fields." But there are also "deserted places" where commerce used to reign.[20] This is a significant change not for historical reasons, but for Montesquieu's rhetorical case. If trade is to be made "honorable," as I argued previously, the case for commerce must not be made in terms of promises that cannot be kept. By contrast to the exuberant Trenchard, Montesquieu does not argue that trade—alone—can produce in human beings superlative virtues that they might otherwise lack in pre-commercial or even pre-political society. If there is a defense of commercial society, powerful enough to reverse the prejudice against trade, it must begin with an honest refusal to grant commerce magical powers that it does not have.

Commercial Morality before Commercial Society

For simplicity, the rest of book 21 can be divided roughly into three major eras. (1) the virtues associated with commerce in the ancient world (XXI.6–12); (2) the disappearance and "destruction" of commerce in medieval Europe (XXI.13–19); 3) the revival of commerce in Europe on the basis of liberty as opposed to ancient political virtue.

Beginning with the first topic, it is worth emphasizing Montesquieu's writing style in his discussion of "the commerce of the ancients."[21] When Montesquieu turns, near the end of Chapter 6, to discuss the pre-modern traders who symbolize the "commerce of economy," he focuses not on the commodities being exchanged but the virtues made necessary for the "long and arduous" voyages along the coasts of the Mediterranean. The Phoenicians did not engage in a commerce of luxury, or trade "as a result of conquest." Their wealth came from their "frugality, their ability, their industry, their perils, and their hardships," which made them "necessary to all the nations in the world." Montesquieu likens their voyages to Homer's *Odyssey*, the "finest poem in the world."[22]

Homer's military epic, the *Iliad*, by contrast, is referenced, but not celebrated. The small bands of merchants, sailors, and explorers remind us not of warrior heroes like Achilles, but of the wily Odysseus. In his *Pensées* Montesquieu admired Fénelon's *Adventures of Telemachus*, as an "enchanting" work that was a "rival of the *Odyssey*."[23] Like Fénelon, Montesquieu seems to have been attracted to the nostalgic, "happy descriptions" of rustic times, described by the ancient poets, who speak to us "of a time even more happy and tranquil."[24] This appreciation for frugality, industry, and courage is evident in the story of the Troglodytes in the *Persian Letters*.

If he shared this aesthetic judgment, Montesquieu did not likewise share Fénelon's political moralism. The account here of the early heroic traders is indeed poetic, but it is not nostalgic. Montesquieu's wariness of historiographical romance—even while he indulges in it—underscores his true admiration of commercial morality before commercial society. Soon the poetry of heroic traders gives way to a deeper admiration for science and modern finance, especially, the technology of shipbuilding, the invention of the compass, and the letters of exchange. Accepting modern science and economics as the source of modern power, Montesquieu implicitly rejects the utopian "moral economy" of Fénelon.[25]

Anticipating Schumpeter's theory of innovation as "creative destruction," Montesquieu jumps to a discussion of the "state of sailing" in the ancient world. The commercial ambition of the early traders fuels the fire of science and technology, which then weakens the virtues that made their voyages worthy of epic treatment. Trade leads to progress in the arts, which correct "both the defect of nature and the defects of art itself."[26]

The problematic relationship between culture and science or technology can be illustrated through the discussion of the Phoenician maritime trading network. The Phoenicians created an impressive commercial system, with colonies reaching the Western Mediterranean, using the galley. The prosperity of the early traders was built not on large profits from the trade in luxury goods, but on the principles of thrift, industry, and incremental gain. Phoenician maritime power and prosperity were absorbed, so to speak, into the larger, luxurious trading empires. In contrast to classical political philosophy, Plato in particular, who described Phoenician vice as a moral defect in their soul connected to the love of money, Montesquieu views the Phoenician example as virtuous, but untenable, because of technological innovation. As he argues later in

Chapter 21, the invention of the compass "opened the universe," with a number of dramatic consequences for European politics.

Before examining the role of technology, however, Montesquieu first turns to the subject of Alexander the Great. Four events under Alexander produced "a great revolution" in commerce: the capture of Tyre, the conquest of Egypt, that of the Indies, and the discovery of the sea to the south of that country.[27]

Alexander the Great: "Chief of Trading Factories"

Alexander is an important, but ambiguous hero in Montesquieu's economic history. To understand Montesquieu's unique treatment of this famous historical figure, it is necessary to detour briefly for a consideration of the historiographical debates surrounding Alexander in Montesquieu's own time. For some, Alexander represented scientific advance, commerce as communication, a uniter of civilizations, and prosperity through open trade. Others viewed in him the modern mania for distant conquests.[28] Thus the scholarly controversy over the "real Alexander" was more than an antiquarian debate; it was also a reflection of the profound ambivalence of Montesquieu's contemporaries in regards to the spread of commercial values and their effect on civilization. Montesquieu, in addressing himself to this interpretative debate, was also self-consciously addressing the larger question of the moral and philosophical implications of commercial modernity.

The attraction to Alexander in the eighteenth century is perhaps best illustrated by reference to the publication, more than 20 years after Montesquieu's death, in 1775, of a large work—a literature review of sorts—on the growing number of sources of the history of Alexander by the Baron de Sainte-Croix.[29] By the time of this publication, there had emerged two distinct interpretative camps, each with a clear and contrasting vision of Alexander's role in world history. On the one side were authors like John Gillies and William Robertson of Scotland. Robertson and Gillies presented Alexander as a model of the civilizing conqueror. They emphasized his aims to facilitate communication, to promote commerce, and to "diffuse civility." Alexander's project, in Gillies words, was to "attempt to enlighten barbarism, to soften servitude, and to transplant the improvements of Greece into an African and Asiatic soil."[30] Opposing Robertson and Gillies were writers and historians who emphasized Alexander's tougher, imperialist side. A French royalist, Baron de Sainte-Croix, read Alexander not as a friendly, cosmopolitan, modernizing hero, but as a heroic conquering general. Sainte-Croix emphatically rejected the idea that Alexander had any policy of progressive "urbanization."

Sainte-Croix was enraged, for example, to find out that this great military genius had been transformed into a humanizing cosmopolite. Gillies was "delirious" and should be condemned for having attempted to reduce Alexander "into a chief of trading factories."

It is not possible in this space to address the extent to which Montesquieu's treatment of Alexander in book 21 influenced later historians like Gillies and Robertson. It is sufficient to note, at the start, that they relied heavily on Montesquieu in formulating their arguments against those who followed Sainte-Croix. Turning back now to *The Spirit of the Laws*, it is easy to see why Montesquieu's "liberal" successors in the historical scholarship on Alexander openly recognized Montesquieu as their inspiration. As John Gillies would say in 1786, it was Montesquieu "Voltaire only excepted" who was "the most distinguished apologist of Alexander."[31]

Gillies was right in the main, but he failed to see that Montesquieu was not merely an apologist. Rather, as can be be easily shown, Montesquieu renovated Alexander's image, updating it to suit his purpose in book 21. This is clear if one compares the image of Alexander in book 21 with the image of Alexander in book 10. There, in book 10, one finds a very different Alexander: a warring general and a master tactician. Alexander's biography in book 21 provides sharp relief. Here, Montesquieu re-imagines Alexander's legacy through the lens of economic history. While not denying the warring, imperialistic legacy of the ancient general, Montesquieu reframes Alexander's legacy in commercial rather than military terms.[32] The conqueror is replaced by the civil engineer.[33] Alexander gets transformed into what Saint-Croix begrudgingly called a "chief of trading factories."[34]

Montesquieu's renovation of Alexander's image fits with the larger purpose of modifying the political economy of honor, explained in the last chapter as the "ennobling" of the eighteenth century *negociant*. Turning now to the invention of the compass and the bills of exchange, Montesquieu now further distinguishes between ancient and modern commerce, significant, as we will see, for undermining the case for resurrecting Rome as an exemplar for modern monarchy.

Compass

Referencing Pliny, Montesquieu takes special note of improvements in navigation. The theme of the following chapters before the collapse of commerce is world exploration, but the hero of this section is not a trader, or a conquering "engineer," but an invention, the magnetic needle.

The introduction of the compass in economic history is significant for a few reasons.[35] First, according to Montesquieu, the compass made it possible to leave the coasts, and to venture out into the ocean under cloud cover, a dramatic change that made navigation safer, but also provided explorers with a liberation from nature, freeing sailors from their dependence on the monsoons.[36] Here is Montesquieu's description of the challenges of open sea navigation, which confined sailors to the coast of Gujarat and Malabar:

> The main problem in sailing around Africa was to discover and weather the Cape of Good Hope...the coast from the Red Sea to the Cape is safer than the one from the Cape to the Pillars of Hercules. For those who set out from the Pillars of Hercules to discover the Cape, the compass had to be invented, so that they could leave the coast of Africa and sail into the vast ocean, either going towards the island of Saint Helena or towards the coast of Brazil.[37]

The compass, however, was evidently a partial liberation. As Montesquieu subtly suggests, this invention did not come without a price.

First, by making the "long and arduous" voyages easier and more routine, the compass diminished both the attraction of—and the need—for the Tyrean virtues. Second, and more importantly, nations like Carthage immediately increased its power "by its wealth" from long distance trade,[38] thus setting up a fateful rivalry with Rome, a nation that Montesquieu believes was inherently disinclined to trade,[39] and yet, historically fearful of the military threat of a rising commercial power in its own backyard: it was "as a rival nation, and not as a trading nation, that [the Romans] attacked Carthage."[40] This development complicates the image of Alexander the Great even further. If Alexander represents the new—however uneasy—combination between the spirit of commerce and the spirit of "preservation,"[41] the rapid military expansion of Carthage, and Rome's subsequent aggressive response, delayed, or made impossible, the potential for a synthesis. The Romans will trade with Marseilles, only as a condition of their acceptance of Roman hegemony.[42] Carthage, Corinth, and Delos and any other trading nation that did not accept Roman sovereignty on such terms, were destroyed.[43] Rome acted *as* destroyers, Montesquieu adds, "in order not to appear as conquerors."[44]

Roman Anti-Commercialism

The significance of Rome in Montesquieu's history of commerce is comparable in purpose to that of Alexander. Just as Montesquieu challenged the conventional history of Alexander, ennobling commerce in the process, so does he challenge the conventional history of Rome, transformed, in this instance, to discredit the popular notion that Rome *honored* commerce. "The truth is that [the Romans] rarely thought about it."[45]

Like Machiavelli before him, Montesquieu seeks in Rome the knowledge of examples from ancients that could provide practical lessons for modern politics. Rome is important for political economy only in a negative sense. Rather it, provides positive lessons for acquiring and maintaining power.[46] Familiar with Machiaveli's *Discourses*, Montesquieu also found Rome useful as an historical example of the theoretical distinction between republics based on expansion, and those like Sparta, devoted to preservation of territory.[47] Unlike Alexander's conquests, which encouraged trade, and the "circulation of peoples," in the spirit *pour tout conserver*[48] Rome "conquered everything in order to destroy everything."[49] Montesquieu had not changed his mind since he wrote the *Considerations*. Rome was appropriate as a model for modern economies built on conquest, "destined for war."[50]

In the *Considerations*, Montesquieu had sketched the consequences. Rome's failure to attend to commercial development and commercial exchange underwrites the whole narrative of its "decline." Destined for war, Rome could not afford to allow its citizens to become "soft" and "cowardly" by participating in commerce and the luxury trade.[51] This suppression of commerce worked in favor of the republic's short-term territorial interests.

In the beginning, Romulus allowed free men to choose only between two kinds of occupations—agriculture and war. "Merchants, artistans, and those who paid rent for their house, and tavern-keepers were not numbered among the citizens."[52] Commerce and the arts were regarded "as the occupations of slaves." Knowing only the "art of war," the Romans ensured that the sole path to magistracies and honor was through cultivation of martial virtue. This served Rome well in the rivalry with Carthage: "Gold and silver can be exhausted, but virtue, constancy, strength, and poverty never are."[53] Virtue drove Rome's ascendancy. Its leaders became "masters of the world" and foreign kings were reduced to silence and "as it were, stupefied"[54] by Rome's military prowess.

While Rome conquered the world, "a secret war was going on within its walls."[55] Roman anti-commercialism had produced a patrician class that had acquired "all the magistracies, all the dignities, and consequently all military and civil honors."[56] Royal authority passed into the hands of the consuls, and the people began to feel "they lacked the liberty they were being asked to love."⁵⁷ Conceding to the demands for a greater share in government, the patricians agreed to share wealth, but not honor. The result, Montesquieu concluded, was an eruption of dissensions within the republic that would spark the wars that would eventually lead to Rome's ruin.⁵⁸

Montesquieu's explanation for Rome's decline in the *Considerations* is retold in the history of commerce in book 21. A few new features are added. The Roman contempt for trade was coupled with a disdain for "seafaring people" (considered inferior to the bravery of the Roman land troops, who could not withdraw, or evade danger).⁵⁹ As the republic expanded, the provinces were increasingly ruled by "harsh" and "tyrannical government," creating a political culture in the outer provinces that was "incompatible with commerce."⁶⁰ Under Constantine, legal distinctions between shopkeepers and undesirables were removed: women who maintained a shop for commodities were no longer socially distinct from slaves, tavern-keepers, "women of the theater," or the madam of a whorehouse.⁶¹

Fearing the rise of a "merchant" morality within, Rome was no less concerned about the dangers of exchange with the barbarians. As Roman greatness depended on keeping the art of war a secret, and preventing barbarian peoples from acquiring "the art of conquering," the emperors made laws "to halt all commerce with the barbarians," including the sale or trade of wine, oil, or liquors "even for them to taste."⁶²

Trade with Arabia and the Indies was not similarly limited. Using Pliny and Strabo, Montesquieu commends Rome's "external commerce" with Arabia and the Indies. Although he questions whether this trade enriched the "empire" (and not merely individuals), Montesquieu admits that Rome's Eastern trade routes procured a number of significant benefits: navigation was improved, the influx of new commodities increased internal commerce (which favored the arts), industry was stimulated, and greater numbers of ordinary people joined professions that allowed them simply to enjoy "making a living."⁶³

According to Montesquieu, historians had mistaken this commerce with Arabia and the Indies as proof that Rome honored commerce. As Montesquieu suggests instead, these trade routes were only one "branch" of commerce, and moreover, their existence coincides, he claims, with the end of the republic, at a time when demand for exotic luxury goods was on the rise.⁶⁴ To summarize a complex argument, Montesquieu is suggesting here that the international luxury market was too little too late. What gains were made at the beginning of the empire by extending commerce were far outweighed by the neglect of domestic commerce in grain, and other products necessary for subsistence.⁶⁵

Destruction and Revival

The last major section of Montesquieu's economic history describes the destruction of commerce in the thirteenth and fourteenth centuries and its subsequent revival as a result of the invention of the letters of exchange.

In chapter 17, three major turning points are highlighted. First, the barbarian tribes began to fill the void left by the collapse of the Roman laws protecting property and trade. The Visigoths regarded commerce "only as an object for their banditry." They honored it "no more than they did agriculture and the other professions of the vanquished people." Second, the nobility, who "reigned everywhere" in Europe, distanced themselves further from the ignoble professions; as vassalage increased, they "no longer [troubled] themselves with [commerce]." Third, and most importantly: the re-emergence of Aristotelian political and moral philosophy, now in the hands of the "Schoolmen." They proscribed lending money at interest, a practice which in the early years of scholasticism was "condemned without distinction."[66]

It is now possible to analyze the peculiar way in which Montesquieu interprets the destruction of commerce in Western and Eastern Europe. By destruction, he does not mean the shut-down of the river-routes, or decline in trade—subjects covered earlier in the sixth chapter. Commerce was destroyed, rather, by a historically unique re-alignment or transformation of moral and cultural values. Most importantly, the Scholastics or "schoolmen" borrowed Aristotle's explanation of "usury" in the *Politics* (esp. book. I, Chapters. 9 and 10 [1256b40–1258b8]) and combined it with biblical arguments against lending money at interest, thus creating the moral basis for condemning moneymaking and finance "without distinction." In Rome, the disdain for commerce was attached to "mean" or lowly classes. With the introduction of the religious case against lending and moneymaking, commerce as a profession became associated with dishonesty.[67]

Scholastic theologians, including Aquinas, would later adopt more nuanced, less hostile, teachings toward trade (distinguishing, for example, between kinds of "legitimate profits" and allowing for an appreciation of property and the value of work). Here, Montesquieu focuses on the early theological equivalence between usury and immorality, largely ignoring the debates about the "commodities" or "incommodities" of the practice in practical terms (the preferred approach of philosophers at least since the time of Francis Bacon).[68] According to Montesquieu, commerce as a profession received a double stigma when it became associated with the Jewish people.[69] The merchant's profession was no longer something simply unbecoming of a gentleman. Christian theologians successfully linked the merchant way of life to the cardinal sins of *avaritia* (avarice) and *luxuria* (lechery).

Ironically, the persecution of the Jews (who became "wealthy by their exactions") initiated a series of events that would culminate in the revitalization of commerce. The pillaging of merchants, the imprisonment, torture, extractions, and forced conversions, did not "relieve" the envy of the people, or hamper trade. Instead,

> One saw commerce leave this seat of harassment and despair. The Jews, proscribed by each country in turn, found the means for saving their effects. In that way, they managed to fix their refuges forever; a prince who wanted very much to be rid of them would not, for all that, be in a humor to rid himself of their silver. They invented letters of exchange, and in this way commerce was able to avoid violence and maintain itself everywhere, for the richest trader had only invisible goods, which could be sent everywhere, and leave no trace anywhere.

The process by which the "letters of exchange" helped commerce return, in Montesquieu's words, "to the bosom of integrity" is ambiguous, and scholars emphasize different functions. The argument can be interpreted literally, emphasizing the personal safety of merchants.[70] Robert Howse, for example, notes that the "letters of exchange" allowed merchants to hide and store their wealth in a moveable or intangible form; they became a means for eluding violence.[71] Other readers have seen in Montesquieu's analysis a broader message relating to the development of limited or moderate government. Thomas Pangle, for example, has noted that the letters of exchange chastened and educated rulers and princes by forcing them to reconsider the constraining power of public finance and the "rules of commerce."[72] Paul Rahe, similarly, observes that Montesquieu had discussed the moral logic of the "letters of exchange" earlier in his career. From his *Pensées*, it is clear that Montesquieu had long considered the ways in which commerce works to inspire moderation ("Montesquieu's watchword") in princes and would-be-despots.[73] More generally still, the invention of the letters of exchange can also be understood in the context of international relations. Stephen J. Rosow, for example, has focused on the international dimension of Montesquieu's argument, noting that moveable wealth encouraged the formation of financial institutions, and hence regular relations and mutual dependency among nations.[74]

These readings accurately portray Montesquieu's understanding of the importance of commerce and moveable wealth in the transfiguring of the merchant class—from a persecuted and contingent enemy of honor, at the start of book 21, to an unsettled, independent social force that would leverage political power through independent wealth creation. Partly as a consequence of the invention of moveable wealth, "great acts of authority" would become "so clumsy" that princes would soon realize that "only goodness of government brings prosperity."[75] In Montesquieu's influential phrase,

> One has begun to be cured of Machiavellianism, and one will continue to be cured of it. There must be more moderation in councils. What were formerly called *coups d'etat* would at present, apart from their horror, be only imprudences. And, happily, men are in such a situation such that, though their passions inspire in them the thought of being wicked, they nevertheless have an interest in not being so.

From a literary perspective, this passage completed the reversal of the figure of commerce, capable only of "fleeing" from oppression, but incapable of resistance.[76] At the end of book 21, commerce no longer simply *evades* the avarice of princes. Commerce in its modern (mobile) form invalidates the logic of despotic "extractions."

As an historical fact, however, Montesquieu's description of the "cure for Machiavellianism" was not particularly novel. At least since the sixteenth century, intellectuals in England had been debating the consequences, dangers, and merits of merchant capital.[77] Many of the social and political anxieties associated with flexible commercial wealth, increasing in France, had already been aired or rehearsed in England. Merchants, it was said, were using their wealth to create social status, reversing the pattern of a land-based social hierarchy in which status created wealth. Moveable wealth created a shadowy network of moneylenders and financiers, undermining political and religious authority. Conservatives viewed these elusive forms of trade increasingly as a potential threat to a world based on land status, honor, and duty.[78]

The intellectual response in England to attempts to restrict the spread of modern commerce may help to put Montesquieu's version of economic history in perspective. In response to restrictive regulations aimed at reducing the spread of the disease of moneymaking and commerce, English writers published a great variety of works in defense of the morally ambivalent activities of the trader. Key among these efforts was the affirmation of the social benefits of credit and free trade. In addition to tracts that highlighted the beneficial *effects* of commerce, English apologists also began to refashion a sympathetic imagery of the merchant, as a counterweight to the stigma of the merchant as social "pariah."[79] Also significant were the many attempts to shape attitudes toward money, commonly regarded as on object of devious manipulators, and usury, the moral legitimacy of which, while not seriously debated in the 1740s when Montesquieu was completing his *The Spirit of the Laws*, was nevertheless treated as suspect by the standards of religious counsel.[80]

Viewed in the context of those debates, one can perhaps better appreciate both the novelty and the rhetorical complexity of Montesquieu's political economy. At least two critical factors make a comparison with his English forerunners in political economy more complicated, however, requiring a longer treatment. The first is religion and culture. While the monolithic influence of the Catholic church in French intellectual life may be overstated, by the same token, scholars of Montesquieu's political economy tend to underestimate the cultural influence of the Church, especially, as it was underwritten by economic power.[81] Similarly, the topic of private property in Montesquieu's political economy has received little attention, despite Montesquieu's famous insistence on the importance of civil laws in reforming politics. It is to these two topics—religion and private property—that we turn to in the following chapters.

CHAPTER 5

COMMERCE AND THE RHETORIC OF TOLERATION

The Religious Roots of Machiavellianism

To appreciate the importance of religion in Montesquieu's political economy, it will be useful to think more broadly about Montesquieu's reference to a "cure for Machiavellianism." We begin by noting a semantic nuance: the "cure" for Machiavellism was not presented as a remedy for Machiavelli's teaching, but for Machiavellianism. Joining Francis Bacon, Voltaire, Rousseau, and Hume, later, Montesquieu separated the two.[1] Letters of exchange, in other words, do not apply to the political philosophy of Machiavelli, but to the failure of Machiavellianism. This leaves open the possibility, in other words, that Montesquieu's political economy preserves part of Machiavelli's adversarial position in regard to the Papacy, or more broadly, the Florentine's criticism of the "preachers of meekness and superstition."[2]

Putting aside the question of Machiavelli's influence on Montesquieu, two practical questions can be raised. First, what specific *ill* does this cure claim to remedy? Second, and more importantly still, what are the political implications of the invention of the letters of exchange?

On this second point, Montesquieu presents the letters of exchange as a cure that not only worked at a discrete moment in time (in medieval Europe) but that will *continue* to operate ("one has begun to be cured of Machiavellianism, and one will *continue* to be cured of it"). Whether or not political action is required is not in fact explained in the twentieth chapter of book 21. The mechanism is described, rather, in two separate accounts, in book 22, Chapter 14, and in book 25, Chapter 12.

Another peculiarity lies in the text. In the famous twentieth chapter, Montesquieu selects examples of "Machiavellianism" from history; notably, examples that predate Machiavelli. The mention of Aaron during the reign of Henry III refers, for example, to an incident in the 1250s. The confiscation of the goods of the Jews who embraced Christianity is dated, as another example, to the edict given at Baville, in 1392.[3]

Putting these two observations together, it is fair to ask: is Montesquieu describing acts here that we can confidently ascribe to Machiavelli the political philosopher? Or, in describing these violent confiscations by thirteenth- and fourteenth-century tyrants, is he not suggesting that the disease called *machiavélisme* has deeper roots—not in the books of the Florentine—but in the moral outlook inspired by the Schoolmen after they combined their precepts with the economic teachings of Aristotle? In using these examples, Montesquieu compels the reader to wonder if these extreme tyrannical acts of King John and Henry III could have been either prudent or profitable if these kings did not have— conveniently at their disposal—the moral sanction of a clergy newly enthused with Aristotle's rhetoric against commerce.

As further evidence, note Montesquieu's emphasis on the reaction of the theologians in the next paragraph:

> Theologians were obliged to curb their principles, and commerce, which had been violently linked to bad faith, returned, so to speak, to the bosom of integrity.

From the foregoing, an additional layer of interpretation is suggested. The invention of the letters of exchange tempers the avarice of the prince and the theologian who supplies the prince with principles.

Side-Effects of the Cure

The mention of Spain at the end book 21 is significant for a few reasons. Spain is a monarchy where the point of honor, according to Montesquieu, is taken to excess. It has a conquering spirit, not incompatible with the Catholic religion, which governs it almost exclusively.[4] In addition, Montesquieu views Spain as a ruthless imperial power, corrupted by its own success abroad, financially ruined by its dependency on its own colonies. Such a combination of political principles, religious uniformity and intolerance, and economic backwardness, preoccupied Montesquieu; he saw in these the ingredients for a monarchy on its way to despotism.[5]

The Spanish example is also a part of a theoretical triad with England and France that Montesquieu had been developing at least since 1724, when he wrote *Considérations sur les richesses de l'Espagne*, an unpublished work that was developed in *Réflexions sur la monarchie universelle* and planned as an "appendix" to *Considerations*.[6]

The relevance of Spain to political economy is understandable further in light of the preceding discussion of Rome. The Spain of the Hapsburgs is painted with the same flaws, including: a disdain for trade, a focus on conquest, ignorance of the sources of genuine prosperity,[7] and a general neglect of the population. Two features make modern Spanish monarchy a "particular case": suppression of "intermediate powers," checked only by the immense power of the clergy,[8] and its historical position as a large conquering state in a world increasingly governed by the logic of modern economics and finance. This modern combination of political, economic, and religious despotism gave urgency to the question, what is wealth?

This topic is explored in book 22, where Montesquieu examines laws and "their relation to the use of money." Book 22 is the most technically difficult book in *The Spirit of the Laws*,[9] and for understandable reasons, is rarely studied. The merits of book 22 from the point of view of economic science or economic history is mixed, at best. Economic historians have interpreted Montesquieu's defense of money as a "sign" as mercantilist, in spirit. Critics have also noted that the epistemological approach to the question of the "meaning" of money went out of fashion as modern economics turned to studying the function and effects of money as opposed to its nature or meaning.[10]

Reconsidered in light of an attempt to make commerce honorable, however, book 22 raises crucial questions for political economy. First, the "nature" of money was linked to the larger question of the nature—and origins—of national prosperity. While scholars still debate the beneficial economic effects of Law's banking and monetary scheme,[11] the effects of the System on the public perception of money and finance were disastrous, from the point of view of liberal reformers. As Kaiser has argued, the debate over money had an important bearing on the debate over the nature of sovereignty.[12] Law's system had tested, to the limit, the theory that money and credit could (or should) be regulated by the crown as part of its "royal authority." In the long run, the Law episode may have proved that "great acts of authority" were imprudent, as Montesquieu had argued. But in the short term, the collapse of the scheme, according to the conventional view of historians, had also destroyed the prospect of establishing a system of public credit in France.[13] Thus turning to the problem of honoring commerce as a *profession*, in book 21, there is an important link, to the issue of public credit, in book 22. One can see Montesquieu balancing a defense of modern finance with a careful avoidance of the (now tarnished) pro-finance vision of Law, "one of the greatest promoters of despotism yet seen in Europe."

In order, Montesquieu examines: "the nature of money" (XXII.2–5); credit and exchange rates (XXII.6–10); John Law's financial system (XXII.10); the problem of political manipulation of exchange rates and finance (XXII.12–13); the relation between "exchange" and despotism (XXII.14–16); public debt (XXII.17–18); and the causes and errors of the religious and political prejudice against loaning at interest (XXII.19–22).[14]

The central political argument is reflected in the title of chapter 14, "How Exchange Hampers Despotic States."[15] Repeating and extending the argument from book 21 (regarding the importance of the "exchange" in putting a check on plundering princes and priests) Montesquieu uses the example of the establishment of commerce in Muscovy as an illustration of the effects of economic institutions in rendering despotic law ineffective: that "the subjects of the empire, like slaves, were unable to leave or to send out their goods without permission." A similar phenomenon is observed in Italy. An increase in the number of independent "exchanges" simplified the transfer of wealth from one country to another, globalizing and augmenting the effects of mobile wealth. As in Muscovy, these new centers of money changing and moneylending circumvent heavy-handed property laws, such as preventing the sale of land or the transfer of wealth to foreign countries (XXII.15).

The central *social* issue—entirely ignored in book 21—is the moral legitimacy of moneylending, a subject which Montesquieu addresses in a group of arguments in the last four chapters"[16] While he admits that it would be "a very fine act to lend one's money to someone else without interest," he adds, "this can be only a religious counsel and not a civil law." The religious counsel is flawed in two important ways. First, it confuses the object of civil law (the "goodness of society") with the object of religion (the "goodness of man.")[17] Second (referring to the "law of Mohammed") it confuses usury with "loans at interest." Such confusions not only hamper commerce. Historically, the attempt to regulate moneylending out of existence increased interest rates, thus naturalizing usury and encouraging predatory lending: "Usury increases...in proportion to the severity of the prohibition; the lender indemnifies himself for his peril in infringing the law."[18]

Montesquieu's purpose was not to defend usury in itself; it was, in his words, to keep it "within just bounds."[19] The Romans had failed not only to achieve such moderation, through policies designed to discourage public borrowing. In the process of the attempt to root out corruption, the "honest means" of borrowing and lending disappeared. Montesquieu argues that the economic and political ripple effects of this unintended consequence were felt especially in the provinces, already "devastated" by harsh and despotic government.[20] Arguing that "extreme laws for good give rise to extreme evil," Montesquieu concludes book 22 by noting that "business must go forward," hinting, in addition, that the social opprobrium attached to moneylending hastened the destruction of the republic.

Underneath the condemnation of moneylending, however, lay a far greater challenge for Montesquieu's political economy. If indeed his goal was to reverse the damage to the image of commerce, it would be necessary, in addition, to disjoin two longstanding ideas: that the pursuit of self-interest in commercial society was unworthy of a soul who might aspire to a virtuous or honorable life; and second, that the increase of riches in a society would necessarily undermine religion.

Interests of the Soul

If books 21 and 22 answer to the aristocratic objection—of trade as a profession of "mean" people, book 23 can be thought of as the beginning of a reply to the religious objection—of trade as a profession of dishonest people.[21] Anticipating the traditional association between the pursuit of profit and the cardinal sin of avarice,[22] Montesquieu develops and clarifies his distinction between "wealth in signs" and "true wealth," which he locates in the labor and productivity of people. Thus, the title of book 23, *The Laws and the Number of Inhabitants* refers not only to the importance of population in an agricultural economy, as scholars commonly assume, but to the vital importance of civil laws, which influence both the productive power of labor and the prospects for human happiness. The true interests of human beings are rooted not in narrow economic interests, but in the things that enhance life: sex and love (XXIII.1), family and children (XXIII.2-4), the mutual sharing of the burdens of society (XXIII.11), the value and dignity of work (XXIII.15), the perpetuation of the human species (XXIII.16), and the provision of public goods for the "old, the sick, and the orphaned" (XXIII.29).

These earthly interests may be "disturbed" in "a thousand ways."[23] Thus Montesquieu turns, in book 24, to the topic of religion, focusing especially on the conflict between commerce, money, and population, and the varieties of religious experience and dogma. While Montesquieu's books on religion take up a mere two of thirty-one books in *The Spirit of the Laws*, his specific views on key elements of Christian doctrine have proved notoriously difficult to untangle. Following Montesquieu's own insistence that he speaks as a political writer, this chapter will not attempt to survey the range of scholarly opinions on Montesquieu's religious beliefs.[24] It is necessary to confine ourselves to ongoing debates on the relation between religion and politics, or in the following, religion and political economy. It has been suggested that Montesquieu's aim in Part 5 is to show that the religious laws have the same basis and are consistent with good political and civil laws.[25] Others have stressed the irreconcilability of religious laws with political and civil laws promoting Montesquieuean liberty. According to Robert Bartlett, Montesquieu's aim was to encourage the formation of a society in which religion "in general" would "fall into desuetude."[26] Montesquieu's anti-religious rhetoric served a radical end beyond simply transformation. The end of Montesquieu's theological political writings is long-range secularization.[27] The *means* for this end is not philosophy, science, biblical or theological criticism, but a kind of moderate materialism, which provides a "recipe to demote religion." It works by removing "the very concern for [religion] from the soul by the gentle means supplied by commerce."[28]

While this view is not uncontestable, it does illustrate, in my view, accurately, the primary importance of commerce or "economy" in the political analysis of religion—a topic that remains, in some respects, neglected in Montesquieu scholarship.[29] Missing from previous liberal analyses, however, is an exploration of the complicated "two-way" relationship between religion and economics. Viewed as a dialectical process, not a one-way interaction, it is clear that Montesquieu did not *present* his argument as a "recipe" for destroying religion.

To appreciate the fuller importance of the two-way or dialectical relationship, consider, first, an alternative and moderate liberal reading, which preserves Montesquieu's skepticism of traditional or revealed religion, while nonetheless maintaining the essential differences between Montesquieu and his irreligious precursors (Hobbes, Bayle) and his contemporaries (Voltaire, Diderot, and the *Encylopedists*).[30] According to Diana Schaub, Montesquieu joins fellow liberals in regarding Christianity as a danger to sound politics. She does not deny the possibility that Montesquieu is agnostic, atheist, or a deist. Book 1, in particular, appeals to the skeptic. Montesquieu's admiration of Bayle is barely concealed. Like his predecessors, Montesquieu was a religion tamer. His breakthrough consists in the elaboration of a commerce as the solvent for fundamentalism. Commerce works through the creation of "substitute satisfactions."[31]

According to this view, however, Montesquieu departed from Enlightenment radicals in significant ways. First, Montesquieu does not make the mistake of underestimating the difficulty of "civilizing" religion. Second, religion is not to be cut out root and branch, at the cost of political moderation:

> While Montesquieu joins his fellows in regarding Christianity as a danger to sound politics, Christianity is not the only threat he sees. He is concerned to ward off despotism of all varieties. Accordingly, he seeks to reform Christianity and solve the theological-political problem, but to do so without augmenting the power of the earthly sovereigns. Montesquieu is not a political centralizer... With Montesquieu, the link between liberalism and absolutism is severed.[32]

In the following, one more difference will be emphasized. Unique among Enlightenment philosophers, Montesquieu embarked on a careful study of the variety of religious beliefs, practices, and institutions. This "comparative religion" was not designed as a "philosophy" of religion, as an aid to comprehending the validity of religious beliefs. It is designed, rather, as Montesquieu claims, with the aim of discovering "the relation to the good to be drawn from them in the civil state."[33]

Previous liberal interpretations, in my view, have not overlooked the *political* effects of religion in Montesquieu's comparative study. Rather, there has been, to this date, little attention to the effect of religion on economy. As a result, the tension between commerce and religion in *The Spirit of the Laws* tends to have been overdrawn, resulting in a Montesquieu that was moderate in every aspect of his writing, save religion, where one would least expect to find Montesquieu departing from moderation as the governing principle of his political philosophy. A closer look at the relation between religion and economy in Part 5 helps to clarify Montesquieu's stated intention to "unite" the interests of "the true religion" with "political interests" (XXIV.1).

Religion and "Real Needs"

Before proceeding, it is necessary to summarize briefly the main questions and themes raised in book 23. In the first ten chapters, book 23 portrays religion in a negative light, as a distorting force that harms or impedes the natural liberty and wellbeing of women in the family, the lack of equal rights to property, enduring patterns of polygamy, paternalism in the rules of love and marriage.[34]

The negative association between religion and individual liberty is subject to a number of significant qualifications. First, Montesquieu had long distinguished between religions that promote life and "real needs," and those which thrive on a denial of this-worldly security and happiness.

Usbek, for example, describes the great clash between monastic religions and commercial society *as* an economic clash:

> The dervishes own and control all the state's wealth; they are a company of misers, who perpetually take and never return; they continually accumulate revenue in order to acquire capital; all this wealth becomes, as it were, paralysed; no longer is there any circulation, or any commerce, or any arts and science, or any manufacturing... commerce brings everything back to life, whereas... monasticism spreads death over everything. (114)

This opposition—between life-giving commerce and poverty-inducing monasticism—might be applied, on a larger scale, to Parts 4 and 5 of *The Spirit of the Laws*. The reader is encouraged to think of extreme forms of religion both as a civic and a civil problem.

To effectively counter the religions of poverty, however, it is not sufficient to redefine money for a society skeptical of its corrosive effect on honor and rank, the subject of book 22. A bolder attempt is made in book 23 to provide a re-evaluation of the value of life. This perhaps explains the significance of Montesquieu's poem in honor of Venus, life-giver (a passage added only in the very last phase of writing, as late as 1747). From a cold, rational look at the least erotic of matters (book 22, the *Laws and the Uses of Money*) he turns to a celebration of the erotic, presumably, one of the conditions of human flourishing (book 23, the *Laws in their relation to the number of Inhabitants*).[35] If money rules the world in book 22, in book 23, it is the charm of Venus, life-giver, who holds the reigns. The desire for unlimited acquisition is common, but the power of Venus is universal: it "sinks love's tingling dart" in every human being, "luring them lustily to create their kind."[36]

The real core of the tension between Part 4 and Part 5 is not, therefore, religion and commerce (or God and money), but religion and the human body (or God and sex).[37] Religion is not, of course, the only force that shapes attitudes toward sex and sexuality. In the next logical grouping of chapters[38] Montesquieu highlights the influence of climate and politics, which compete, so to speak, with religion in bending and shaping individual erotic drive.[39] The analysis points at an idealized balance: between local economic and political needs (the second grouping of chapters) and local religious laws (the first grouping). If religion plays an over-sized role, in regulating matters of sexuality, climate plays an increasingly trivial role, as societies develop.

The importance of *eros* in political economy is further explored in the third and last grouping (XXIII.17–29).[40] In the last 13 chapters of book 23, Montesquieu returns explicitly to the relationship between religion and sexuality. The rhetoric *against* monasticism and otherworldliness is ratcheted up considerably. Not to offend the ecclesiastical censors, Montesquieu once again returns to Rome. While Roman–republican foreign policy was ruinous and self-defeating (a cause of the "depopulation of the universe" XXIII.19), pre-Christian civil law provides relevant examples. In particular, the middle republic prioritized population growth, a "nursery" of citizens, supported by laws that avoided "useless marriages." A number of these laws (inducing the citizenry to have large families) are, in retrospect, tyrannical, ridiculous, or both, sometimes producing tragi-comic unintended consequences.[41] Still, it is generally true that Montesquieu is much more sympathetic to the pre-Christian emperors—Caesar and Augustine—than he is to Rome after Constantine's conversion. Christianity, he says, gave Rome an "idea of perfection" which led the citizens to a "speculative life" and produced a "distance from the cares and encumbrances of the family" (XXIII.21). Religious—in a word, celibacy—made "multiplication" no longer one of the "cares" of the state.[42]

This particular aspect of Montesquieu's critique of Christian Rome can easily be misunderstood.[43] Readers have claimed, for example, that Montesquieu was caught up in what scholars have termed the "depopulation delusion."[44] The problem as it is stated in *The Spirit of the Laws*, however, is not merely that Europe is *in fact* suffering from depopulation; but rather, that Europe is in danger of *repeating* Rome's mistake after Constantine. According to Montesquieu, Constantine's policy hurt population growth by reversing laws favorable to propagation. When Montesquieu concludes, in Chapter 26, that Europe is in danger of depopulation (it is "an instance of the case in which laws are needed to favor the propagation of the human species") he is not attempting to give demonstration to a demographic trend.[45] The criticism is lodged in the context of a larger story about the historical rise of Christianity and its diverse effects on society. Understood in broad historical terms, Montesquieu's analysis of population is preparatory, that is, for a critical re-examination of religion, carried out in Part 5.[46] It is clear, moreover, from the *Persian Letters*, that depopulation was not only an effect but a *symbol* of religious fanaticism. The "depopulation of the universe," he argued, was the "most terrible catastrophe the world has ever experienced." But it was not from accident, plague, or famine. The root cause he described as an "internal defect, a secret, hidden poison, a decline afflicting the human race."[47]

The final two chapters of book 23 contain a message about the stakes of reform. Depopulation has natural sources (accident, plague, famine) and political ("internal vice" or "bad government"). Natural depopulation contains its own correction. Surviving populations either perish or revive the spirit of "work and industry." Cultural depopulation due to an "internal vice" is harder to remedy because its cause is largely invisible to the "common people": "The clergy, the prince, the towns, the important men, and some principal citizens have gradually become owners of the whole region; it is uncultivated, but the ruined families have left their pastures to them, and the working man has nothing." The chain of reasoning connects depopulation to feudalism, and feudalism to a combined monastic and aristocratic abhorrence of industry and commerce.

Commercial society generates its own iniquities. In a commercial economy, security is attached to professions, and wealth is generated through competition and industry. "When there are such a great number of branches of commerce, it is not possible for some branch not to suffer and, consequently, for its workers not to be in some temporary necessity." As a result, Montesquieu views welfare for the old, sick, and the orphaned, a necessary obligation of the state: "A few alms given to a naked man in the streets does not fulfill the obligations of the state, which owes all the citizens an assured sustenance, nourishment, suitable clothing, and a kind of life which is not contrary to health."

At the close of book 23, Montesquieu evokes Henry VIII, famous, among other things, for his dissolution of the monasteries in the late 1530s. This rude intrusion of the despotic founder of the Church of England[48] is an unsubtle, but effective, reminder of the alternative to moderate reform in France. Henry's brutal violation of the Clergy's authority and holdings "liberated" the "spirit of commerce" and industry in England.

Book 23 thus ends with two equally unpleasant alternatives. A failure to address the "internal vice" and "bad government" of feudal political economy would result, Montesquieu predicted, in languor, poverty, desolation, and despotism—setting the stage for violent struggle, and a necessary redistribution of property, repeating the history of imperial Rome in its decline.[49] The second alternative is direct confrontation. Would it be necessary to launch a precipitous attack on the economic power base of the Catholic church, following the example of Henry VIII?

Montesquieu's Audience

The remaining section of this chapter outlines Montesquieu's assessment of the historical and economic conditions necessary for religious transformation and reform. We will then address (in the final chapter) Montesquieu's related project for transforming the civil law, concentrating especially on the problem of property in the context of pre-revolutionary France.

Having raised the *stakes* in book 23 of religious reform, Montesquieu now turns directly to his comparative study of religion. Henry VIII is manifestly a foil. Modeling his own proscription for moderation, Montesquieu embarks on a sociological study of the earthly effects of religious beliefs, practices, and institutions. Implicitly rejecting militant anti-clericalism, the sociological approach to religion in Part 5 focuses attention instead on social utility. Addressing his audience as a political writer, and as an historian, not as a theologian,[50] Montesquieu's avowed rhetorical purpose is to seek out religions—including the false ones—that are "most in conformity with the good of society, the ones that, though they do not have the effect of leading men to the felicities of the next life, can most contribute to their happiness in this one."[51] Later, Montesquieu reflected on the delicacy of this approach. He had attempted to avoid flattering those with "more piety than intelligence," while at the same time, doing nothing that might discredit himself in the eyes of philosophy (those with "more intelligence than piety").[52]

Unique among the *philosophes*, Montesquieu's study of the social utility of religion includes an analysis of the relationship between religion and economy.[53] Calling believers back to the common social utility of their beliefs is not a breakthrough, nor obviously was it original to Montesquieu.[54] Echoing the seventeenth century natural law tradition, Montesquieu asked readers to voluntarily disengage from the question of the truth of religion, and to consider, as he does, religion "only in relation to the good to be drawn from them in the civil state."

Yet, few writers went as far as Montesquieu, I will argue, to emphasize the economic costs and benefits of religious law and belief. Religion is reconceived in Part 5 comparatively, inviting or indeed demanding a cost-benefit analysis. To put this more simply, religion becomes a choice among competing spiritual products. Faith is transfigured into a commodity, making it possible to suggest that Montesquieu inaugurated the study of religion as a two-way interaction with political economy.[55] Religion is viewed variously as the "dependent variable," with economic development and modernization shaping attitudes and belief. But it is also explored by Montesquieu as the experimental variable, a driving factor in the formation of individual characteristics, including industry, honesty, and thrift—factors that are explicitly linked by Montesquieu with economic performance and prosperity.[56]

None of this is suggestive of a science of fine calibration. All that can be generated are crude but suggestive hypotheses: Christianity is more suitable to moderate government; Islam's military history discourages "soft mores"; Protestantism is more likely to foster independence and republicanism; speculative religions detract from production and distribution of basic needs; predestination encourages an aversion to work.[57]

Montesquieu was surely aware of the limits of religion as sociology. In the first chapter, "religions in general," the enterprise is characterized as a humorously futile science, insofar, that is, as it involves "poking around" among abysses and shadows to find which one is the deepest.[58] The analogy of the project as an attempt to "sound out" the depth of abysses is not unimportant, however. Using the deliberately humorous language of shadow-measuring, Montesquieu suggestively avoids the bolder, more radical language in currency, that is, of Enlightenment.

It becomes clear in the second chapter that Montesquieu's ideal reader is not the wavering believer. Appearing to oppose Bayle's claim that it is "better to be an atheist than an idolater" and that "it is less dangerous to have no religion at all than to have a bad one," Montesquieu in fact strengthens Bayle's argument, in the following ways.[59] First, Montesquieu tacitly concedes to the premise of Bayle's "sophistry." Earlier in his life, Montesquieu had more or less supported Bayle in the latter's criticism of the idolatry of pagans. As early as 1716, Montesquieu had been staunchly opposed to the presumption that pagans merited eternal damnation. He did so on the grounds of the theological plausibility of arguments for evil and for grace. Here, the much older Montesquieu opposes Bayle for incorrectly enumerating the evils religion has produced. One reasons incorrectly, he writes, to "collect in a large work a long enumeration of the evils it has produced, without also making one of the good things it has done." Even if it were useless for the *subjects* to have a religion, "it would not be useless for princes to have one and to whiten with foam the only bridle that can hold those who fear no human laws" (XXIV.2).

As above, Montesquieu's silence on the theological question of grace is carefully sidestepped. But in opposing Bayle's *conclusions*, Montesquieu clearly affirms the utilitarian premise. Bayle has simply made a reckless accounting error. Presenting himself as a defender of true religion, Montesquieu serves in fact as a friendly tutor. His reader is asked to judge only the facts: who is the more discerning auditor of the true good and evil of religion?

In the third chapter, Montesquieu provides an apology of Christianity that rests on this-worldly standards of humanity, liberty, and peace. Christianity is superior on the grounds of humanity (in particular, Montesquieu opposes Christianity to "Mohammedanism," which he argues is less gentle and humane and contributes less to happiness in this world [XXIV.3]). It is admirable for its positive role in preventing despotism and bridling the cruelty of princes. Finally, in a phrase often quoted, Montesquieu defends Christianity because of its positive contribution to international legal norms that have helped to reduce the human costs of war:

> We owe to Christianity both a certain political right in government and a certain right of nations in war, for which human nature can never be sufficiently grateful.[60]

Deftly avoiding the topic of reform, Montesquieu returns to take on Bayle.

Bayle had proposed a second, more challenging paradox. "[Bayle] dares propose that a state formed by true Christians would not continue to exist." In his *Pensées*, Montesquieu terms this "foolish," that is, "to say that a republic of good Christians could not last."[61]

The reply to Bayle in *The Spirit of the Laws* depends on a number of shaky assumptions: that Christian citizens would be "infinitely enlightened about their duties," that their "zeal" to perform them would be augmented by Christian views of the "rights of natural defense" and more, that "the more they believed they owed to the religion, the more they would think they owed to the homeland." These Christian principles would be "infinitely stronger than the false honor of monarchies, the human virtues of republics, or that servile fear of despotic states."

This series of arguments is misleading. In the abstract, there appears to be no tension between the city of God, which needs no gates to defend itself against invaders, and the earthly city, which does. The rationale for Christian patriotism in book 24 depends on the assumption that Christian piety will replace republican virtue, monarchical glory, and despotic insecurity or fear.

This abstract defense of Christian patriotism in book 24 should be considered in relation to Montesquieu's considerably more complex view of Christian patriotism, in book 19. There, in the context of commercial England, Montesquieu suggests that religious principles were quite insufficient. Famously, Montesquieu argues that England combines religious and pecuniary interests to preserve external liberty. Bayle's "paradox" from the perspective of historical reality is a red herring. The real question, already raised in book 19, was how a large commercial republic might be expected to sacrifice their "goods, ease and interests" for their liberty.[62] The English patriot performs a calculus, not dissimilar to the faithful. Except, she does not think: "The more I think I owe to Christianity, the more I think I owe to the homeland." Rather, "The more I think I owe to commerce and business, the more I think I owe to the homeland."

Read in light of the previous discussion of England, it is clear that Montesquieu had developed two distinct responses to the second of Bayle's paradoxes. A pure Christian republic may not lack for courage. The harder question that Bayle did not ask—and the question that mattered infinitely more in light of national survival—was whether such a nation would lack for credit.[63]

Putting Religion Back to Work

Montesquieu had explored the question of whether Christianity and commerce might be compatible in the *Persian Letters*. He described the tension in terms of a suggestive metaphor, a power struggle between the king's "confessor" and his "mistress," the one representing religious morality, the latter representing the allure of pleasure and luxury—rivals for the "king's mind."[64] Young monarchs are more susceptible to the influence of the latter, Rica argued, adding further that with age, these two powers "become reconciled, and join their forces."

This playful anecdote is formalized in the book 20 maxim: "the laws of commerce perfect mores for the same reason that they destroy mores. Commerce corrupts pure mores: this is the subject of Plato's complaints; it polishes & softens barbarous mores, as we see every day."[65] Importantly, that maxim lacked any explanatory content, however. It also left unexplained the reverse causal relationship of religion and commercial activity and society. Part 5 addresses this reverse causation. It creates as it were a "science" of the chemistry between religion and commerce.[66] But to create the conditions for a successful match, Montesquieu outlines a number of amendments to the methods in which philosophers have traditionally debated the utility of religion.

First, Montesquieu collapses an important distinction between revealed religion and philosophy. "The various sects of philosophy among the ancient could be considered *as kinds of* religion."[67] Claiming that he will "cease to think" of himself as a Christian, momentarily, Montesquieu laments the decline of the Stoics, noting that the destruction of Zeno's sect was "among the [great] misfortunes of human kind." Stoicism "alone made great men; it alone made great emperors."[68]

If revealed religion and pagan philosophy could be fairly compared, it was not a big leap to suggest, as Montesquieu does next, to introduce a standard by which to judge all religions regardless of their natural or divine source. "Men, being made to preserve, feed, and clothe themselves, and to do all the things done in society, religion should not give them an overly contemplative life."[69] The active life of Stoicism provides, by contrast, a healthy counterpoint to the contemplative, grave, otherworldliness of monasticism. The example of Stoicism also illustrates Montesquieu's inner conviction that life is not reducible to satisfaction of base desires, or toil for its own sake: viewing "wealth, human greatness, suffering, sorrows, and pleasures to be vain things," the Stoic aspiration is to avoid a life devoted merely to labor (dull and inhuman) while also rejecting a life of public self-sacrifice for the sake of honor or "greatness."

If contemplative religion is harmful to the extent that it leads to indifference of human needs, does Montesquieu's stance also reject philosophy as a way of life? One of the revealing ironies of Montesquieu's study of religion, in Part 5, is that it requires boundless curiosity, and an awe-inspiring speculative effort, not merely a labor in the sociological effects of religion, but also, a deep investigation into the psychological content and meaning of various systems of metaphysics. Shinto mythology, its view of heaven and hell, for example, is examined in relation to the history of civil laws in Japan. Divine destiny in Islam (*qadar*) is examined in relation to the effect on industry and attitudes toward work. The cosmological doctrines in Taoism are analyzed in relation to care of the body.[70]

As these examples demonstrate, Montesquieu does not clearly distinguish between the effects of religious belief on citizenship and the effects of religious belief on commerce or economy. Presumably, Montesquieu views them as inseparable in his study, although he does assume at least three necessary conditions for both. First, the religion must have a place of reward and punishment. A doctrine of the afterlife that is devoid of reward or punishment may not only be useless to the state; in some cases, it may provide a vacuum in the justice system, encouraging the legislator to compensate by enacting more repressive civil laws.[71] Second, free will is preferable to predestination from a civic *and economic* point of view. A religion that "fixes" the fate of the individual without regard to action in this life is worse, he claims, than having no religion at all.[72] Finally, Montesquieu is highly critical of descriptions of the afterlife that, for lack of a better word, promise sensual or erotic rewards:

> Almost everywhere in the world, and in all times, the opinion that the soul is immortal, wrongly taken, has engaged women, slaves, subjects, and friends to kill themselves in order to go to the next world and serve the object of their respect or love.[73]

This last condition occupies a central place in the political economy of religion as presented in *The Spirit of the Laws*. Readers of the *Persian Letters* will be reminded of the fantastic description of the afterlife, narrated by a Persian woman named Zulema, whose vision of heaven is filled with "sublime men," including male slaves waiting on every desire, where everything is "designed to fill her senses with rapture," and where the "purpose of so many pleasures was purely to lead her gradually to greater pleasures."[74] This vision of heaven, Zulema implies, leads her to "disdain death," which would "mark the end of her sufferings and the beginning of her felicity."[75] One will notice that this same argument is made in book 24 in *The Spirit of the Laws*, although with an added emphasis not on the sexual rewards of the afterlife, but on the degree of *certainty* that one will be rewarded: "Men who believe in the certainty of rewards in the next life will escape the legislator; they will have too much scorn for death. How can one constrain by the laws a man who believes himself sure that the greatest penalty the magistrates can inflict on him will end in a moment only to begin his happiness?"[76]

In the time between the *Persian Letters* and *The Spirit of the Laws* Montesquieu played with possible reforms. Perhaps the most significant proposal, found in book 24, is a de-sensualization of the soul's existence after death.[77] Montesquieu consistently argued that religious moderation depends on a strong emphasis on a specifically incorporeal spirit: faith should "[make] us hope for a state that we believe in, not a state that we feel or that we know."[78] The soul is an ontological reality, and it is not strictly unconnected from the body. But the appetites should not remain, nor presumably, should the organs that exist to satisfy them. A "pure" Montesquieuean soul seems to have mental properties, but it neither performs intentional actions or—most importantly—experiences sensual pleasure in the base sense. Denying the resurrection of the body, Montesquieu further distinguishes between three dangerous "dogmas" related to the immortality of the soul: pure immortality, a "simple change of abode," or metempsychosis. Each has their disadvantages, although "a simple change of abode"—the one Montesquieu associates with Christianity—is particularly harmful, when it is "wrongly taken" to imply a resurrection of the body.[79]

To summarize, Montesquieu's vision of a reformed civic theology is minimalistic, but not relativistic. Industry and citizenship are improved by the promise of a place of reward. Although a lake of fire, including permanent torture, is not recommended, Montesquieu does speculate on the utility of a place of punishment (heaven *without* hell is considered more dangerous to civic stability than outright non-belief). Finally, Montesquieu rejects religious determinism, appearing to opt for a system that emphasizes free will, although he takes no sides in the finer controversies of conditional, temporal, or other species of predestination.[80] If there is one inflexible doctrine that is central to a Montesquieuean metaphysics of the soul, it is Montesquieu's outright rejection of the wishful thinking of enthusiasts who believe that death will answer all the erotic prayers that go unanswered in this life.

The Economics of Toleration

After surveying the range of effects of belief on citizenship, Montesquieu begins to focus attention on the causes of religious diversity in practice. Respect for the diversity of religious belief is not rooted in a respect for diversity itself, but in the following chapters, as a reflection of historical utility and the socio-economic root causes of "local religious laws."[81] The danger of religious intolerance, explored in book 13 in light of personal freedom, is analyzable here by the standards of peace, security, and prosperity. Civil peace and political stability are upset when religion inspires "horror" for indifferent things, including the consumption of beef or pork.[82] Prosperity is affected in various ways, for example, by an excessive attention to "festivals," or through local ordinances that do not distinguish between the "useful" work done in towns and the "necessary" work in the country.[83] Importantly, Montesquieu recommends a study of the historical causes of local religious laws, not merely to better understand the economic influence—say, of a religious ban on the consumption of certain kinds of livestock—but of the economic rationale behind the formation of practices themselves. So for example, Montesquieu believes that the phenomenon of the Holy Cow can be explained by considering the costs and benefits of the relatively unpalatable meat, as opposed to the much greater economic prestige of milk and butter.

At the end of book 24, Montesquieu has travelled a long way: first, from the question of the truth or falsity of religion; to an appraisal of religious beliefs as they affect attitudes and incentives toward justice and work; and finally, to a particularized "sociological" account of the material causes of religious practice. Two rhetorical shifts are worth highlighting before we turn to book 25. First, Montesquieu has *broadened* the scope of religious debate by drawing the reader's attention away from the high stakes disputes between Protestant and Catholic, Jesuit and Jansenist theology. The controversy of Christian metaphysics is replaced with a colder, rational examination of "world religions." In broadening the discussion, Montesquieu's analysis necessarily becomes more shallow, reducing the study of religion, some would say, offensively, to a series of testable propositions about the economic and sociological origins and effects of comparative philosophies of the soul.

But is this shallowing not at the same time a deliverance of the promise in book 1? Montesquieu has explained why the belief in an immortal soul, and the "idea of a creator" is a natural law; that is, in the sense that it is of great "importance" to all human beings. Furthermore, Montesquieu's treatment of religion in book 24 is consistent with his earlier claim that religion is the "first" natural law, not in the temporal sense, but in the sequence of human development.[84] Religion for Montesquieu is manmade, not a product of God's disclosure to man through revelation. But it is not irrational. It appears to be like any other human institution, a product of climate, history, culture, politics, and occasionally, good economic sense.

Book 25: Attachment and Detachment

Perhaps it was Montesquieu's view that religious war would be less common, and religious disputes less disruptive, if the study of religion could be reduced to a "thin" sociology. In book 25, however, Montesquieu presents a more sophisticated approach. Even from a reductionist starting point, the study of religion has to take into account not only the *roots* of belief (what Hobbes called the "seeds of religion") but the *persistence* of belief, even after religion has ceased to serve its original function.

In turning to this question, of the persistence of belief, the political economy approach takes on added significance. If economic decisions are a factor in the sources of religious custom, to what extent might they play a role in the selection and perpetuation of religious institutions?

Montesquieu starts the book, like the last, by putting up a guard, although it is posed in the form of a slight against the hypocrisy of the atheist:

> The pious man and the atheist always speak of religion; the one speaks of what he loves and the other of what he fears.[85]

The title of the chapter "On the Feeling for Religion," underlines Montesquieu's skepticism; the object of piety is a feeling, or a desire. While he reverses the Hobbesian emphasis on religion as the *"feare* of power invisible, feigned by the mind, or imagined from tales publiquely allowed," Montesquieu nonetheless retains the Hobbesian emphasis on the passions as the source of religious enthusiasm.

Montesquieu distances himself from the Hobbesian explanation, at the same time. If piety in general is hope or love, an "appetite for obtaining" as Hobbes might say, then *particular* religion, which is to say, religious diversity, is a result of reason and passion together. Particular religion arises out of differences in our "way of thinking" (XXV.2). It follows from these opening two paragraphs that religion is not merely superstition, a "panic" or "terror" of the unknown. But more reasonably, a product of natural passion *and* reasonable calculation. What stands out in Montesquieu's framework here is his analysis of the range of motives for attachment and detachment. Presumably, if one can better understand the ranges of attachment, such information would not be useless in "changing religion."[86]

No space is wasted in identifying a list of potent ingredients in the rational and emotional concoction that makes up a commanding belief. Most importantly, a religion that portrays a "supreme spiritual being" who responds to and comprehends earthly desires, while also encouraging "sensible" practices of worship, has great staying power.[87] Combining perfection with an understanding of earthly desires produces a more "invincible" attachment, while also producing a "more zealous...propagation."[88]

The flattering idea of being chosen matters. "When an intellectual religion also gives us the idea of a choice made by the divinity, and of a distinction between those who profess it and those who do not profess it, this attaches us greatly to the religion."[89] Further, it helps also to have "many practices," since one is attached "to the things that continually occupy" our time. Hence, according to Montesquieu, barbarians and savages are somewhat flexible in their religious evolution. Hunting and warring make it impossible to "burden themselves with religious practices."

Hell is a significant attraction. While Montesquieu does not explain why, here, he does elaborate, in article 122 of the *Spicilège*, on a terrifying description of hell taken from Marsollier's *History of the Inquisition and its origin* (1693). There, the existence of a metaphysical hell provided existential justification for the *question*. The practical implication being that a religion with a hell is more fearsome and better able to justify cruel punishment in this world.[90]

A fifth important condition is related to a longing for "pure morality." Men may be "rascals one by one," Montesquieu observes, but when they get together, "they love morality." Successful religions are like morality plays. There is justice in the end.

Moving now to the strictly economic, Montesquieu argues in a penultimate paragraph that religious durability correlates directly to the "externals of worship." Powerful religions are often "magnificent" temporally as well as spiritually. The outward wealth not only flatters the believer. "Wealth in the temples and the clergy affects us greatly," he explains, for more basic reasons: "The very poverty of peoples is a motive attaching them to that religion, which has served as a pretext for those who have caused their poverty."[91] The third chapter entitled "On Temples" describes the importance of building a "house for god," a critical space for reassurance that prayers are answered, but also a "natural idea" for people who cultivate the land.[92] "Peoples who have no temples have little attachment to religion," argues Montesquieu, citing Genghis Khan's "scorn" for mosques.[93]

Does Montesquieu's analysis contain a recipe for secularization and/or dis-attachment? It is worth bearing in mind a few complicating factors. In book 19 he insists, for example, that the legislator is to "follow the spirit of a nation," adding, "for we do nothing better than what we do freely and by following our natural genius."[94] It was also claimed as "a maxim of capital importance" that mores and manners, especially in despotic states, are not safely "overturned."[95] Reformation through the instrument of law "would appear to be too tyrannical." Instead, Montesquieu insists on reformation at the level of what we call civil society, that is "by other mores and other manners."[96] It is preferable to "engage the peoples to change them themselves."[97]

Chapters 4–8 continue what may be considered the *indirect* strategy of Part 5. They present a number of related commercial and economic means to reduce the grip of religious fanaticism. He recommends leaving the "right" of property ("sacred and inviolable") of the Church, but removing the "fact," that is, by allowing the "necessary domain" of the clergy to be "fixed and eternal" but appropriating new domains. Monasteries should not receive special privileges, to buy and sell "for life," which allows the clergy to "gamble with the people" while "holding the bank themselves."[98] Following the enlightened Plato, the state can regulate the profiting of superstition, extractions from the peoples on the pretext of flattering the gods with lavish gifts.[99]

In short, Montesquieu clearly supports the radical Enlightenment goal of detachment from superstition. Yet Montesquieu can still be distinguished from radical reformers and debunkers. First, resurrecting arguments directly from Plato's *Laws* (716e–717a; 885b), Montesquieu emphasizes the limits of rational demonstration. Plato's stranger had said "all of the most sensible things that natural enlightenment has ever said on the subject of religion." In the next few chapters, Montesquieu outlines a new strategy for promoting "toleration in religious matters." It involves the broad dissemination of a commercial worldview, making it possible, without shocking the "spirit" of the nation, to reduce "pernicious opinions" without relying on rational argument alone.[100]

The Longer Road to Toleration

Montesquieu provides a minimalist reconstruction of the eighteenth-century debate on the necessity of toleration.[101] In part, this is because

Montesquieu had written on toleration in the *Persian Letters*; specifically, on matters relating to the 1685 revocation of the Edict of Nantes, the exile of Huguenots, the forced conversion of Armenians living in Persia, and the negative economic effects on commercial and industrial development in those communities.[102] In book 25, his thoughts are distilled into two general ideas. Toleration in a religiously diverse society is necessary for civic order. The state must guard against religious interference with political laws as jealously as it guards private religious liberty.[103]

Montesquieu's view on toleration is more sophisticated than is generally acknowledged, however. The brevity of Montesquieu's remarks on toleration illustrate, by example, his belief that a principled defense of tolerance is difficult to translate into political practice. If a state adopts the principle of toleration (an "open door" policy of tolerating all religions) it may leave itself defenseless on rational grounds against the spread, internally, of intolerant sects. On the other hand, legal or political discrimination (the "closed door" policy) also has its problems, as other scholars have noticed.[104] Few legislators are in the fortunate position of being "the master of the state's accepting a new religion or not accepting it" (XXV.10). Moreover, it is difficult to imagine a case where a liberal society might without contradiction "quash" religions *perceived* to be intolerant (or in Montesquieu's words "greatly zealous to establish themselves").

To the extent that Montesquieu has a practical solution, it is understandable only in light of his deeply held conviction in the slowness of historical change. In Montesquieu's own words, true or lasting change depends on "preparing the spirits" (XIX.2–6). In relation to religious change, this is suggestive of a project to deliberately cultivate religious "indifference."[105] Toleration depends not on the refinement of public opinion (or, following Bayle, challenging the received notion that comets were an augury of disaster through historical science) but a "forgetting" of the concern for the soul after death.[106]

In this sense, one can better understand the absence in *The Spirit of the Laws* of a well-developed theory of toleration. Still, two chapters remain crucial for understanding not only Montesquieu's strategy for encouraging religious tolerance, but the core significance of commercial and economic development to that end.

To clarify Montesquieu's intentions, it is useful again to return briefly to Hobbes.

Laurence Berns summarizes Hobbes' solution to religious toleration aptly as follows.[107] For Hobbes, peace in civil society depends on the sovereign possessing the power of life and death over his subjects. Religion teaches that there are other powers capable of granting infinitely greater rewards than life, but also more devastating punishments than death.

Naturally, they will tend to obey the supreme judge, over against the earthly sovereign. Therefore, the truth or falsity of the doctrines concerning the Kingdom of God should not be decided "by any but those that have the sovereign power."

In Chapters 12 and 13 of book 25, Montesquieu rejects Hobbes' solution. Hobbes solution, ironically, was not realistic enough, and in at least two ways. First, Hobbes' political psychology mistakenly identified fear as a natural solvent for religious fervor. In particular, Hobbes erred in assuming that a fear of a violent death can be manipulated—by the sovereign—to help detach men from their fear of powers invisible. This will not work, argues Montesquieu, because the magistrate is unlikely to succeed by *compounding* one fear on another, that is, by merely "filling [the soul] with this great object [of fear]" (XXV.12).[108] The compounding of fears only brings human beings closer to the moment of death—thus adding more fuel to the fire of zealotry. Hobbes' mistake, in Montesquieu's words, was to bring people "closer to the moment when [they] should find religion of greater importance" (XXV.12).

Fighting religious fear with political tyranny is also a losing proposition from the perspective of the stability of the state.[109] At best, subjects will be more confused about their duties. At worst, the two fears may effectively cancel each other out, leaving the state not only with bad believers but bad citizens as well (XXV.12). Montesquieu's rejection of Hobbes' political psychology in this chapter is followed by an unstated acknowledgement of Locke's alteration of Hobbes' blunt teaching. Following Locke, Montesquieu revises Hobbes' solution to religious civil war, not only with a gentler political psychology but also with a more sophisticated political approach to taming religious extremism.[110]

The penultimate expression of the Montesquieuean alternative is found at the end of Chapter 12:

> A more certain way to attack religion is by favor, by the comforts of life, by the hope of fortune, not by what reminds one of it, but by what makes one forget it; not by what makes one indignant, but by what leads one to indifference when other passions act on our souls and when those that religion inspires are silent. General rule: in the matter of changing religion, invitations are stronger than penalties.

The Limits of Remonstrance

One more step is needed to appreciate Montesquieu's unique contribution to the debate on toleration. According to historian David A. Bell, the French Enlightenment spoke with a single voice on two political causes: reforming the system of criminal justice, and establishing religious toleration.[111] In both cases, argues Bell, the principle weapon used was "the judicial *cause celebre*" of highlighting an "individual case of persecution and justice" before the "tribunal of public opinion." The most famous of these, in the 1760s, came from the pen of Voltaire, who led the way in fighting for the "posthumous rehabilitation" of Jean Calas, a merchant, from Toulouse, gruesomely executed after having been falsely accused of murdering his own son. As Bell concludes, the *philosophes* brought these cases widespread attention, using pamphlets, judicial briefs, and newspapers, often by means of sympathetic lawyers. The success of this campaign is still regarded as one of the key reasons for the reform of criminal justice in the old regime (especially sanctioned torture) and, in 1787, limited toleration of Protestants.

It is in this context that we may now examine Montesquieu's famous chapter, "Very humble remonstrance to the inquisitors of Spain and Portugal."[112] The chapter opens as follows:

> An eighteen-year-old Jewess, burned in Lisbon at the last auto-da-fé, occasioned this small work, and I believe it is the most useless that has ever been written. When it is a question of proving such clear things, one is sure not to convince.[113]

It is worth noticing, first, that Montesquieu makes use of a framing device to separate himself from the speech. He does not separate himself from the point of view of the Jewess, however; only from the *manner* or ultimate persuasiveness of the arguments within it.

The "author" of this "humble remonstrance" is also a Jew, but not unfriendly to Christianity:

> The author declares, that, although he is a Jew, he respects the Christian religion and that he loves it enough to take away from princes who will not be Christians a plausible pretext for persecuting it.

Here, we need only to observe that the author is not a partisan polemicist writing singly to embarrass or scold the Church for the Inquisition. The author raises a different kind of question. How might reformers speak to the enemies of free conscience, the "Inquisitors" of humanity who are least likely to be moved by rational argument?

The rest of the "humble remonstrance" provides an outline of an answer. In it, the Jew, self-aware of the limits of his own rationalism, provides three distinct kinds of argument.[114] The first is grounded solidly in Christian moral principles. A direct appeal is made to the

Christian principles of love, compassion, and mercy (XXV.13; 3–5).[115] The Inquisitors, he notes, are "much more cruel" than even the emperor of Japan, who burned "all the Christians in his state...by a slow fire." Similarly, the writer invokes the common ideals of peace, charity, and universality.[116]

The argument, up to this point, works on the internal logic of Christian morality. It is framed in a manner that aims to protect Christianity, not against its foes, but against itself. One could call it, simply, the "ideal" remonstrance. It is a call for the Inquisitors to imitate the example of their own prophet:

> We entreat you, not by the powerful god we both serve, but by the Christ that you tell us took on the human condition in order to give you examples you could follow; we entreat you to act with us as he himself would act if he were still on earth.[117]

As the speech proceeds, however, it becomes evident that the thoughtful writer does not put a great deal of faith in this first "ideal" remonstrance. Abandoning this line of argument, the writer turns to an appeal to natural justice:

> But if you do not want to be Christians, at least be men; treat us as you would if, having only the feeble lights of justice that nature gives us, you had no religion to guide you and no revelation to enlighten you.[118]

At the end of the remonstrance, the writer changes course once more. If the "feeble lights of justice" are not themselves sufficient, perhaps the zealot may be moved by a lower motivation, never in short supply: human vanity.[119] Claiming that he will now speak "plainly," the writer admits that he has taken sanctuary in a simple, although seemingly hopeless, appeal to pride; presumably, the only remaining option when other forms of remonstrance fail.[120]

CHAPTER 6

THE PROBLEM OF PROPERTY IN
THE SPIRIT OF THE LAWS

The question before us now is not whether Montesquieu was a proponent of the modern Enlightenment project.[1] The more useful question, arising out of this study in political economy, is whether Montesquieu's philosophy of liberalism can properly be understood as part of the radical Enlightenment, as distinguished from the moderate mainstream, or conservative Enlightenment.[2] Bound up in this interpretive question is the larger question of Western intellectual inheritance: that is, the way in which modern political rationalism, liberalism, and capitalism might be better understood by returning to the eighteenth-century intellectual battles over the meaning of commercial modernity.

As argued in the previous chapter, on the topic of religion, one can find evidence for both views. Defenders of Montesquieu's radicalism on religion focus especially on the chapter "on Penal Laws" in book 25, where Montesquieu argues that "a more certain way to attack religion is by favor, by the comforts of life, by the hope of fortune, not by what reminds one of it, but by what makes one forget it." Critics of the idea of Montesquieu as radical commonly point to Montesquieu's commitment to the values of toleration and moderation. They focus especially on Montesquieu's claim in book 24, that it is possible to "unite" the true religion with political interests. Opposing the revolutionary liberal view, they argue that Montesquieu's writing on religion in *The Spirit of the Laws* should be interpreted as an attempt to "reconcile" the ends of religion and politics, to uncover the common principles that would prevent religious conflict and promote sociality.[3]

The purpose of the following chapter is to extend the liberal-revolutionary reading of Montesquieu by way of a detailed examination of the problem of property[4] in *The Spirit of the Laws*.[5] While it is not possible to address the full political implications of Montesquieu's subversive views of the civil laws, arguably the foundation of Montesquieu's revolutionary political economy, it is possible in the following to clarify his complicated stance on property, a topic which has so far attracted little attention.[6]

Property as Convention

A condensed version of Montesquieu's theory of property is found in book 26, in the wider context of Montesquieu's conception of civil law. Perhaps the most striking aspect of Montesquieu's treatment, here, is the explicit denial of a right of property in the state of nature: "As men have renounced their natural dependence to live under political laws, so have they renounced the natural community of goods to live under civil laws."[7] From this passage, readers have concluded that Montesquieu's view of property is rooted in positive law. There is no natural "mine" or "thine," before civil society; property is to be understood as the creation of the sovereign state.

In this key passage, Montesquieu also appears to subordinate civil laws to political laws. While the civil laws should almost never be ruled by "canonical right," or the laws of religion,[8] Montesquieu nonetheless describes property or "domain" as a legitimate object of the state.[9] In the initial presentation, there appears to be no limits on the needs of the public over and above the liberty of the individual.

Decades later, critics would object, precisely on this basis, that Montesquieu's *The Spirit of the Laws* was dangerously absent of a support for private property. Looking back after the revolution, Montesquieu was seen as partly responsible for the socialist confiscations at the end of the eighteenth century and, stretching the argument even further, the social and economic upheavals of 1848.[10]

Carefully examined in its original historical and political context, however, Montesquieu's philosophy of property radically undermines the "positive law" conception of property. In no way did Montesquieu believe that property was merely a creation of the sovereign, an artificial product of a convention decided on by consent. While it is true that Montesquieu breaks from the natural law tradition, at least in the attempt to ground property in the state of nature, the following chapter demonstrates that Montesquieu did not abandon the Lockean or natural right understanding of property. Admittedly, Montesquieu does not attempt, anywhere in his writings, to justify "posession" in Lockean terms. Instead, Montesquieu justifies a right to property *internally*, and in a way consistent with the psychological requirements of Montesquieuean liberty. This argument will be made more clear by re-examining the concrete examples of property and related subjects in *The Spirit of the Laws*, including: communal ownership, property and criminal justice, property and taxation, marriage, family and inheritance laws.

Communalism and Utopianism in the Old Republics

Montesquieu's views on communal ownership can be clarified by reference to the larger debates in France on communal ideals of property. 1767, Scottish Jacobite James Steuart published *Inquiries into the Principles of Political Economy*. In it, Steuart imagined a revival of what he called "the most perfect plan of political economy...anywhere to be met with, either in ancient or modern times."[11] By "perfect," Steuart was referring to the legendary political economy of Lycurgus, available in Plutarch's *Parallel Lives*. In France, the political economy of Lycurgus was perhaps a more difficult sell, but as historians have shown, the example of Lycurgus' economic philosophy was not a foreign or novel idea. In fact, French advocates of social justice in the 1760s and 1770s often referred to the classical models as inspiration for promoting enlightened monarchy. As Gross argues:

> [Lycurgus] took on the appearance of an enlightened eighteenth-century monarch whose every economic gesture was exemplary: the basic necessaries for all (barley, olive oil and wine in ample measure); luxuries shunned, decorative crafts made redundant; coins minted from iron instead of gold and silver; shelter provided by log shacks crudely fashioned with saw and hatchet.[12]

In other words, the possibility of reviving a "perfect system" using Plutarch's account of Lycurgus in modern monarchy was not at all fantastical. Discussions of a "cult of Plutarch" included all the big names, monarchists and republicans alike: Saint-Pierre, Rousseau, Brissot, Condorcet, Robespierre and Saint-Just. According to one historian, these figures rarely delivered a speech without paying tribute to the legendary economic revolution, initiated by the ancient legislator.[13]

Decades earlier, Montesquieu presented his own views of Lycurgus' political economy, in books 4 and 5 of *The Spirit of the Laws*.[14] Even a cursory glance at those books show, conclusively, that Montesquieu read the account as a dangerous and hyperbolic fantasy. Furthermore, Montesquieu interpreted the communalist reforms of Lycurgus not as an end in itself (equality), but a means to a different end, virtue. The ancient Greeks, persuaded that popular government requires virtue, *required* a love of equality. To develop that passion was difficult: it would require self-renunciation, and the construction of "singular institutions" to guard against inequality, luxury, and decadence. Economic policy was designed, in short, to promote virtue and limit ambition. In Montesquieu's words, the economic systey of Lycurgus was designed to promote "the single desire, the single happiness, of rendering greater services to one's homeland than other citizens."[15]

Did Montesquieu view the economic system of Lycurgus as a viable model for modern states, monarchical or republican? Privately, Montesquieu makes the following remark:

> I am not one who regards Plato's Republic as an ideal and purely imaginary thing which would be impossible to put into practice. My reason is that the Republic of Lycurgus seems to be just as difficult to put into practice as Plato's, and yet it was so well put into practice that it lasted as long as any republic known, in its strength and splendor.[16]

Montesquieu seems to have changed his mind, however, at least, when it comes time to evaluate the merits of Lycurgus in *The Spirit of the Laws*:

> When you see, in the Life of Lycurgus, the laws he gave the Lacedaemonians, you believe that you are reading the history of the Sevarambes. The laws of Crete were the originals for the laws of Lacedaemonia, and Plato's laws were their correction.[17]

The comparison of Lycurgus, in Plutarch, to Plato, is not a new addition. As Montesquieu wrote earlier in the *Pensées*: "One has to reflect on Aristotle's *Politics* and on Plato's two *Republics* if one wants to have a clear idea of Greek laws and mores. To look for them in the historians is as if we wanted to find ours by reading the wars of Louis XIV."[18] The system of communal property in Sparta, in other words, is complemented by a study of Plato's "two republics." In writing, Plato "corrects" the historical laws of Lacedaemonia.

What is entirely new in Montesquieu's presentation, in 1748, is the reference to the obscure "history of the Sevarambes." This is a highly significant modern reference. The "history of the Sevarambes" was published in 1675, under the name, Denis Verais, with the following full title (which Montesquieu does not include): "The History of the Sevarambians: A Utopian Novel."[19]

According to Céline Spector, an outspoken critic of the "liberal" or Straussian interpretation of *The Spirit of the Laws*, Montesquieu did not view the "communal property" arrangements as utopian.[20] Referring to a passage in book 4, Spector quotes the following passage as further evidence: "Those who want to create similar [democratic] institutions will establish the communal property of Plato's *Republic*, the respect he required for the gods, the separation from strangers for the preservation of mores, and the city engaging in trade, but not the citizens."[21] While Spector admits that there are limitations on Plato's recommendations (it will only work in a small, homogeneous participatory republic), she concludes nonetheless that Montesquieu "advises following Plato's recommendations respecting the use of property."

Spector's conclusion is simply not supported by the evidence. First, one needs only to recall the context of the passage. Scholars working on the history of Utopian literature have placed the "History of Sevarambes," now all but forgotten, alongside Thomas More's *Utopia* and Jonathan Swift's *Gulliver's Travels*.[22] Immanuel Kant had apparently read the book, grouping it with Plato's "Atlantis" and Harrington's *Oceana* as one of the greatest utopian works.[23] Montesquieu's contemporary, David Hume, needed no introduction to the work when he heard of it,[24] although he dismissed it lightly as "an agreeable romance."[25]

The recommendations on property in Plato and Lycurgus are not only regarded as a fantasy, by Montesquieu; in fact, these examples seem to have repulsed him. In the same book in which Montesquieu compares Lycurgus to the utopian fiction of Verais, Montesquieu provides a punishing critique of Plutarch's great legislator, arguing that he had successfully brought into existence a regime that "succeed[s] in *mixing* [virtue and moderation]" with "larceny," and with the "harshest slavery," and with "the most heinous feelings."[26] Did Montesquieu view these evils as necessary expedients in establishing a perfect regime?

The policies that Montesquieu targets are instructive in light of this discussion of property. First, Lycurgus "removed all the town's resources, arts, commerce, silver, walls." The citizens were encouraged to have military "ambition" but little material comforts (they lived without the "expectation of bettering oneself").[27] To achieve the goal of producing in the citiznes a love of equality, it was, in the final analysis, necessary to attack the foundation of the family. Citizens would be encouraged to have "natural feelings" but not to think of themselves as "child, husband, nor father." And herein lies the devious genius of Lycurgus. True equality required drastic provisions for eliminating not only the market (commerce and "silver") but all private attachments, as well, especially that most precious bond between father, mother, and child. Only then, Montesquieu notes, did Lycurgus succeed in leading Sparta "to greatness and glory."[28]

In *modern* times, two legislators have tried to imitate the old republics: "Mr. Penn," whom Montesquieu calls a "true Lycurgus," and the Jesuits of Paraguay. In Montesquieu's view, the latter community succeeded only by denying all pleasures in life "[except] the pleasures of commanding." Are these examples proof of the viability of Lycurgus' program in the eighteenth century?

An answer to this requires, first, a recognition of Montesquieu's warning not to ignore the essential difference between Crete and Sparta and the modern experiments of Mr. Penn.[29] Mr. Penn is a "true Lycurgus" not because he mirrors the ancient legislator in economic matters. Rather, because "he has had peace for his object as Lycurgus has had war."[30] Might this suggest, then, a synthesis of the old with the new, a modification of the ancient political economy? Correctly observing this difference between a political economy dedicated to a warring democracy, and an economic philosophy supportive of a virtuous Christian community, readers have suggested that Montesquieu may indeed have entertained the revival of ancient political economy, but in the context of a virtuous Christian republic. According to Nannerl Keohane, for example, Montesquieu's praise for William Penn is sincere: it is a remarkable example of the creation of a virtuous community "amidst the dregs and corruptions of modern times." Citing Montesquieu's praise also for Berne, Keohane suggests that Montesquieu "was convinced that there were certain conditions in which such models (of democracy) might become relevant for a people and certain extraordinary men who might put them into effect."[31]

Keohane is surely not wrong to point to Montesquieu's admiration of William Penn, even if it is colored by a tone of incredulity. In the following section, however, we will see a revealing shift in Montesquieu's views on private property. Leaving behind the question of the *possibility* of a revival of primitive communism, Montesquieu began to analyze the benefits and *grounds* of private property rights in modern commercial societies.

Property and Criminal Law

Book 6, relating to crime and punishment, is a significant book on the topic of property. Here, Montesquieu starts with an assertion that both denies the superiority of ancient republics in securing property, while re-asserting the advantages of modern monarchy. Royal justice assumes, and indeed, requires, that "the citizen's property and life are as secure and fixed in monarchy as the very constitution of the state."[32]

That the judicial system *should* protect property in monarchy is not in itself a revealing statement. Nothing meaningful can be gleaned from this statement without asking the prior and more interesting question: what did Montesquieu mean by property? Addressing this question is crucial to understanding Montesquieu's bifurcated defense of property rights in a specifically monarchical context, that is, in a fragmented, feudal, and corporatist political culture.

Property, like commerce, is related to the constitution. At various points in his major writings, Montesquieu refers to "property" in the sense of noble privileges, and feudal prerogatives. At other times, Montesquieu uses property in the sense which came to dominate French politics in the years before the revolution, that is, of property as an "inviolable and sacred right" attaching to all people, regardless of rank or station.

Keeping this distinction in mind, it is clear that Montesquieu did *not* mean to suggest that modern monarchy *should* or *does* protect *individual* property, in the revolutionary or "liberal" sense. As Montesquieu explains, property in monarchy is inseparable from honor and social status: "In a monarchy, the administering of a justice decisions not only about life and goods, but *also about honor, requires scrupulous inquiries.*" The differences between people (rank, origin, condition), in other words, require a justice system that distinguishes not just among things but among people: "There must be privileges in governments where there are necessarily distinctions between persons." So, the normative statement, monarchies *should* protect property, is theoretically unimportant. It only means that from the standpoint of stability, the judicial system must respect *existing* property arrangements. At most, the first chapter of Book 6 only advances a rather basic claim that property rights, in monarchy, are necessarily more complex than in despotic government.

Somewhere in between despotism and monarchy is the "moderate" state. In the moderate state, property takes on a different meaning. Montesquieu refers to "property" in a moderate monarchy more broadly, as including not only material goods, but in an expansive sense, including "life" and "honor."[33] Note, for example, that Montesquieu switches to this "liberal" conception of property—inclusive of property, life and honor—in his vivid comparison of the criminal law in Turkey.

> [In this country] one pays very little attention to the fortune, life, or honor of the subjects; all disputes are speedily concluded in one way or another. The manner of ending them is not important, provided they are ended. The pasha is no sooner informed than he has the pleaders bastinadoed according to his fancy and sends them back home.[34]

This passage is revealing of Montesquieu's broader understanding of property in *The Spirit of the Laws*. In the turn in book 6 to criminal law, justice, and punishment, the topic of property begins to emerge as a necessary condition of the moderate state. In the moderate state, the "goods" of the citizen are threatened "only after long examination." While due process applies primarily to life, it is important to note that for Montesquieu, protection of life applies *regardless* of social status or other perceived standards of merit or virtue. In the moderate state, "the head of even the lowest citizen is esteemed."

One may reasonably object that Montesquieu's defense of property here is thin, or that such a claim does not match up to a robust version of Lockean self-ownership. To appreciate Montesquieu's fuller defense of property, it is worth pausing to review the rhetorical difficulty in *The Spirit of the Laws*.

In the liberal tradition, property has been generally thought to describe a legal or customary relationship between a person and *a thing*.[35] William Blackstone, for example, in his *Commentaries on the Laws of England* defined property as "that despotic dominion that one man claims and exercises over the external things of the world, in total exclusion of the right of any other individual in the universe." If property is a right in relation to external objects, it is easy to see why property law, in the Anglo-American context, evolved toward an understanding of property not as an abstract principle of possession, but as a "bundle of rights." Conceived as a collection of particular legal claims, property in the liberal tradition is divisible into rights of possession, of use, management, the right to capital, the right to security, transmissibility, et cetera.[36] There are two key assumptions here: the owner is an abstract individual, and ownership means essentially the same thing in different legal systems.[37] We can illustrate, borrowing from A.M. Honore's famous example of ownership of an umbrella:

> ...the owner [of an umbrella in a modern liberal state] can, in the simple, uncomplicated sense, use it, stop others using it, lend it, sell it, or leave it by will. Nowhere may he use it to poke his neighbor in the ribs, or to knock over his vase. Ownership, dominium, propriete, Eigentum, and similar words stand...for a type of interest with common features transcending particular systems.[38]

The problem of property in *The Spirit of the Laws* consists in the fact that Montesquieu is not analyzing ownership of umbrellas. Nor is Montesquieu comparing like systems, with common assumptions about rights to possession or the nature of the person.

To put this another way, in *The Spirit of the Laws*, the distinction between property in "things" and property in "persons" is ambiguous. *Propriété* in *The Spirit of the Laws* often refers to things, goods or "possessions" that require some "title" or legal recognition.[39] But as we have already seen, property in the non-liberal state includes important distinctions among persons, due to rank, origin, or condition. Attention to this rhetorical problem is crucial for understanding Montesquieu's larger intentions for reforming the civil law.

In continuing to distinguish between *persons*, Montesquieu was not promoting or reflecting French civil law. This distinction (between persons and things) was also key for Montesquieu's history of the civil laws. Montesquieu relied heavily on the language and distinctions in Roman law; specifically, the sixth-century *Institutes* of Justinian. There are extensive references to *Corpus Juris Civilis* (of which the Institutes was one unit), reflecting Montesquieu's larger interest in connecting the current property system in France to its origins in Roman law.[40] This does not mean that Montesquieu was not aware of the development of the liberal tradition on property. Montesquieu often looks across the channel to the example of England, where the law of "persons" was becoming vestigial.[41]

Instead, Montesquieu clearly is attentive to the fact that the political situation in France required a rhetorical strategy consistent with the principles of monarchy. For example, Montesquieu was conscious of the historical exploitation of property rights by the crown. He admits that the king's domain was not absolute as it once was.[42] Indeed, Louis XIV had once considered that he had "*la disposition pleine et entire*" of all the property in his kingdom. But it was not impossible to imagine a reversal, or even, a resurgence of the old doctrine of "inalienable domain." Simply put, the language of an "absolute" right to property was itself part of the problem in a reformed monarchy. The language of an absolute right to property was dangerous, especially, in modern states where the clergy, the prince, and *les villes* and *les grands* had emerged as the "*proprietaries de toute la contree.*"[43] In a revealing passage, Montesquieu argues that the concept of "inalienable domain" is in fact "a very modern thing," neither "known" among the ancients in theory or practice.[44]

The resurgence of property as an absolute right attached to the crown had implications beyond the sphere of monarchical sovereignty which, he noted sharply, had become to be thought of as simply a "great fief."[45] The concept of inalienable domain did not only apply to monarchy. Since the time of Louis XIV, there had been a remarkable growth in the size and reach of the bureaucracy, as well. Montesquieu refers often to these "great offices" attached to the king, and in the context of a threat to individual freedom.[46]

Of particular concern for Montesquieu was the historical rise in the "goods of the fisc." While there were notable linguistic variations between, for example, "benefices," "honors," and "fiefs," complicating the historical picture, Montesquieu specifically warned of the pernicious relationship between absolute property rights and the growth of an artificial aristocracy. The nobility, he argued, had come to believe that it had not only the right to "draw all the fruits and emoluments" from their own lands (now hereditary), but as Montesquieu explained in book 30, also exclusive privileges. Some privileges were merely "useful" rights like tax exemptions, but more importantly, Montesquieu warned that property rights also entailed *social* rights, rights that were becoming "honorific," including, to take two notable examples, pensions and occupational entitlements.[47]

We should keep in mind that the growth of ecclesiastical property raised the stakes even further. It was clear enough, historically, how the nobility came to possess their property and entitlements. Property rights were doled out in exchange for fighting and for bearing arms. The warrior nobility provided horses, vehicles, and the obligation to go to war.[48] Later, Montesquieu explains, the nobility began to do "double service," both with arms and through judicial service in the lord's court.[49]

It was less clear, however, precisely how the extension of Church property rights could be justified, or if it could, and on what grounds. The obligations of the Church in return for "Territorial justice" and the extremely lucrative rights attached to them—to render justice, to exact *freda*, and to levy tithes—confused even the bishops, Montesquieu observes, who quarreled over the details of the bargain, especially, the obligation to go to war.[50]

Montesquieu recounts the dramatic increase in Church holdings in book 30. More specifically, Montesquieu provides a useful explanation of how "possession" evolved into the idea of "fixed estate." Originally, lands ("great fiscs") were provided to the clergy for two main reasons: it was easier for the "census" or for tax collection purposes, and because, in Montesquieu's words, "the owners of lands believed that by their servitude they participated in the saintliness of the churches."[51] Over time, the ecclesiastics became increasingly involved in campaigns, employing vassals with their own armies.[52] The documented records establishing the "patrimonial" justice of the churches in their territory were then reinterpreted by the absolutist (revisionist) histories of intellectuals like Abbé Dubos.[53] As historians revised or covered over the historical record, corruption set in, and kings increasingly gave out land or property as favors.

The parcelling out of the royal domain was accompanied by political promises to preserve "honors" and ranks forever.[54] In addition to these causes, Montesquieu also describes the growth of bureaucratic interests (XXXI.4), the conversion of ecclesiastical goods into fiefs (XXXI.9), and the establishment of tithes.[55]

While it is not possible to analyze Montesquieu's history of property in the old regime, the above examples are sufficient to make two simple observations. First, Montesquieu's historical approach to the "origins" of property in France explains the causes—but does not defend—the distinction between the law of persons and of things. Second, Montesquieu's description of the evolution of property law helps to explain his apparent disagreement with Locke, in book 26, on the origin of private property. That is to say, the history of property in France renders the attempt to ground property on a philosophical basis impractical, at best. When, for example, Montesquieu argues that property is a result of positive law, he does not mean to endorse the "conventionalist" philosophy, according to which there is no basis for property in nature. Rather, the historical *distribution* of property merely shows, in the French case, that the philosophy of a "fixed estate" attaching to the king, nobility, and clergy, emerged after the fact. That the real origins of property in France are the product of force, corruption, and cunning, hardly matters. The language of "rights" was, as I have argued, tainted in France, to an extent that is hard to exaggerate, and which has important implications for our understanding of Montesquieu's case for private property.

Thus, we can begin to better appreciate Montesquieu's unique approach to the problem of property in *The Spirit of the Laws*. Montesquieu's approach is unique because he emphasizes the historical contingency of the language of "right" in the old regime. Attention to the rhetorical problem of property complicates our understanding of *The Spirit of the Laws*, but it also provides two significant theoretical advantages and at least one practical benefit.

First, Montesquieu's adoption of the "positive law" view of property *undermined* rather than supported the historical footing or foundation of feudalism. Second, it allowed for a revolutionary re-evaluation of property laws in a government where property adhered to persons and not only to things.[56]

As a practical issue, the notion of property as "convention" also provided lawyers and intellectuals an important place in the emerging new social order.[57] As legal historians Kelley and Smith have argued elsewhere in detail, lawyers, not philosophers and statesman, were the pivot of the revolution; it was the legal class, after all, that would prove essential in assessing or authenticating titles, renewing leases, contracts, and other claims during the upheavals. In Smith's words, it was the lawyers who held the balance of power in the early days of the revolution, because it was the lawyers, ultimately, who provided the rationale for "denying anything with feudal taint."[58]

The strategy of the eighteenth century jurists, in treating property as purely the creation of civil law, contained a number of obvious flaws in application. In one sense, it could be viewed as a partial surrender to the old regime reactionary philosophy according to which "property" exists only by virtue of the sovereign. And, as the eighteenth century drew on, it became increasingly clear that this "positive" view of property was also a significant threat to the new class of owners, including the legal profession, as the revolution moved leftward.[59] The acts by the Assembly in 1793 to declare land associated with *feodalite* as forfeit cut both ways. The Assembly's decision to act on the "belief that the conventional basis of property made it subject to legislative decision" both weakened the old regime and, as Montesquieu would have predicted, made "confiscations" and other attacks on the new orders inevitable. Indeed, the revolutionaries, emboldened partly as a result of a weak theoretical commitment to property, extended "confiscations" far beyond the initial targets (feudal property) to uncultivated fields, the seizure of the property of emigres, and the establishment of wage and price controls.[60] The possibility of legislative tyranny raised the question to liberal philosophers in the nineteenth century anew: where was the concern, respect for, and theoretical basis of property and liberty after the revolution?

Montesquieu, as will now be argued, did not in fact follow the positive law jurists all the way. In the following section, we will see that Montesquieu did not abandon the natural right foundation of property. Instead, what we see in Montesquieu's writings is an attempt to combine what appear to be incompatible arguments: a conventional or positive law account of property in the context of monarchy, with a principled understanding of self-ownership.[61] This attempt to balance judicial rhetoric with limits on legislative tyranny is illustrated, in the following, through an analysis of the topics of suicide, taxation, family law, and laws governing inheritance.

Montesquieu's View of Property as Qualified Self-Ownership

The most dramatic illustration of Montesquieu's broader, more principled case for property can be found in his discussion of (what was called at the time) "self-murder." [62] We start here because this topic provides the most dramatic example of Montesquieu's principled stance in favour of a broad understanding of natural right and self-ownership.

THE PROBLEM OF PROPERTY 125

Aquinas had condemned suicide on three main grounds or for three reasons: suicide was a crime against oneself, against society, and against God.[63] Montesquieu, in effect, replied to all three of these objections in the *Persian Letters*.[64] Usbek, a Persian, arrives in France, and finds, to his shock, that the families of suicides are punished harshly by the law. In Europe, suicides are "put to death a second time," dragged ignominiously through the streets, "declared infamous, and all their goods confiscated." Expressing an obvious inclination for the primacy of individual sovereignty, against the Thomistic view, Usbek notes: "When I am crushed by physical pain, by poverty, by scorn, why should anyone wish to prevent me from ending my suffering?"[65]

But is suicide a crime against society? Usbek's second argument recalls Locke's argument for a right of rebellion. "Society is based on mutual advantage," notes Usbek. When society becomes a burden, he asks rhetorically, "why should I not renounce it?"

Finally, Usbek defends the heretical opinion that suicide is not a crime against God. According to Usbek, self-disposal does not violate the laws of either "creation" or "conservation." Viewing the person as a sovereign authority of his own body, Usbek claims that suicide is a legitimate choice, because the individual is simply using a right that has been given by the creator: "[I am]Simply using a right I have been given...I can interfere to my heart's content with the whole of nature, without anyone being able to claim that I am opposing the purposes of Providence."[66]

If Montesquieu appears to agree with Usbek, in the *Persian Letters*, that suicide is not unnatural, Montesquieu does also appear to revise his opinion in 1754. As Waddicor notes, "Montesquieu had either changed his belief or decided to disguise it more carefully." He does this by adding a new letter from Ibben to Usbek. In the revised version, Ibben argues that it is more "obedient" to God to maintain civil laws against suicide as a deterrent.[67] In *The Spirit of the Laws*, Montesquieu had provided conciliatory footnotes. At the end of a sentence describing the preponderance of suicide among the English as an effect of a "distemper," caused by their climate, thereby appearing to excuse the act, Montesquieu added: "the act of those who kill themselves is contrary to natural law and to revealed religion."[68]

We should also note that it is true that, given the opportunity to defend his views of suicide, in his 1750 *Defense*, Montesquieu backs away from the strong self-ownership argument of Usbek, focusing instead on justice. Adopting a more neutral legal tone, Montesquieu attacked the *criminalization* of the act, largely avoiding the moral controversies raised in Usbek's response to St. Thomas.

A brief summary of Montesquieu's writings on slavery confirm, however, that Montesquieu did not abandon natural right arguments in relation to the broad conception of property as life and liberty.[69] Indeed, as Montesquieu's readers know well, the anti-slavery polemic in *The Spirit of the Laws* is one of the clearest examples of Montesquieu's affinity with natural rights philosophy in his writing. The polemic is deeply ironic, or rather as one scholar has suggested, "antiphrastic" (meaning that the audience hears what they expect to hear).[70] But this does not take away from the force or persuasive power of these passages. Montesquieu demonstrates a profound commitment to natural right and natural equality.[71]

The core of Montesquieu's writings on slavery are found in book 25 Part Three, as part of a general examination of servitude.[72] Book 15 divides into two main parts.[73] The first ten chapters examine the nature of slavery, its different forms, and where (or if) slavery is ever legitimate. The next ten chapters address the practical question, "What the laws ought to do in relation to slavery."

We will concentrate first, primarily, on Chapter 5, where Montesquieu produces a hypothetical defense of race slavery, from the perspective of the slaveholder.[74] The first two arguments appeal to economic utility or necessity. Europeans have made slaves of Africans because they were short on labor (having "exterminated those of America"). Second, sugar would be too expensive if Europeans had to work the plantations themselves.

In the next series of arguments,[75] Montesquieu then ridicules the argument from racial superiority, in the process, bolstering a commitment to the natural equality of all human beings as such. Racial slavery denies natural equality on the basis of a number of considerations that were meant to elicit a dark-humored laugh: pigmentation, facial structure, hair color, and primitive reasoning skills (some cultures, for example, value "glass necklaces" above gold).[76] Piling on, Montesquieu argues that the slaveholder finds it "impossible" to assume that these people are men. If that were true, European Christians could not call themselves Christian.[77] Critics of slavery, on the other hand, are described as "petty spirits" that exaggerate the "injustice done to the Africans."

While few of Montesquieu's readers were duped by this core chapter on racial slavery, far more of Montesquieu's critics have focused on Montesquieu's problematic "concessions" to slavery in its other forms. While insisting that slavery is opposed to natural law and to Christianity, Montesquieu nonetheless concedes that there are "natural reasons" for its existence. Slavery may be "more bearable," for example, in despotism, where "one is already in political slavery."[78] Slavery he says is "less counter to reason" in certain climatic conditions, where the heat enervates the body and weakens courage.[79] In addition, Montesquieu counsels against immediate emancipation, even in republics, where the institution would seem to be least compatible with natural right and most contrary to reason.[80]

On inspection, the above concessions are insubstantial and do not present any difficulties to a natural right reading of *The Spirit of the Laws*. Montesquieu claims that there is only one *just* origin of slavery, or to use his own words, the only justification "conforming to reason":

> Herein lies the just origin, the one conforming to reason, of the very gentle right of slavery that one sees in some countries, and it has to be gentle because it is founded on the free choice of a master, a choice a man makes for his own utility and which forms a reciprocal agreement between the parties.[81]

In other words, there is no moral argument for slavery that does not reduce to free choice, short-term utility, or contract.

The question to ask is whether slavery can be rationalized in any other circumstance.[82] Making novel use of Aristotle,[83] Montesquieu concedes that there may be one more exception: "Aristotle wants to prove that there are slaves by nature, and what he says scarcely proves it. I believe that, if there are any such, they are those whom I have just mentioned."[84] To understand this oblique reference to Aristotle, we should recall the basis of Aristotle's own qualification of the natural slave; namely, that it depends on a peculiar circumstance, the existence of a person who "shares" or "perceives" reason but lacks enough of it to be self-sufficient (1254b20).[85] But we have seen that Montesquieu's own exception renders Aristotle's qualification moot. Can a natural slave, *lacking* reason to be self-sufficient, consent to sell himself for his own utility? In Chapter 1, Montesquieu clearly stated his reason for rejecting precisely this hypothetical: even provided that such a being exists, that relationship would be "useful neither to the master nor to the slave."[86]

But perhaps we can imagine a person only so intelligent to adduce that the utility of enslavement might outweigh the benefits of freedom. Recall Aristotle's extra qualification: that such a person must also be without courage or will (so as not to be bothersome to the master). Here, Montesquieu's theory of climate drastically undercuts that remaining rationale. Only a combination of climate *and* despotic government can produce a being "enervated" in body and so "weakened in courage" that slavery would be preferable. *Even* then, Montesquieu argued, slavery exists only as a result of the threat of violence ("fear of chastisement").

Montesquieu's treatment of slavery, in short, can be read as a methodical dismantling—not of Aristotle's defense of natural slavery—but of Aristotle's qualifications for the *existence of* the natural slave. In this sense, the historian Fletcher was right when he said, "there are perhaps no pages in the whole of the *Esprit des Lois* which reflect more completely the genius of Montesquieu than those relating to slavery."[87]

Domestic Servitude, Property, and Family Law

The books on slavery are followed by a book on "domestic servitude" (XVI) and "political servitude" (XVII). Turning to these topics will further illustrate the extent of Montesquieu's self-ownership view of natural right.

In summarizing this vast topic, it is necessary to focus only on three aspects of Montesquieu's treatment of property and civil law. These are: Montesquieu's critique of paternalism; his treatment of property in relation to marriage and sexual relations; and his discussion of primogeniture and the laws governing inheritance. The civil laws in each case are subject to variation, but it is clear that they are not reducible to convention or to expressions of positive law.[88]

If slavery is impossible to justify even on Montesquieu's flexible understanding of natural right, can the same thing be said about paternalism? Recall the view, of Filmer, in England, and Bossuet, in France, that royal authority could be analogized to paternal authority, thus strengthening the divine right of kings through natural law. Montesquieu did not attack this line of argument directly, as we will see. Instead, he used the example of despotic China to construct the foil: in China, he wrote, "the prince is regarded as the father of the people."[89] There the state is constructed on "the plan of a family."[90]

Unlike the dismantling of slavery, above, Montesquieu does not attempt to pull out the arguments for paternal right root and branch. For example, there are scattered comments on paternal power in the *Persian Letters* and in his notebooks[91] where he admits of important distinctions between state paternalism and institutional or individual paternalism; the latter provides plenty of examples where interference with individual liberty and property may be justified. For example, Montesquieu argues that there is a "degree of paternal power" established "by nature" within the family.[92]

Yet, while nature may establish paternal power of the father, for example, over the child, Montesquieu explicitly rejects the view of those who "have thought that government by one alone is most in conformity with nature."[93] Are there any exceptions? As often with Montesquieu, the exceptions tend to prove the rule. Paternalism may have politically salutary consequences in severe governments, he argues, where there are fewer laws: "nothing maintains mores better" than the extreme subordination of the young to the elderly in a republic.[94] Or paternalism may strengthen the father's (delusional) belief that his family *is* his property (indeed, in many places, fathers make no distinction between his family and his goods).[95] Paternalism can be useful in traditional monarchies, where "purity of morals" is not as strict as in republics.[96] Extended to property law, paternalism proved critical for the preservation of the monarchical structure: paternalism was viewed as essential to preserving the loyalty of the nobles to the prince, who himself depends on the "fixed property" of hereditary estates for protection and security.[97]

Such considerations must be weighed in balance with Montesquieu's attacks on absolute paternal power, his attempts to *limit* paternalistic property laws, and his principled defense of individual rights. In Montesquieu's *Traité des devoirs*, for example, he shows that paternal power can never be absolute, and he makes a further distinction between paternal power based on the idea of "possession" or property and paternal power as temporary interference for the sake of the well-being of the dependent. These basic ideas are clarified in *The Spirit of the Laws*. Following Locke, Grotius, and Pufendorf, Montesquieu repeats the common view that paternal power must be limited[98] by age of the child, who does not have an independent "will" of their own. Montesquieu's purpose in these passages is further illuminated by his choice of historical examples, especially in the Roman republic. Paternal power is "very useful" in democracies "for maintaining mores."[99] In republics lacking the "repressive" power of monarchy, it is necessary to supplement the force of state authority with paternal right. In Rome, "fathers had the right of life and death over their own children. In Lacedaemonia each father had the right to correct the child of another."[100] Paternal right extended to property: "the father [remained] the master of his children's goods during his life," a right, Montesquieu argues that is "not in the spirit of monarchy."[101]

Clearly, Montesquieu severed paternal right from political right.[102] The harder question is whether paternal power could be separated from civil right. To help answer that question, it is useful to turn to Montesquieu's complex analysis of family law, in particular, the legal status of women in marriage.[103]

Montesquieu's book on civil slavery in book 15 is followed by a book on "domestic slavery." The argument in book 16 extends and *applies* the formal instances of "natural equality" in *The Spirit of the Laws*.[104] It prepares the ground as it were for the eradication of slavery within the family.[105]

Not surprisingly, scholars still argue about the meaning of Montesquieu's arguments for female equality, and for the same reasons they have debated the meaning of his criticism of slavery. Like slavery, Montesquieu appears to have provided *justifications* of female inequality, which appear to be contingent on circumstance. For instance, Montesquieu argues that women enjoy a compensatory "form" of equality in monarchical government because of their "natural advantages" that otherwise prevents them from claiming true or natural equality to men.[106] He suggests that situation of women varies with government and with climate.[107] Women are linked, somewhat problematically, with luxury and corruption.[108] While slavery for women is no more appropriate than for men, domestic subordination is not unconnected to reason and nature.[109] Men are superior not only in strength but in reason.[110]

Famously, Montesquieu also provided a controversial apology for polygamy in the first five chapters of book 16. The objections to Montesquieu's account can be distilled down to two. First, Montesquieu undermined the attempt to uphold the Christian prohibition of polygamy. And, according to one critic, Montesquieu went beyond the pale by refusing to make a moral distinction between polygamy and polyandry.[111]

One may legitimately wonder about the purposes of the investigation into the "various circumstances" (XVI.4) in which polygamy might be "somewhat tolerable" (XVI.6). According to Montesquieu, polygamy may be less "opposed to reason" in a society where marriage norms are very weak, that is, where "it is very simple" for "a man to leave his wife to take another" XVI.2. And he argued that there were "fewer reasons" to reject polygamy where economic circumstances allow for the wealth of one individual to be "spread out" in support of a larger family (XVI.3). Polygamy could also be justified as an *affaire de calcul*, a rationalization of sex and birth differentials. The state might for example make "calculations" to offset a certain misfortune where there are "more boys than are girls" or "more girls...than boys" (XVI.4).

Considering polygamy "in general," Montesquieu argued unambiguously that it was an "abuse" on moral grounds but also "not useful to mankind" (XVI.6). "A father cannot love twenty children as a mother loves two," he noted, underscoring the effect of the practice on the young, which he viewed as "injurious" especially to children. As for the religious arguments for the possession of multiple wives, Montesquieu viewed them as inconsistent, both with doctrinal and scriptural arguments for the equal treatment of women (XVI.7).[112] But on the individual level, Montesquieu's final view was that plural marriage made the ideal of self-ownership unattainable. His hypothesis was based in his view of human nature: the more the family becomes extended, public, and shared, the more the private self, the small, and the desire for autonomy and independence reasserts itself in resistance. Reverting back to consequential grounds, he added that polygamy often presupposes separation or "enclosure," which is to say, it leaves women more vulnerable to attack and to abuse (XVI.8). The system of polygamy provides a new arena for men to exercise a new "empire" over women (XVI.9). Under such conditions, the individual's right of commerce or "communication" with the larger society is naturally threatened (XVI.11). Importantly, the "feeling" of autonomy within the domestic sphere decays, as feelings and attachments become focused, Montesquieu argues, on the "family within a family."[113]

Turning to divorce, one finds the same pattern of argument, grounded in moral considerations related to self-proprietorship. Strong arguments are made in both the *Persian Letters* and in key passages in *The Spirit of the Laws*, where divorce is analyzed from three angles.[114]

The first extended discussion of divorce laws is found in book 16. The general argument is that the liberalization of divorce laws is a key component of the resistance to slavery in general (XVI.18). A second major discussion of divorce appears in book 23. Here, Montesquieu analyzes the historical progression of divorce laws through three "eras": Greco-Roman laws, medieval laws, and the era of reform and Enlightenment. The final major discussion of divorce appears in book 26, where Montesquieu defends liberalization from the point of view of the happiness and fulfillment of the individual. It is possible here only to touch on the salient points in these three separate accounts.

Self-ownership and Divorce Law

In book 16, Montesquieu distinguishes between divorce and repudiation, and in the process, defines divorce: "A difference between divorce and repudiation is that divorce occurs by mutual consent on the occasion of a mutual incompatibility, whereas repudiation is done by the will and for the advantage of one of the two parties, independently of the will and the advantage of the other."[115] Implying that divorce *should* occur by mutual consent, and on the occasion of "mutual incompatibility" was not an unusual claim. As Carol Blum has argued, Montesquieu's more radical suggestion was on the subject of repudiation, which he said could be *initiated* by the wife. This was a provocative stance.[116] First, domestic servitude depended on an imbalance between husband and wife in terms of initiating proceedings.[117] And perhaps more obviously, argument ran up against the Catholic doctrine of indissolubility.[118]

Keeping these points in mind, one can appreciate Montesquieu's turn to ancient history in book 23.[119] The principle of "mutual incompatibility" among the Romans is viewed positively by Montesquieu (compare XVI.15), although it is important to note that the grounds of divorce were not based in a concern for individual happiness in the ancient republics. Carvilius Ruga, consul, was forced by the censors to repudiate his wife "because of her barrenness" (XVI.16). He had taken an oath that he would give "children to the republic." Population concerns, then, not individual liberty, provided the distinct character of classical republican laws regarding rights in marriage.

Continuing to side with the controversially pre-Christian view, Montesquieu then argues that divorce laws in the West moved from political to religious causes, away from utilitarian considerations until they finally obtained an "inflexible" character. Christian jurisprudence became "mixed" with old Roman laws (XXIII.20, 449; compare the account in book 26, XXVI, 503). The transformation had mixed results. The modern era had freed itself from the obsessive concerns with population growth, but married life had also become more "harsh," resulting in a "sorry liberty" (XXIII.21), especially where the forbidding of divorce was made for strictly theological reasons (see XXIII.6).

These "liberal" views are supported and consistent with Montesquieu's views on marriage. One of the "great objects" of marriage, he argues, is to remove the uncertainty of infidelity (XXVI.13). Secondarily, and historically speaking, marriage facilitates the propogation of the species (XXIII.21). That Montesquieu subordinates propogation to other purposes is significant. Primarily, it distinguishes Montesquieu's view from the older classical republican view, which, he argues, focused primarily on "increase" in population. Montesquieu's view is modern in that he did not defend "propogation" in exclusion to other inducements: marriage is also made because of a "natural obligation" of the father to nourish his children (XXIII.2), for love and "fancy" (XXIII.8), and for mutual aid and comfort (XXVI.10). In book 26, this broadened set of considerations undergird his defense of divorce liberalization. Take the following passage, for example, where consent provides the bridge between divorce initiation and divorce made "in conformity with nature":

> If divorce is in conformity with nature, it is so only when consent is given by the two parties, or at least one of them; and when neither the one nor the other consents to it, divorce is a monster.[120]

The emphasis on consent here is minimalistic, but important, especially insofar as it helps to distinguish Montesquieu's views on marriage from traditional religious views.

Religious laws have improved and strengthened marriage, most of all, by providing for a public belief in the "sanctity of marriage" (XXVI.9; XXVI.6; see also PL 112). The Christian religion, specifically, has contributed to a sense of the "sublime" importance of marriage, while also supporting the "form" of marriage and its various ceremonies (see XXVI.14). Moreover, religion favors the ideal of a "spiritual state" between the husband and the wife (XXVI.9).

On the other hand, Montesquieu is critical of religious laws that he finds to be in tension, both with natural laws, like self-defense,[121] and the civil laws (which should have in view "the general good of society").[122] The difficult question for interpreters of Montesquieu is the political one. When these spheres of law conflict, who should decide between them, and on what grounds?

Generally, Montesquieu provides a classical liberal standard: he recommends that religion yield to natural law and natural right (XVI.7). In rare cases, he admits, civil right must yield to the principles of the laws of religion (XVI.9).[123] But on questions like divorce, there is less ambiguity: religion plays an informative but clearly subordinate role (XXVI.13).

The foregoing summary of Montesquieu's views on women, divorce, and marriage, has been necessary for two reasons: as a reminder of Montesquieu's principled views on property in the broadest possible sense, and second, for a broader appreciation of the crucial importance of inheritance laws in Montesquieu's political economy.[124] Turning now to Montesquieu's views of inheritance, the following section summarizes Montesquieu's views on what I will refer to as private succession. The bold confrontation of the institution of primogeniture makes more clear the underlying commitment to a version of self-ownership in Montesquieu's *The Spirit of the Laws*. Montesquieu's foray into primogeniture also provides necessary background for understanding the larger political issue at stake, namely, the controversy over political succession and the inheritance of thrones.

The Tangled Logic of Primogeniture

Unlike the books on slavery (formally outlawed by Louis X), and the divorce debate (already well underway in France) Montesquieu was breaking new ground with his study of the history of inheritance laws.[125] Indeed, in the opening passage of book 27, which focus on the Roman laws of inheritance, Montesquieu makes claim to a discovery, boasting, for example, that he has discovered something "no one has seen before" (XXVII).

At stake in this discovery, as we will now see, is the legitimacy of the very foundations of the French constitution (XXX.21). In the guise of a history of the French civil laws, Montesquieu will reinterpret the founding event of the monarchy, clarify the nature of sovereign power, and in the process, undermine the intellectual supports of both the royal and traditional noble claims to property.[126]

Confusion resulting from Montesquieu's ambiguous treatment of primogeniture goes back to Montesquieu's own generation.[127] Did Montesquieu favour the status quo? What di Montesquieu discover about the history of the convention, and were these discoveries related to his political views?

The subject of private succession or private inheritance is particularly difficult to sort out. Contemporaries of Montesquieu often simply selected examples that suited their criticism of Montesquieu. Just to take one example, some critics latched on to Montesquieu's criticism of the noble historian Comte de Boulainvillier as evidence for his conservative monarchical tendencies—as proof that Montesquieu was attempting a recovery of a "monarchical-constitutional" theory. Some even claimed that this was the basis for a conservative "Montesquieu's school."

These one-sided accounts not only overshot the meaning of Montesquieu's arguments in favor of primogeniture. More significantly, they failed to account the wide range of criticisms of primogeniture. As we will see, Montesquieu's criticisms ranged from a radical re-evaluation of private succession in the Roman laws, to proposed reforms in the order of royal inheritance.

Taking monarchy as it is, not as it should be, Montesquieu started by treating the reasons for the practice of primogeniture. At the individual or family level, first-born inheritance laws helped to prevent the subdivision of estates, thus ensuring stability and also preserving the "nature" of monarchical government, inequality. On the political level, primogeniture was commonly viewed (positively) as a means for fixing the laws of succession, necessary to avoid uncertainty, and to ward off the inevitable slide from monarchy to despotism.[128] Socially, the principle first-born inheritance provided the nobility with economic autonomy. "Power was another degree further removed," Montesquieu noted, from influence.[129] Large inherited estates interrupted the "communication" of power, opening what Montesquieu called "intermediate channels" where it could flow and be dispersed throughout society.[130]

Montesquieu also explored the benefits of primogeniture in relation to "honor," the principle of monarchy. Within the family, primogeniture encouraged the youngest sons of the nobility to seek preeminence or honor in careers in the military, government, or the Church. It was believed, moreover, to strengthen paternal attachment, that is, by providing the father with additional motives to build a fortune and perpetuate the family name. For Montesquieu, this was not unimportant, given his less than idealistic views of fatherhood.[131] In short, the family name connected honor to property. Names were especially important in a monarchy, where virtue was not the principle motive: primogeniture encouraged the creation of ambitious dynasties that would outlive the individual.[132]

There was then a powerful if perverse logic sustaining the convention, and Montesquieu keenly perceived this legal custom to be an essential pillar of monarchical rule. But as we will see now, this did not prevent Montesquieu from exposing the arbitrariness of the "institution of heredity," a system, he argues in book 31, that led to the regrettable passage from political to feudal government (XXXI.31). It was, in the end, a system that could not ultimately be reconciled with a self-ownership society.

The Liberal Argument against Primogeniture

Montesquieu's arguments against primogeniture have not adequately been summarized, partly, no doubt, because they are scattered and far-ranging. Property and private succession are tackled from a comparative, sociological, economic, and historical perspective (esp. XXVII). In organizing Montesquieu's survey of the variety of laws of succession, we can show that Montesquieu had planned, deliberately, to stockpile a wide variety of arguments against first-born male inheritance.

The bulk of Montesquieu's discussion of succession laws from a comparative point of view are found in book 26. He begins with the classical republican perspective, which envisages the father and son not as a "family" but "simply as two citizens." The property between them is therefore strictly considered from a civil point of view (XXVI.5). From the political imperatives of ancient democracy, arise the Voconian law, which does not permit the appointment of female heirs (XXVI.6). Saint Augustine and Saint Marcouf found this both unjust and impious, on the grounds of natural law. Montesquieu sides with their revulsion, but does not share the same natural law perspective. Natural law orders fathers to feed his children, not "to oblige them to make them their heirs." Natural *right* however, covers protection, not inheritance.[133]

Montesquieu's objection to the Voconian law contains a rejection both of the *a priori* simplicity of natural law theory, and a sophisticated rhetorical strategy. Surveying alternatives for property and inheritance arrangements in despotic regimes, Montesquieu selects examples that underscore liberal principles. In China, for example, there was an experiment in which the Emperor's brothers succeeded to the throne, ahead of the first-born son. This simple example illustrates not only the absurdity of eldest male property rights. It highlights the liberal principle of merit, which in this case, depends on "experience," not bloodline.[134] As another example, Montesquieu points out that relatives inherited property in ancient Numidia. In Arabic countries, an uncle or some other relative is chosen. In polygamous nations, property passed to the sister of the deceased, thus avoiding impossible quarrels among numerous children. In each case, Montesquieu's selection of examples points to a pattern: merit as a replacement for hereditary succession.

Before turning to book 27, it is necessary to briefly recount Montesquieu's treatment of the inheritance laws of France in book 18. There, Montesquieu traced the origins of primogeniture in France to the Salic laws; significant, according to Montesquieu, because it is here that one finds the first codification of the rule in European history that women should possess nothing and that the son must "inherit the father's legacy."[135]

In book 18, the Salic laws are interpreted by Montesquieu in their original economic context. Laws restricting female inheritance were based in a particular accident relating to the terrain—and to the Germanic understanding of *property*. As Montesquieu states, "In order to know what these Salic lands were, one must discover *what property was* and what the use of the land was among the Franks before they left Germany" (XVIII.22; italics added). Salic, according to Montesquieu, comes from the word *sala*, meaning "house." According to Tacitus and Caesar, the Germanic people understood property as extending only to the "house" not the *land* surrounding it.[136] The land was given to the owners for one year, after which time it became public again. Because the early Franks did not have stable ownership in the land, it was therefore expedient, economically, for them to extend patrimony to the males, only. The males could inherit the house, but the daughters married and "entered other houses."

Montesquieu's account of this historical development contains a revealing twist. This "purely economic" understanding of the law soon became outmoded (XVIII.22). As the Franks acquired "new properties" and began cultivating the land, they began to extend the idea of property from the house to the land, and ultimately, to moveable property ("slaves, herds, horses, arms"). The original Salic laws which privileged the males was soon deemed to be "harsh" and unjust not only for the daughters, but for the younger brothers and closest relatives on the female side.[137]

Montesquieu views this change in attitudes as a critical turning point in European history. The Franks, no longer trusting in the justice or utility of male first-born privilege (see XVIII.22) attempted to change the laws to permit fathers to pass property down to the daughter. Interestingly, that early attempt at legal reform of family law was "silenced." The Frank's liberalization scheme was abandoned, while the practice of limiting female inheritance continued unchallenged. And yet, centuries later, the rule of primogeniture remained essentially unchallenged. The establishment of fiefs further entrenched male economic privilege, while adding further legal limits on female inheritance.

The Salic laws, to summarize, have their origins in an obscure Germanic understanding of property. Centuries later, French historians were mistakenly relying on the Salic custom to justify male inheritance of the French crown.

In book 27, Montesquieu performs a similar archeological or critical method, but focuses on the origins of inheritance laws in Roman history. Unlike the Salic laws, the original laws restricting the rights of women to inherit derive not from economics, but from the classical republican political imperative to maintain an equal division of lands. Referring to the Law of the Twelve Tables, Montesquieu discovers the origins of legal male privilege in the attempt to prevent the transfer of large parcels of land from one family to another. The Law of the Twelve Tables called for "agnates" (relatives on the male side) to inherit only. Interestingly, these laws did *not* restrict female heirs on the male side. This, according to Montesquieu, is a significant historical finding, one that has "not been seen before." But why?

Such findings are to serve as a model for interpretive jurisprudence. Legal historians only had to put the accounts in book 18 side by side with the account in book 27. In doing so, they could not but conclude that neither version of primitive successional laws logically support the current exclusion of females in the order of inheritance. That is, neither the Salic laws nor the original Roman inheritance laws provide non-arbitrary arguments in favor of male first-born inheritance.[138] Even the Voconian laws (enacted later during the Punic wars and which further restricted female inheritance) was not based on discrimination between male and female, Montesquieu notes. The restrictions on inheritance were made on the basis of class, according to the imperatives of republican egalitarianism.[139] But even this law, Montesquieu concludes, "opposes natural feelings," as it sacrificed the citizen and the man and "thought only of the republic."

Montesquieu's conclusion in book 27 is that the Roman laws on inheritance were appropriate for the spirit of ancient republics, not modern monarchies (XXVII). Justinian, moreover, had disposed of the distinction between male and female. As for the Salic laws, we have already seen that they could hardly be used to justify current property arrangements. Montesquieu then presents three books on the history and "revolutions" of the civil laws in France. Taken together, these three books do not simply describe the origins of "moderate monarchy" as an evolution of either French or Roman civil law. They also present a direct but unique challenge to the French monarchic state.

The approach to the dynastic controversy in these books is consistent with Montesquieu's arguments against primogeniture. Montesquieu's critique of dynastic succession is more targeted, however, and should be compared to three important works dating from the late sixteenth century to the early seventeenth century: Francois Hotman's *Le Gaule Francoise* (1574), Jean Bodin, *Six books of the Commonwealth* (1576), and Bernard de La Roche-Flavin in *Treize livres des Parlements de France* (1617). According to Iris Cox, these three books contributed to the live debate on the future of the French constitution: "All three authors accepted the fact of kings at the head of state, but their different ideas on the succession to the throne, and on the legitimate exercise of authority, set the scene for the discussions of the French constitution up to the revolution."[140]

Hotman's view drew on the long history of the tradition of French Gaul. Kings should be elected, deposed if necessary, and the laws should be composed by the Estates.[141] Bodin concluded that absolute sovereign power was limited only by an obligation "to obey the laws of God." La Roche-Flavin, by contrast, argued that the Parlement of Paris, and secondarily, the regional Parlements, were the "true successors" of the early *Assemblees des Grands*, the original source of sovereign—and therefore lawmaking—power in French history.[142]

In book 30, Montesquieu makes a personal confession, noting that he has—to this point—ignored the importance of the debates on the origins of the feudal laws.[143] Thus far he has only observed the "leaves" and the "trunk" of civil law. In his last two books, conceding that it would be impossible to write a comprehensive history, and admitting that he finds himself in a "dark labrynth full of paths and detours,"[144] Montesquieu describes his own purpose using a suggestive metaphor: the work before him is to dig up the tree *from the roots*. Given this claim, and given his subsequent argument that he himself "holds the end of the thread" out of the labrynth, it is hard to agree with those who have summarized the last two books as merely an historical appendix.

I propose here to re-examine the significance of the final two books of *The Spirit of the Laws* by focusing on one subject: the evolution of property and inheritance laws. While Montesquieu's history of France contains more than a few sub-plots, the primary storyline is not hard to identify. In chapter 19, Montesquieu argues that this is a narrative of how the French people lost independence in civil government.[145] The evolution of inheritance laws is a key part of that story.

In the opening chapter, Montesquieu admits that the feudal laws diminished the power of kings, but not without great consequences for individual liberty: when "domain" was ceded and the weight of "lordship" passed away from the kings, there appeared "various kinds of lordship" over "persons." This process—of the creation of property in offices and in people—began long before the establishment of fiefs, that is, among the Germans. Among the Germans, there were vassals, but not fiefs: "There were no fiefs because the princes had no lands to give, or rather fiefs were war horses, weapons, and meals."[146] Thus Montesquieu's claim is that vassalage originated in a contract unconnected with land, but more importantly, in a time where there were not fixed estates.[147]

The beginning of the idea of a fixed estate, which entailed servitude to *land*, thus benefitting the apologists for modern feudalism, did not begin with the Franks, Montesquieu argues, but with the Romans.[148] "It is not true," he argues, that "the Franks, on entering Gaul, occupied all the lands of the country in order to make fiefs for them. Some people have thought this, because they have seen that near the end of the reign of the Carolingians, almost all the land had become fiefs, under-fiefs, or dependencies of one or the other, but this had particular causes that will be subsequently explained."[149] During the first invasions, Montesquieu continues, fiefs were revocable. No king had the disposition of the fiefs, "the only property," as this would have provided them with a "power as arbitrary as is that of the sultan of Turkey." Montesquieu added, "this upsets all of history."[150]

Two implications follow. First, and most broadly, history could not support the dynastic arguments of either of the absolutists or those, including the nobility, who saw themselves as the defenders of the "fundamental laws." Neither of the historical schools, usually associated with the *these royale* or the *these nobiliaire*, were justified in appealing to historical civil laws to support their position. Montesquieu clearly distinguished himself from those schools by arguing that the civil laws, especially relating to succession, are a matter of political not civil law. The absurdity of using civil law to justify either vision of monarchical authority is expressed by Montesquieu as follows: "It is absurd to claim to settle the rights of kingdoms, nations, and the universe by the same maxims used to decide a right concerning a drainage pipe disputed between private individuals."[151]

Montesquieu's proposed solution was to regard the invention of the modern property in persons as an historical bargain, which served the purposes of the time. The Burgundians were pastoral, the Romans predominantly were agricultural. The Burgundian who grazed his herds "needed much land and few serfs," while the Romans, who cultivated the land, needed comparatively less land "and a greater number of serfs."[152] The arrangements to divide fallow and fertile land were not made "in a tyrannical spirit," nor with the intention of formally establishing "servitude" to the land.[153] What we now call serfdom, Montesquieu hints, arose out of a contract of "mutual needs" between the two codes of two peoples inhabiting the same country.[154] Servitude was not "peculiar" to the Romans, or "liberty and nobility a thing peculiar to the barbarians."[155]

Montesquieu's account undercut two opposing views: the Count of Boulainvilliers' and the Abbé Dubos each, according to Montesquieu, who had constructed history in the form of a "conspiracy." Boulainvilliers' treatise was a conspiracy against the "third estate," while Dubos', according to Montesquieu, "was a conspiracy against the nobility."[156] Thus Montesquieu's re-examination of the civil laws situated him between the "Romanists" and the "Germanists." This position, as we will see, was relevant not only as a reinterpretation of the origin of the distribution of intermediary powers, and therefore, the existing "number of servitudes" that persist in the property laws of the old regime. It also implicated modern politics or "Political right" since the knowledge of the history of civil laws was equivalent to knowledge of the foundation of the monarchy. Concentrating on property law, Montesquieu could explain the artificial origins of modern "orders."

The emergence of feudal distinctions among persons could be traced to a few primary causes, one especially important: the conquest of the Franks, Burgundians, and the Goths. In chapter 11, Montesquieu describes the "ravages" in terms of an Hobbesian state of war: "[the barbarians] took all the gold, silver, furniture, clothing, men, women, and boys, that the army could carry; everything was put together and the army divided it."[157] A settlement was reached with the inhabitants. Importantly, Montesquieu rejects the notion that the "settlement" between the conquered inhabitants and the tribes involved an agreement to give up civil or political rights in exchange for preservation. The inhabitants resisted and rebelled. Centuries of servitude arose not through invitation or contract, but from resistance to a brutal and unforgiving "right of nations."[158]

The remainder of the book describes the extension and entrenchment of various forms of feudal servitude. Abusive taxation increased simultaneously with other legal burdens for serfs. Exemptions multiplied for privileged orders and freedmen.[159] Many of these exemptions were arbitrary, but some had peculiar causes, which historians have overlooked. For example, Montesquieu argues that the "release" of the burdens from taxation for freemen was, in part, *compensation*, or a reward, for a promise that they would go to war, provide patrols, horses, and equipment to defend the frontiers (thus they "would not be constrained to pay any other census"). In the confusion of war, linguistic and cultural mingling, and countless layers of legal history, Montesquieu attempts to show that these "obligations" were then slowly forgotten. The establishment of the "census" further obscured the origins of those so-called "privileges" of the kings, the ecclesiastics, and the lords. Old conventions became law, and law became "rights."[160] Forgetting the original purposes, in short, it soon became customary to understand, indeed, to define "freemen" as "free from public burdens." In a reverse of the old system, only serfs now had "to pay the census."[161]

Throughout book 30, Montesquieu emphasizes the melding of economic rights into political rights. The grant of land through vassalage shifted power again to owners of real property.[162] Major changes in the administration of justice necessarily followed. According to Tacitus, for example, the German peoples originally had few civil laws. Property, understood in its most narrow sense, left each family "in the state of nature." Satisfaction was often violent, punishment was corporeal and rarely pecuniary.[163] Gradually, the German peoples put a "just price" on crimes, shifting corporal punishment increasingly to pecuniary fines.

Importantly, Montesquieu regards this as a positive development. And yet, the shift to pecuniary punishment took an extraordinary twist. Now justice was, with increasing frequency, attached to the *status* of the person. At the same time that corporal penalties were being phased out, there was now, at the same time, much "greater security" for a free man than for a serf. Settlements for wrongs and injuries involved two calculations: one for the wrong or injury itself, and one for the guilty party, who could pay for a certain "right" in exchange for protection.[164] The remarkable result was an increase in the power of the lords. They now owned the "fief" but also the "justice," *and the revenues* from it. Montesquieu describes this new privilege as a very "lucrative right" that was at the heart of the "patrimonial" system of the courts.[165] From these causes, three great consequences: first, the church "acquired very considerable [property]."[166] Second, the nobles, with the power of judging, gained powers of "immunity." Third, the system of justice was "arrogated" to the vassals, within the fiefs. In short, as property became more "fixed," among the lords, so too did their privileges.

Montesquieu's account of the evolution and growth of feudal property is anything but simple, but it contains two easily identifiable lessons. On the one hand, Montesquieu illustrates the internecine connection between the evolution of property rights in France and the origins of the legal codes. Putting these together, he is able to explain the emergence of the highly artificial distinctions among estates. Second, Montesquieu is able to distinguish himself both from the Count of Boulainvilliers,[167] and the monarchists. Indeed, the broader purpose, the "general idea," in his words, of book 30, is focused on destroying the historical account of Abbé Dubos, whose "three deadening volumes" had tried to prove that the nobility had usurped its privileges.[168]

To understand Montesquieu's critique of Dubos, it is useful to recall the political aims of Dubos's treatise. In short, Dubos tried to justify monarchical privilege by arguing that Justinian had assigned to the children and grandchildren of Clovis "all the rights of dominion over Gaul." Yet as Montesquieu had already shown, the Frankish monarchy was not a gift from an emporer. It was "was already founded," that is, as a compound of the "rights of persons" and contracts among "the mutual needs" of two peoples.[169] Critical to Dubos's thesis was the argument that there was, at the time of the founding of the monarchy, "one order of citizens among the Franks." Book 30 dispells that illusion by revealing the many layers of property rights that grounded the infinity of legal distinctions that would later become the foundation of the monarchical orders.

From one perspective, then, book 30 could be read as a pro-noble treatise, insofar as it justifies the existence of seigneurial justices, and therefore, the fixity of the nobility in its privileges and rights. But in studying the foundation of the French constitution, it is well known that Montesquieu also clearly distinguished his position from the rival history of Boulainvilliers, who, as above, Montesquieu charged with leading a "conspiracy" against the third estate. Boullainvilliers may have been right to emphasize the rights of the nobility as a limitation on royal absolutism. Yet, as Montesquieu argues, he clearly overstated the case in arguing that noble rights were either perpetual, or hereditary. If seigneurial justices did not exist from the beginning of the monarchy, it would be impossible to claim that the power of the feudal aristocracy was original, or in the language of the dynastic controversy, that noble rights and freedoms were "primordial."[170]

If book 30 challenges royalist revisionism through scrutiny of the evolution of civil law, book 31 provides a direct challenge to the principle of heredity among the nobility.[171] As in book 30, property is the touchstone. The opening chapter describes changes "in the offices and fiefs" as a key turning point in understanding the "revolutions" of Frankish monarchy. As the nobility acquired absolute property in their domains, the balance of power that supported moderate government dissolved: "the tree extended its branches too far, and the head withered."[172]

The "modern concept" of "inalienable domain" had a number of fateful consequences. According to Montesquieu, the triumph of absolute property resulted in a transformation from political government to feudalism. Further, as offices became permanent, corruption seeped in, resulting in "successive abuses" as it became clear that property in land was no longer the only road to power. Land could be given away, but renouncing the "great offices was to lose power itself."[173] At first, the "mayors" and ministers did not recognize the profound implications of giving out small favors, including the "preserving" of honors and ranks in perpetuity (XXXI.3–7). During the first century of the Merovingian rule under Childeric (c. 457 AD–481 AD) the fiefs became hereditary, and the kings were increasingly relegated to a ceremonial role. At that stage, the concept of "inalienable domain" was still "unknown" both "in theory and in practice" (XXXI.7). The consolidation of power—and the transformation of hereditary offices—happened under the Carolingians, in the time of Charles Martel (c. 688–74). Martel founded new fiefs, setting a precedent of making "gifts perpetual."

The Church of course played an important role in this legal and social revolution. As the practice of giving gifts in return for military service grew, it became more common for the kings to transfer lands to the churches. Pepin, Montesquieu argues, had made himself "master of the monarchy by protecting the clergy" (XXXI.9). He jokingly adds that the clergy received so much property during the reigns of the Merovingians, Carolingians, and Capetians they must have been given the "whole of the goods of the kingdom several times."[174]

The story of growth of the theory of absolute property in France is not linear. After the arrival of the Normans, for example, the church lost enormous sums of real property. Charlemagne considered re-appropriating the fortunes from the warriors, but decided instead to allow for the establishment of tithes. Tithes are described by Montesquieu as "a new kind of good" which pleased the church not only for financial reasons. It also made clear that usurpations would be more recognizable in the future."[175] While the establishment of tithes—as compensation for loss of land during the invasions—did not restore the church's wealth, it did set in motion a new dynamic power, which led to a new era of political independence for the church (XXXI.13–14). The monarchy also backed away from naming candidates and electing bishoprics and "other ecclesiastical benefices."

These changes in offices are of minor interest, historically. But they are of major significance to an understanding of Montesquieu's political economy. In short, they reveal Montesquieu's deep opposition to the traditional theory of dynastic inheritance, and hence, his more general opposition to the status quo. But this argument could be proved even without the foregoing summary. Within the history of the civil laws, Montesquieu leaves subtle clues but also explicit and radical suggestions for reform. At the beginning of the Carolingian reign, for example,

Montesquieu notes that the crown was a mix of elective and hereditary principles.[176] When Hugh Capet (c. 941 – 996) was crowned, the monarchy lost this elective principle, becoming instead a "a great fief" (XXXI.16). For Montesquieu, this loss was a very troubling and significant departure from the French constitution under the Carolingians, especially, Charlemagne (c. 742/748 – 814), whom Montesquieu clearly admired, as this passage from his notebooks demonstrates:

> Charlemagne's continual victories, the moderation and justice of his government, seemed to found a new monarchy. He avoided squabbles and often assembled the nation. Arts and sciences seemed to reappear. It seemed that the French people were about to destroy barbarianism.[177]

In *The Spirit of the Laws* Charlemagne is further praised for preserving popular elements of monarchy; specifically, the "faculty of electing" by removing the restriction on choosing among the children of kings. Charlemagne also kept the power of the nobility within its own limits, curtailing both the "oppression of the clergy and the freemen" (XXXI.18).[178] Charlemagne may have been "too susceptible to pleasure with women."[179] But Charlemagne is nonetheless held up as a model of political and economic prudence. He "regulated his expenses admirably; he developed his domains wisely, attentively, and economically; the father of a family could learn from his laws how to govern his household."[180] Montesquieu also feels obliged to mention the monarch's magnanimity, noting that he sold eggs from the farmyards of his domains, and the "unused vegetables" of his gardens, while redistributing the wealth of the Lombards and the "immense treasuries" of the Huns who had "despoiled the universe."

After Charlemagne, however, the "rampart" of authority collapsed, beginning with the disorder brought upon by Louis the Pious, and successors. In order to maintain their power, the emperor's children solicited the clergy, giving them "rights unheard of" before Charlemagne. The prince weakened the monarchy further, as Montesquieu says, through "dissipating" crown domains.[181] While Louis gave "immense gifts" to the churches from his domains, his sons "distributed the goods of the clergy to the laity."

In chapter 28, Montesquieu finally arrives at the most revolutionary changes, those that "occurred in the great offices and in the fiefs." In the earliest days of the monarchy, it was highly uncommon for fiefs to be sold in "perpetuity." The crown had never "alienated the great offices in perpetuity." Charles the Bald, the grandson of Charlemagne, extended the hereditary principle more than any previous king. "It would be difficult to follow the progress," Montesquieu notes, "of the abuses resulting from this and from the extension given to this law in each country."[182] One notable consequence was the change in the understanding of the principle of succession. Each fief became "like the crown," that is, elective and hereditary. The idea of the perpetuity of fiefs was now seemingly fixed forever.[183]

What were the results? First, the inheritance of fiefs and the "general establishment" of perpetual property rights "extinguished political government and formed feudal government."[184] Second, Montesquieu argues, the crown itself came to be understood as "a great fief."[185] It followed, third, that the right of the eldest, or "of primogeniture," was "established among the French."[186]

The story of primogeniture reaches its climax, in book 31, with Montesquieu's final attack on the royalist understanding of property. When fiefs had been revocable, or for life only, the civil laws were subordinate to political laws, which could have in its view the common good.[187] When fiefs became permanent or hereditary, great estates now could be "given, sold, or given as legacies." The idea of property, in other words, as a concern of *both* civil right *and* political right, lost its meaning. Property in large estates now became solely a matter of civil law: "considered as a kind of good in commerce, it was a concern of civil right." Unlike the Roman right and the Salic laws discussed earlier, French civil law had become untethered from politics and therefore, from considerations of the common good. With the advent of fiefs "in perpetuity," the only question that mattered was the enlargement or persistence of the fief.

Montesquieu ends *The Spirit of the Laws* by noting that his treatise on fiefs "closes" where most authors "have begun it."[188] This passage does not represent his final thoughts on property, however. In book 26, Montesquieu had provided an apparently revolutionary principle, a rule, for deciding what should be done when a "certain order of succession becomes destructive of the political body."[189] When the political law "destroys the state, decisions must be made by the political law that preserves it, which sometimes becomes a right of nations."

As the printer was putting the finishing touches on Montesquieu's book, small capital letters were added, apparently, to underscore the principle on which a right of rebellion might be justified. When the political law becomes destructive, there must be "no doubt," Montesquieu continues, that "another political law can change that order." This new law will not be in opposition to the first. Rather, it will be "at bottom entirely in conformity with it, because both will depend on this principle: THE WELL-BEING OF THE PEOPLE IS THE SUPREME LAW."[190]

CONCLUSION

In recent years, Montesquieu scholarship has seen a number of attempts to explain, critique, attack, or revise Montesquieu's philosophy of liberalism. Today, scholars are less likely than they were in the past to take extreme positions, defending him either as the hero of the liberal tradition, or, even less plausibly, a "rationalizer of reaction."[1]

Yet, questions still remain, and scholars continue to press the question, "Was Montesquieu a liberal republican?"[2] Despite the revival of the liberal reading of Montesquieu by Thomas Pangle in the 1970s, and despite major recent advances, including the masterful work of Paul Rahe in his 2009 *Montesquieu and The Logic of Liberty*, the "liberal" reading seems not to have weathered well.

This study has presented a case against what I believe to be an overcorrection in the literature. The cause, I have argued, is rooted in a lingering confusion regarding the political significance of Montesquieu's writings on commerce. This confusion has generated a number of interpretative errors and ambiguities, which continue to cloud the revolutionary implications of *The Spirit of the Laws* in obscurity. These include: an over-emphasis on Montesquieu's optimism for the pacific effects of commercial exchange; a misunderstanding of the *reasons* for Montesquieu's separation of the nobility from trade; neglect of Montesquieu's history of commerce, which has as its primary goal the ennobling of the profession of the merchant; insufficient attention to the "two-way" relationship between commerce and religion; and a general unwillingness to engage with the natural rights basis of Montesquieu's complex theory of property.

If there is a revolutionary-liberal project in *The Spirit of the Laws*, these and similar topics must be accounted for. How, or to what extent, Montesquieu consciously revised the political philosophy of what we now call "classical liberalism" is a question that I do not pretend to answer in this book. Here it is appropriate to defer to an argument first presented in *Montesquieu's Philosophy of Liberalism: A Commentary on The Spirit of the Laws*. Montesquieu not only adopted the principles of his predecessors—Hobbes, Spinoza, Locke—but importantly, as Pangle argued, subjected those principles to a "new analysis," based not in the abstractions of Enlightenment political theory, but in "political experience as revealed by the history of the European nations and the accounts available to him of non-European peoples."

Montesquieu's political economy is useful in this specific sense. It consists not only in a modification of the common arguments for commerce in the eighteenth century. More importantly, it presents the alternatives to modern commerce, and economic liberalism. Thinking through these alternatives is perhaps the most interesting reason to reflect on Montesquieu's economic and political thought. This book has explored only a few: the "perfect system" of Lycurgus, the modern communalism of the experiment of Penn, the philosophy of mercantilism in seventeenth- and eighteenth-century European monarchies, Enlightened economic despotism, and the transitional, emerging doctrines of Montesquieu's contemporaries, the physiocrats.[3]

In following what Montesquieu once called the "Longer road," there is value, too, in revisiting the Enlightenment philosopher's apprehensions, or reservations, regarding the cultural perils and political pitfalls of commercial modernity. One of the most striking features of Montesquieu's political economy is his ability to comprehend both the future promise and the real weaknesses of liberal capitalism and commercial society—a concern that was evident in his earliest works. There is an exchange in the *Persian Letters* worth reflecting on, by way of conclusion.

Rhedi, a Persian traveler, questions whether commerce—and the arts and science that usually follow—is good for mankind. Rhedi had begun his journey abroad in the *Persian Letters* with great optimism. In Letter 29, he is barely able to contain his excitement upon his arrival in the dazzling commercial society of Venice. Rhedi describes his "delight" in "living in a city where every day my mind is improved" and where it is possible to "[learn] about the secrets of commerce, [and] the affairs of princes." Venice not only delights his senses; it is the source of his understanding and Enlightenment; it allows him, in his words, to finally "cast off the veil that covered my eyes in the land of my birth."

As time passes, Rhedi's mood darkens, especially as he begins to reflect more deeply on the dangers of commercial civilization. Note the profound change, for example, in Letter 102, where Rhedi, after having lived for an extended period of time in the bustling commercial towns, appears to have lapsed into a gloomy cynicism. The experience of living in commercial society leaves the young man positively yearning for the "innocence of ancient times."[4] In a long and thoughtful letter to Usbek, Rhedi then makes this statement, a confession that my resonate with many young readers today: "I'm not convinced that the benefits [that the arts and science and commerce] bestow compensate man for the evil purposes to which they are turned every day." Rhedi, we find out, has come to suspect that commercial civilization is—as Montesquieu suggests above in his discussion of English restlessness—a greatly disappointing illusion.[5]

The older Usbek replies to Rhedi.[6] First, he notes that Rhedi has "exaggerated" the evils of commercial society, noting, with some subtlety of argument, that it is only in a free and commercial society where one is "free to educate [oneself]" that a spirited person—precisely a spirited person like Rhedi—is free to openly question the commercial way of life. Echoing a common charge against today's critics of capitalism, Montesquieu notes that it is precisely in those states where there is the most freedom and where intellectuals enjoy the greatest benefits of commerce that both commerce and freedom are considered "pernicious."

Usbek also reminds Rhedi of the importance of thinking through the alternatives: a world without commerce would be a world without science. He rethe "miserable, brutish conditions that would follow the loss of all branches of human knowledge." As for the dangers of modern war, Usbek suggests, albeit optimistically, that these weapons, once discovered, will be "buried" by those who discovered them; their use will be limited by "international public law." Usbek concedes that wars will be deadlier. But he adds that they will also "end sooner than they did in the past" and that the absence of "hand-to-hand-fighting" will make the battles themselves less cruel and bloody.

Will commerce and the arts "emasculate nations"? Usbek argues that Rhedi need not worry about the "ruin" of modern empires due to the "softening" effects of commerce. Nations pursuing commerce and trade will be stronger—more independent. Most significantly, they will be able to pay for their wars without tyrannizing their own people and destroying their own economies through excessive taxation.[7]

The unpredictability of commercial society will make life "hard" and force people to work more. Cities, like Paris, "the most sensual city in the world," will be overcrowded, and many people will find urban existence degrading or inhumane. And yet, because of the passion to work, and as a result of the spread of the desire to acquire more wealth, the spirit of industry will affect people in "all conditions" in positive ways as well (not wanting to be "poorer than the man he's just seen, whose situation is by a mere hair's breadth inferior to his own"). Idleness, and softness, concludes Usbek, in a sentence that underlines Montesquieu's view of the relationship between philosophy, science, and commercial civilization, are "incompatible with the pursuit of the arts."

It is on this last point that one may come to fully appreciate the significance of Montesquieu's political economy. Political liberty, according to Montesquieu, is the "opinion" that each one has of his or own security.[8] In order to secure this liberty, government must be such that "one citizen cannot fear another citizen." With this object in view, or in mind, we have seen that Montesquieu turned to political economy, not narrowly conceived, but broadly imagined as an integrated study of the variety of conditions under which political and civil liberty—combining to form the experience of liberty—could be realized.

The study of political economy, for Montesquieu, does not provide the ends, the "object" or the "purpose of various states."[9] It does, however, perform an essential service in narrowing the range of objects, assuming, as Montesquieu does, an unrelenting increase in global trade, cultural exchange, and the replacement of conquest with wealth as a basis for modern security and prosperity. Montesquieu's political economy is unique therefore in at least two ways: it is in its essence a rejection of mercantilist philosophy, and, perhaps more significantly, a powerful repudiation of the emerging "new science" of political economy, a term introduced by the admirers of Quesnay, and signifying the abandonment of the study of constitutions to a search for economic laws, applicable to all constitutions.[10]

From a Montesquieuean perspective, the shift in modern thought from an integrated political economy to theoretical economics is concerning. Today's separation of disciplines ignores the importance of politics, but in addition, the psychological element of liberty, which Montesquieu repeatedly referred to as a "philosophical state" rather than "a civil state." In the *Pensées*, Montesquieu wrote: "A free government can be compared to a great net in which the fish roam about and do not think they are caught."[11] The Ancients, according to Montesquieu in a separate passage, compared laws "to spider webs, which, being only strong enough to stop flies, are broken by birds."[12] Montesquieu's revision of the ancient metaphor is revealing; the fish are not free, but "think they are free."

In using this metaphor, Montesquieu did not mean to suggest that liberty is merely an illusion or a state of mind. Indeed, the study of political economy demonstrates that human beings are free—within a certain latitutde—to choose their political and social arrangements, despite the natural and historical forces that often seem to overwhelm our best efforts Montesquieu does not deny, in his words, "that there are very good and very bad governments, and even that a constitution is *more imperfect* in the measure that it draws away from this philosophical idea of liberty that we have."[13] A philosophical idea of liberty implies a free soul, which itself presupposes a free government, one capable of correcting itself by its own laws. But self-correcting governments are rare, and vulnerable to decay. Herein lies the significance of Montesquieu's pathbreaking study of political economy. Modern democratic states must avoid the harmful belief that commercial modernity chooses us, and not the other way around.

NOTES

Notes on Texts

1. This translation is based on the 1721 edition of the *Persian Letters*. For an explanation of the decision to rely on the 1721 version (rather than the 1754 version, also approved by Montesquieu), see Mauldon (2008, xxxi). For our purposes, the major practical difference relate to the *number* of letters in each edition. The 1721 edition contains 150 letters. The 1754 edition contains 11 "supplemental" letters in addition to Montesquieu's own "Some Reflections on the *Persian Letters*." This has created some confusion, since the 1758 (unauthorized) version *combines* all of the letters into one sequence (making 161 letters—a combination that Montesquieu did not himself authorize). To avoid confusion, I will use the original (1721) numbering. In the endnotes, references to letters will be denoted as, for example, *PL* #1.
2. Basia Carolyn Miller, and Harold Samuel Stone, trans. and eds. 1989. Cambridge: Cambridge University Press.

Introduction   Economic Liberalism before Adam Smith

1. See Nicos E. Devletoglou. 1963. "Montesquieu and the Wealth of Nations." *Canadian Journal of Economics and Political Science* 29 (1); Devletoglou. 1969. "The Economic Philosophy of Montesquieu." *Kyklos: Internationale Zeitschrift* 22 (3): 530–541; CatherineLarrère. 2005. *Montesquieu, oeuvre ouverte 1748–1755 actes du colloque de Bordeaux, 6–8 décembre 2001, Bordeaux, bibliothèque municipale*. Napoli: Liguori; Blancheton, B. 2005. "Les faux bilans de la Banque de France dans les années 1920." In *L'enterprise, le chiffre et le droit*, eds. J. G. Degos and S. Trébucq. Bordeaux: Université Montesquieu; and Joelle Grospelier. 2005. "What Could Have Prompted Keynes to Call Montesquieu 'The Real Equivalent of Adam Smith, the Greatest of French Economists?'" *Student Economic Review* 19: 3–15. <http://www.tcd.ie/Economics/SER/pasti.php?y=05>. Of these, Devletoglou's two articles are the most helpful in terms of understanding Montesquieuean economics in isolation (i.e., from his political, social, and moral writings). Devletoglou is particularly important because he provides a readable and detailed

summary of Montesquieu's views on agriculture, industry, enterprise, saving, money, inflation, interest, international trade, and population. He also identifies six French works to consult, the "only studies that we have of Montesquieu's significance as an economist." These include Pascal Duprat's "Les Idées Économiques de Montesquieu" (1870); Joseph Oczapowski, "Montesquieu économiste" (1891); Tournyol du Clos, "Les Idées Financières de Montesquieu" (1912); C. de la Taille-Lolainville, *Les Idées économiques et financières de Montesquieu*; and Alain Cotta, "Le Développement Économique dans la Pensée de C.S. de Montesquieu." Devletoglou returns to these themes and greatly expands on them in "The Economic Philosophy of Montesquieu."
2. I will not rehearse the entire literature on Montesquieu "as economist." I follow Catherine Larrère's advice: "One should not look for the 'economic theory' of Montesquieu in the fourth part of the *Spirit of Laws*. Reading [*L'esprit des lois*] retrospectively to compare the first faltering steps with the certainties of established science is, on the whole, an approach that is open to criticism. This is particularly true when the author is Montesquieu. It is pointless to look for the equilibrium of Pareto in his work."
3. Keynes seems to be alone among experts in economic history. Montesquieu barely merits a mention in two classic works: Blanqui's *History of Political Economy in Europe* and Schumpeter's *History of Economic Analysis*.
4. Important works in English that address commerce in its political aspect include: Thomas Pangle, *Montesquieu's Philosophy of Liberalism*, esp. Chapter 7 (from here on out designated by MPOL); Pangle's *The Theological Basis of Liberal Modernity in Montesquieu's Spirit of Laws* (henceforth noted as TTB); Hulliung's *Montesquieu and the Old Regime*; Hirschman's *The Passions and the Interests*; Desserud's "Commerce and Political Participation in Montesquieu's letter to Domville"; Larrère's essays; the works of Céline Spector, especially, *Montesquieu: Pouvoirs, richesses et societies,*; Clark's *Compass and Society: Commerce and Absolutism in Old-Regime France*; Rahe's *Montesquieu and the Logic of Liberty* (designated MLL); and Cheney's *Revolutionary Commerce*. This is not an exhaustive list. Also consult: Cotta, "Le développement"; Mason, "Montesquieu, Europe and the Imperatives of Commerce"; Morilhat, *Montesquieu: politique et richesses*; Manent, *The City of Man*; Catherine Larrère, "Montesquieu on Economics and Commerce" and "Montesquieu économiste? Une lecture paradoxale"; Carrithers et al. *Montesquieu's Science of Politics: essays on "The Spirit of Laws"*; Céline Spector, *Montesquieu et l'émergence de l'économie politique*.
5. XXX.2.
6. Albert O. Hirschman. 1977. *The Passions and the Interests: Political Arguments for Capitalism before Its Triumph*. Princeton: Princeton University Press, 3. (This will be designated as PAI.)

7. In addition to the economic philosophy of Montesquieu, Hirschman also introduced Sir James Steuart, and John Millar to a wide audience.
8. The interpretation goes back at least to Carcassone's *Montesquieu et le Problem de la Constitution*. But see Spector, "Was Montesquieu Liberal? The Spirit of the Laws in the History of Liberalism," in Rosenblatt *French Liberalism from Montequieu to the Present Day*, Cambridge: Cambridge University Press.
9. Devletoglou, "Montesquieu and the Wealth of Nations."
10. Clark, Henry C. 2006. *Compass of Society: Commerce and Absolutism in Old-Regime France*. Lanham: Lexington.; Hulliung, Mark. 1976. *Montesquieu and the Old Regime*. Berkeley: University of California Press; Paul Rahe. 2009. *Montesquieu and the Logic of Liberty*. New Haven: Yale University Press.
11. David W. Carrithers, Michael A. Mosher, and Paul A. Rahe, eds. 2001. *Montesquieu's Science of Politics: Essays on the Spirit of Laws*. Lanham: Rowman & Littlefield.
12. Binoche Bertrand. "Despotism." <http://dictionnaire-montesquieu.ens-lyon.fr/en/article/1367168359/en.> See also Robert Shackleton. 1988. "Les mots 'despote' et 'despotime.'" In *Essays on Montesquieu and on the Enlightenment*, ed. David Gilson and Martin Smith, 109–116. Oxford: Voltaire Foundation; and Sharon Krause. 2001. "Despotism in the *Spirit of Laws*." In Carrithers et al., *Montesquieu's Science of Politics*.
13. See Spector "Montesquieu's The Spirit of the Laws in the History of Liberalism," 1.
14. Ford, in *Robe and Sword*, 243, mistakenly argues that this does not apply to blacks.
15. Pangle, MPOL, 11.
16. Ibid., 11.
17. Ibid., 11.
18. See, esp. ch. 7 entitled "Commerce and the Charm of National Diversity."
19. Pangle, MPOL, 2.
20. Ibid., 4.
21. Pangle, MPOL, 242; compare Hirschman, PAI, 70.
22. See especially Catherine Larrère, "Montesquieu économiste?" (Citations in this book are to an English version). See also MPE. See Boesche's essay, "Fearing Monarchs and Merchants," who has argued that Montesquieu's deepest fear in the Spirit of Laws was not just monarchs, but "merchants." More reasonably, some have argued that Montesquieu was simply ambivalent about commerce and commercial society. See D. Desserud. 1999. "Commerce and Political Participation in Montesquieu's Letter to Domville." *History of European Ideas* 25 (3): 135–151. For a sophisticated analysis of Montesquieu's ambivalence, consult Paul Rahe, MLL, 98–108. A recent assessment is also provided in Pangle, TTB, 128–129.

The last can be read as a reply to criticisms, but also an expansion on the earlier hypothesis of Montesquieu's "prophetic vision" for commerce.
23. Montesquieu's economic theories are not separable from his "Conceptualization of Commerce," which is ably dissected into its core elements. See Larrère, "Montesquieu on Economics," 337.
24. Larrère, MPE. 6.
25. In a unique and perhaps controversial move, Spector then provides her own positive vision of Montesquieu's political philosophy. "Honor" and not economic interest, provides the best substitute for political virtue. Honor provides "a distinct path for modernity, one that is less demanding than ancient virtue but irreducible to the interest of commercial societies."
26. XI.6; XII.2.
27. Peter Groenewegen. 2002. *Eighteenth Century Economics.* New York: Routledge.
28. Ibid., 62–63. This argument might be compared profitably to Isaiah Berlin's 1955 essay entitled "Montesquieu," where a similar argument is suggested. According to Berlin, the "liberal aspects of [Montesquieu's] teaching" had "degenerated into commonplaces of liberal eloquence" by the middle of 1800s.
29. This view economic claims simply were subsumed in the deluge of writings on political economy at the end of the eighteenth century. The policy issues Montesquieu raised in the *Spirit of Laws* were either solved or deemed not to be puzzles. "Many of the trade problems of the pre-1750 literature faded away," says Groenewegen. Notable examples includee "concern over the adequacy of the money supply and the balance of trade." Both were shown to be "non-problems at least in the long run." Groenewegen, *Eighteenth Century Economics,* 63.
30. Schumpeter mixes his criticism of Montesquieu *as* economist with great praise for the political parts of the work, referring to the book as a whole as "the profound work of Montesquieu." J. A. Schumpeter. 1954. *History of Economic Analysis.* New York: Oxford University Press.
31. According to Althusser, it was precisely because Montesquieu had "little knowledge of political economy" that he could not "comprehend the totality of society." *Politics and History,* 57.
32. Schumpeter, *History of Economic Analysis.*
33. Voltaire, ed. Sheila Mason. 2009. *Commentaire sur L'Esprit des lois.* Oxford: Voltaire Foundation.
34. Following Shovlin, "I use the term "political economist" to refer to individuals who published books and pamphlets dealing with any aspect of economic life. "Citizens of the French Re- public of Letters used the epithet in no more specific a sense than this." See John Shovlin. 2000. "Toward a Reinterpretation of Revolutionary Antinobilism: The Political Economy of Honor in the Old Regime." *The Journal of Modern History* 72 (1): 39–42 (noted as TRRA).

35. See Phillippe Fontaine. 1996. "The French Economists and Politics, 1750–1850: The Science and Art of Political Economy." *The Canadian Journal of Economics* 29 (2): 379–393,for a helpful overview.
36. Peter Groenewegen. 2008. "Political Economy." In *The New Palgrave Dictionary of Economics, Second Edition*. <http://www.dictionaryofeconomics.com/article?id=pde2008_P000114>, 1859.
37. Ibid.
38. See James Bonar. 1966. *Philosophy and Political Economy in Some of Their Historical Relations*. New York: A. M. Kelley, 6.
39. Quoted in Gilbert Faccarello. 1998. *Studies in the History of French Political Economy: From Bodin to Walras*. London: Routledge, 19.
40. Approximately 60 percent of all references to Enlightenment thinkers during the late eighteenth century can be traced to Montesquieu, with the frequency of these citations increasing during the 1780s when the US Constitution was formulated. See John R. Vile. 2005. *The Constitutional Convention of 1787: A Comprehensive Encyclopedia of America's Founding*. Santa Barbara: ABC-CLIO, 495; see also Donald S. Lutz. 1984. "The Relative Influence of European Writers on Late Eighteenth-Century American Political Thought." *The American Political Science Review* 78 (1): 92.
41. For a discussion of the framers' interpretation of Montesquieu in context, see William Allen. 2000. *The Federalist Papers: A Commentary*. New York: Lang, 227–228.
42. For more on Jefferson's reception of Montesquieu, see Carrithers, "Introduction: An Appreciation of the *Spirit of Laws*," 4–5. Also see James F. Jones. 1978. "Montesquieu and Jefferson Revisited: Aspects of a Legacy." *The French Review* 51 (4): 577–585.
43. See William B. Allen. 1975. "Review of *Montesquieu's Philosophy of Liberalism: A Commentary on the Spirit of the Laws* by Thomas Pangle." *Journal of the History of Philosophy* 13 (2): 256–259. Hamilton, of course, was not referring only or merely to Montesquieu's economic writings. The issue in question is the necessity of a "contracted territory for a republican government." Yet it serves as a good example of the problem of reading Montesquieu, and therefore the necessity of being "apprised" of Montesquieu's other sentiments in other parts of the work (*Federalist* 9).
44. Jefferson himself was highly critical of Montesquieu, and therefore unclear exactly what aspects of Montesquieu's economic writings he thought valuable. Jefferson writes, in a letter to Thomas Randolph: "In political economy, I think Smith's *Wealth of Nations* the best book extant; in the science of government, Montesquieu's *Spirit of the Laws* is generally recommended. It contains, indeed, a great number of political truths; but also an equal number of heresies; so that the reader must be constantly on his guard." See "Thomas Jefferson to Thomas Mann Randolph, Jr., 30 May 1790."
45. Antoine Louis Claude, Comte Destutt de Tracy. "http://oll.libertyfund.org/people/antoine-louis-claude-comte-destutt-de-tracy.

46. Jefferson, "Translation of Destutt de Tracy's Commentary on book 2."
47. Jefferson, "Thomas Jefferson to Destutt de Tracy, 26 January 1811."
48. Humorously, Pierre Samuel Du Pont de Nemours, a famous French economist, and a protégé of Dr. François Quesnay, whose *Physiocratie, Ou Constitution Naturelle du Gouvernement le Plus Avantageux au Genre Humain* influenced Adam Smith, did not know that it had been written by a Frenchman. Assuming it to be Jefferson's own correction of Montesquieu, he set about translating it back into French. Jefferson denied authorship, and then sent a copy of it to the late President of William and Mary college, who adopted it as the "elementary book of that institution. "Thomas Jefferson to Destutt de Tracy, 28 November 1813." For an overview of Jefferson's relation to Tracy and this work, see the Liberty Fund edition, ed. Jennings 2011. Jefferson did not like everything that he found in the "other parts" of *The Spirit of the Laws*. He wrote, for example, in a letter to Thomas Rudolph that Montesquieu's thought "contains, indeed, a great number of political truths; but also an equal number of heresies; so that the reader must be constantly on his guard." Jefferson nevertheless expressed his enthusiasm for the work, as a whole, writing to his publisher as follows: "The merit of this work, will, I hope, place it in the hands of every reader in our country."
49. Judith N. Shklar. 1990. "Montesquieu and the New Republicanism." In *Machiavelli and Republicanism,* ed. Gisela Bock et al., 265–280. Cambridge: Cambridge University Press.
50. Johnson Kent Wright. 2006. "A Rhetoric of Aristocratic Reaction? Nobility in *De l'esprit de lois."* In *The French Nobility at the End of the Old Regime*, ed. Jay Smith, 227–251. Pennsylvania State University Press.
51. See Shklar, "Montesquieu and the New Republicanism" for how these differed among the Discourses, *The Social Contract,* and *Emile*.
52. Wright, "A Rhetoric."
53. 1906 Volume I, 103 fn. 2; 149 fn. 1; 828 fn. 1.
54. These studies are valuable to anyone interested in the specifics of economic history, but they do not, in my view, capture the full political and cultural importance of Montesquieu's economic thought. Devletoglou, in "Montesquiu and the Wealth of Nations," has made an interesting investigation into the applicability of this remark, by Keynes. Grospelier has also made an effort to justify the accolade bestowed on Montesquieu by Kenyes. But see Larrère's MPE, where she is more skeptical, arguing that Keynes' remark is a result not of Keynes' reading Montesquieu closely, but rather, "Keynes reading Keynes."
55. I am grateful to Grospelier for making this connection.
56. Montesquieu is incorrectly understood as a proto-physiocrat, an *économiste*, a forerunner of the "sect" of Quesnay.
57. XX.5–7.
58. XX.8–23.

59. David Hume, in a letter to Montesquieu, confirms this reading. See *The Letters of David Hume*, 134–135.
60. Montesquieu's battle plan against religious extremism contains—as part of the overall strategy—within it a moderating lesson. This chapter will look at select passages from books 24 and 25 to show why Montesquieu's aim is not, in fact, to destroy religion, but to tame its excesses. Here this study departs from previous "liberal" readings. See esp. Robert C. Bartlett 2001. "On the Politics of Faith and Reason: The Project of Enlightenment in Pierre Bayle and Montesquieu." *The Journal of Politics* 63 (1): 1–28 (henceforth designated OPFR) and Pangle, TTB.
61. See OC-II, 1358. I borrow this from Albert Hirschman, PAI, 77.

1 Montesquieu *économiste*

1. See, for a useful starting point of biographical sources, François Cadilhon. "Biography of Montesquieu." <http://dictionnaire-montesquieu.ens-lyon.fr/en/article/1376476261/en>; see also Pierre Ferdinand Barrière. 1951. *L'Académie de Bordeaux. Centre de culture internationale au XVIIIe siècle (1712–1792)*. Bordeaux: PUF; Robert Shackleton. 1961. *Montesquieu: A Critical Biography*. London: Oxford University Press; Louis Desgraves. 1985. *Montesquieu*. Paris: Mazarine; François Cadilhon. 1996. *Montesquieu ou l'ingrate réalité du quotidien bordelaise*. Mont-de-Marsan: Éditions inter-universitaires.; Ehrard, Jean. 1998. *L'Esprit des mots: Montesquieu en lui-même et parmi les siens*, Genève: Droz.
2. See *Pensées* #1946.
3. Minuti, Rolando. "Spicilège." http://dictionnaire-montesquieu.ens-lyon.fr/en/article/1377668580/en.
4. Shackleton, *Montesquieu*, 14.
5. Mauldon, Margaret and Andrew Khan, eds. 2008. *Persian Letters*, Introduction. Oxford: Oxford University Press.
6. Shackleton, *Montesquieu*, 15.
7. David W. Carrithers and Patrick Coleman, eds. 2002. *Montesquieu and the Spirit of Modernity*. Oxford: Voltaire Foundation. 161.
8. For more see Michael Sonenscher. 2007. *Before the Deluge: Public Debt, Inequality, and the Intellectual Origins of the French Revolution*. Princeton: Princeton University Press.
9. XIX.27.
10. XX.10; see also XXII.17–18.
11. See *PL* #252.
12. XIII.17.
13. Jean Ehrard has compared Montesquieu's plan to the other proposals; quoted in Carrithers, David W. 2002. "Montesquieu and the Spirit of French Finance: An Analysis of His *Mémoire sur les dettes de l'état* (1715)." In Carrithers and Coleman, *Montesquieu and the Spirit of Modernity*, 161.

14. See Carrithers, David and Patrick Coleman, eds. 2002. *Montesquieu and Modernity,* Oxford: Voltaire Foundation, 177. For some commentators, the plan was too cautious, in that it left the privileges of the intermediary bodies unmolested.
15. See Joel Felix. 2001. "The Economy." In *Old Regime France: 1648–1788,* eds. William Doyle. Oxford: Oxford University Press.
16. On this basis, scholars have suggested that Montesquieu's *Mémoire sur les dettes de l' état* is both economically unsound, and politically "conservative." See Carrithers, "Montesquieu and the Spirit of French Finance," 182. See also Shackleton, *Montesquieu;* this document is the first "exclusively political" writing to be published in this era of Montesquieu's life.
17. Scholars have interpreted Montesquieu's moderation in this early essay as a reactionary or conservative economic position that "all out war" on public debt. This is argued by Carrithers, "Montesquieu and the Spirit of French Finance," 187.
18. Colin Jones. 2002. *The Great Nation: France from Louis XV to Napoleon 1715–99.* New York: Columbia University Press.
19. William J. Bernstein. 2004. *The Birth of Plenty: How the Prosperity of the Modern World Was Created.* New York: McGraw-Hill.
20. Doyle, *Old Regime France,* 25.
21. Ibid., 26.
22. If Montesquieu's only aim was to effect a revolution in French finance, he obviously fell short. But this is a moot point, since it is unlikely that suggestions made their way to the Regent's desk. Yet one may still consider the effect it had on the trajectory of Montesquieu's political economy; and there is no good reason to discount the possibility that Montesquieu's letter *could* have been taken seriously, at the highest levels. The most interesting suggested reform—levies on financiers—was in line, in spirit at least, with the attempts by Orléans in the years following to streamline the state's financial machinery and to cut down on corruption. In fact, Orléans went farther than the young Montesquieu—who detested financiers until his dying days—would have been willing to go. Auditing procedures were put in place to cut down on waste (while increasing tax yields). In 1716, Orléans directed duc de Noailles to resurrect the *Chambre de justice,* the purpose of which was to punish fiscal wrongdoing and to attempt to create an atmosphere of trust. These reforms, in retrospect, have been judged ineffectual. They let the big fish swim away, and the punishments seem only to have made things worse—causing financiers to hoard and spend instead of investing. For more, see Carrithers "Montesquieu and the Spirit of French Finance."
23. Felix, "The Economy," referring to Quesnay and the physiocratic school.
24. *PL* #57.
25. *PL* #22.

26. *PL* #113.
27. *PL* #118.
28. *PL* #113.
29. *PL* #118; 111.
30. *PL* #57.
31. Felix, "The Economy," notes that there was an absence of large-scale war between 1715 and 1740.
32. Ignoring the introduction of special military taxes, the capitation, and the huge increase in the average tax burden; Felix, "The Economy," 14.
33. *PL* #22.
34. *PL* #18.
35. *PL* #11; 113.
36. *PL* #113.
37. *PL* #130.
38. Usbek responds to these concerns in *PL* #103.
39. *PL* #132.
40. Ibid.
41. Felix, "The Economy," 30.
42. Ibid.
43. Felix notes that at one point, tax collectors and more than one hundred thousand agents of the "general farm" were employed to provide information on the economy; this included the growth of a central bureau of trade that would collect information from merchants, chambers of commerce, and major ports. See Felix, "The Economy," 31.
44. For his gambling see Jones, *The Great Nation*, 62. For Laws' admission of despotic power, see 2004. "Montesquieu's Paradoxical Economics." Paper presented at Gimon Conference on French Political Economy. <http://www-sul.stanford.edu/depts/hasrg/frnit/gimon_ papers.html>, 14.
45. Jones, *The Great Nation*, 62.
46. Larrère, MPE, 14.
47. See Jones, *The Great Nation*, 63.
48. II.4.
49. See Larrère, MPE, for the original source.
50. XX.10.
51. As Larrère points out, this was noticed before Montesquieu by Samuel Bernard, in 1709; see MPE, 14.
52. *PL* #136.
53. Mauldon and Khan, *Persian Letters*, xii.
54. It is worth noting that Montesquieu's skewering of Law in *The Spirit of Laws* was hardly controversial. In 1721, by the time the *Persian Letters* was in print, the Scotsman had already been chased out of Paris, traveling with need of an armed guard to protect him from rioters and lynch mobs. See Jones, *The Great Nation*. In 1720, Jones notes, cartoonists had already inflicted a satisfying measure of public revenge. One memorable image pictured Law as a balloon, leaking air uncontrollably from various

orifices. Another painted him as a lunatic, who had led the nation to subscribe to an "economics of the madhouse."
55. See Antoin E Murphy. 1997. *John Law: Economic Theorist and Policy-Maker.* Oxford: Clarendon Press, 5. Some historians think Hume missed the mark here (see Jones, *The Great Nation,* 71). But Jones is slightly off in suggesting that Montesquieu "bemoaned" the social mobility, as a result of the system.
56. See *PL #126.*
57. The most brilliant analysis, and by far the most intricate, is Sonenscher's *Before the Deluge.*
58. See Phillippe Fontaine. 1996. "The French Economists and Politics, 1750–1850: The Science and Art of Political Economy." *The Canadian Journal of Economics* 29 (2): 383.
59. Larrère, MPE, 2.
60. The most obvious connection has to do with their preference for freedom over regulation in foreign trade. See, Céline Spector, "Commerce," in Montesquieu Dictionary, http://dictionnaire-montesquieu.ens-lyon.fr/en/article/1378153189/en. A more important connection is noted by Larrère. Melon dedicates a chapter to Montesquieu, signaling his debt to Montesquieu for the distinction between "the spirit of conquest" and the "spirit of commerce." Larrère, MPE, 8.
61. See Anne M. Cohler, Basia C. Miller, and Harold S. Stone. Eds.1989. *The Spirit of the Laws.* Cambridge: Cambridge University Press, xv; and Jones, *The Great Nation,* 113, for the intendants as police.
62. Cohler, SOL, xv.
63. Quoted in Cohler, SOL, xvi.
64. Sonenscher, *Before the Deluge.*
65. See Sonenscher, referring to Melvin Richter. 1977. *The Political Theory of Montesquieu,* Cambridge: University Press, 41–45; and Paul Rahe. 2005. "The Book That Never Was: Montesquieu's Considerations on the Romans in Historical Context." *History of Political Thought* 26: 43–89.
66. Sonenscher believes that Montesquieu took a "second change of course," a move "against Voltaire," in the years after the publication of the *Considerations.* It was not, he correctly notes, a reversion to Fénelon's concept of monarchy in *The Adventures of Telemachus, Son of Ulysses.*
67. By 1726, Montesquieu's fortune was estimated at 550,000 *livres.* By the year after his death in 1756, the whole of his estate could be estimated at 654,000 *livres.* Perhaps, then, Montesquieu was a miser—but such an accusation cuts both ways in the context of monarchy. Was not Montesquieu simply being consistent with his criticism of the Parisian pursuit of luxury? Indeed, he avoided the "ostentatious mores" of the 1720s, which he had satirized in the *Persian Letters.* See Cadilhon, "Biography of Montesquieu."
68. After all, the sale freed him financially to travel to England, and it was in England, apparently, that Montesquieu strengthened his interest in

political philosophy, although he had claimed to have discovered his principles in 1728, *before* his voyage.
69. Cohler, SOL, xix.
70. Montesquieu was taken by the possibility of converting iron into copper, and made notes on a steam pump, which he would later present at the Academy of Bordeaux.
71. V.8.
72. Ibid.
73. Ibid.
74. See *Pensées* #2141.
75. XX.1.
76. See Shackleton, *Montesquieu*, 124. This was Montesquieu's version of the traveling motto, "When in Rome," after describing a prank, in which Montesquieu is the main victim.
77. Ibid., 78.
78. *PL* #130.
79. Shackleton, *Montesquieu*, 118.
80. He stayed here from November 1729 to early 1731. He kept a journal, of which all that survives is the *Notes on England*. See Iain Stewart, 2002. "Montesquieu in England: His Notes on England, with Commentary and Translation." *Oxford University Comparative Law Forum* (6).
81. See Cecil Courtney, 2001. "Montesquieu and Natural Law." In Carrithers et al., *Montesquieu's Science of Politics*.
82. That Montesquieu pulled his *Reflections on Universal Monarchy in Europe*, the planned "sequel" to *Considerations on the Causes of the Greatness of the Romans and Their Decline*, is also well examined.
83. Stewart, "Montesquieu in England": Even there, in England, where satire was more or less sanctioned, and where the King's solution to criticism was to levy a tax on insults in the papers (so he gets paid every time he is insulted).
84. Montesquieu's revision of Hobbes is well-known. Yet Montesquieu appears to have come to appreciate an important pillar in Hobbes philosophy. Hobbes had argued that "every man who has power tends to abuse that power; he will go up to the point where he meets with barriers." Considering Montesquieu's apparent rejection of Hobbes, it is all the more interesting to observe that Montesquieu carried, in his notebook, a scribbling that he had copied an English phrase he had read, from 1730, during his stay in England; it was a passage from *The Craftsman*, Bolinbroke's journal. Here it was: "The Love of power is natural; it is insatiable; almost constantly whetted, and nevery cloyed by possession" (OC-II, 1358). See also Simone Goyard-Fabre. 1980. *Montesquieu: Adversaire de Hobbes*. Paris: Minard. It is clear that his interest in Hobbes did not leave him; he came to own an edition of the Latin works of Hobbes, including the French translations of *De cive*. From 1725 to 1750 Montesquieu constantly referred to the "terrible system."

85. John Locke and Peter Laslett. 1988. *Locke: Two Treatises of Government*. Cambridge: Cambridge University Press, 12–13.
86. Cohler, SOL, xix. "Montesquieu's interest in England seem primarily to be political." Although this is true in comparison to his travels in Italy, where he remarked a lot on art and architecture, there are some critical passages from his voyage to England that deserve scrutiny.
87. The question of the accuracy of Montesquieu's description, or non-description, of the cabinet, political parties, and the monarch's veto, is interesting but not relevant here.

2 Commerce in *The Spirit of the Laws*

1. Readers will notice that the explanation for gentleness in mores is directly related, in Montesquieu's view, to the transmission of knowledge. So to be accurate, there are three major arguments contained in these opening paragraphs, not two: commerce is the vehicle of knowledge, it softens mores, and leads to peace.
2. XXI.1.
3. Albert O. Hirschman. 1977. *The Passions and the Interests: Political Arguments for Capitalism before Its Triumph*. Princeton: Princeton University Press, 60.
4. Ibid., 61.
5. Erik Gartzke. 2007. "The Capitalist Peace." *American Journal of Political Science* 51 (1): 170. Michael Doyle. 2004. "Liberal Internationalism: Peace, War and Democracy." *Nobelprize.org*. <http://www.nobelprize.org/nobel_prizes/themes/peace/doyle/index.html> points out that Montesquieu was one of the most important early proponents of the second doctrine. Montesquieu, Gartzke concludes, was the real source of Cobden's conclusion that trade was a "grand panacea." And he was the inspiration for Mill's conclusion, in 1902, that commerce was in fact in the process of "rendering war obsolete." Doyle gives Montesquieu credit for this argument, but he also denies to Montesquieu any level of sophistication or insight. He argues that Montesquieu focused too narrowly on a "single feature" of economic liberalism, that is, "trade." Doyle also criticizes Montesquieu for failing to critically examine the arguments he was advancing in favor of a "liberal peace."
6. A good example, although by no means representative, is Roger Boesche Boesche, Roger. 1990. "Fearing Monarchs and Merchants: Montesquieu's Two Theories of Despotism." *The Western Political Quarterly* 43 (4): 741. For opposing examples, at the other extreme, compare Stephen J. Rosow. 1984. "Commerce, Power and Justice: Montesquieu on International Politics." *Review of Politics* 46 (3): 346–366. and Peter T. Manicas. 1981. "Montesquieu and the Eighteenth-Century Vision of the State." *History of Political Thought* 2 (2): 313–347.
7. See Paul Carrese. 2006. "The Machiavellian Spirit of Montesquieu's Liberal Republic." In *Machiavelli's Liberal Republican Legacy*, ed. Paul A.

Rahe, 121–142. Cambridge: Cambridge University Press for an example of Montesquieu's sophistication as a writer and thinker.
8. For example, *PL* #88; 98; V.17–18; XIX.27; *Pensées* #1041.
9. As Pierre Manent has noted, see *The City of Man*. Princeton: Princeton University Press, 36.
10. Rosow, "Commerce, Power and Justice," 356, compares Montesquieu's view on capitalist interdependence, in passing to More's *Utopia*.
11. Thomas Pangle, arguably one of the greatest proponents of Montesquieu's philosophy of liberalism, is sharply critical of Montesquieu on these grounds. Montesquieu's claim that commerce would lead to peace represents a "failure" to see ahead to the "full effects of weapons technology and commercial imperialism." See *Montesquieu's Philosophy of Liberalism: A Commentary on the Spirit of the Laws*. Chicago: University of Chicago Press, 211. Others are more blunt; Montesquieu was just plain wrong, in hindsight. Two world wars, economic upheaval, and the rise of a bipolar world eventually dissolved the optimism for a "capitalist peace." As Gartzke explains, scholars turned away from the "liberal peace" hypothesis during the Cold War and began to focus their attention on more realistic problems and strategies, such as balancing and deterrence. See "The Capitalist Peace," 170.
12. Carrithers has noted the lack of scholarship on Montesquieu's economic thought as a whole; see David W. Carrithers. 2001. "Democratic and Aristocratic Republics." In *Montesquieu's Science of Politics: Essays on the Spirit of Laws*, eds. David W. Carrithers, Michael A. Mosher, and Paul A. Rahe. Lanham: Rowman & Littlefield, 370. Since 1950, only a handful of studies have been devoted to it, including Nicos E. Devletoglou. 1963. "Montesquieu and the Wealth of Nations." *Canadian Journal of Economics and Political Science* 29 (1); Nicos E. Devletoglou. 1969. "The Economic Philosophy of Montesquieu." *Kyklos: Internationale Zeitschrift* 22 (3): 530–541; and André Garrigou-Lagrange. 1956. "Montesquieu et les Economists." In *Actes du congrès Montesquieu: réuni à Bordeaux du 23 au 26 mai 1955 pour commémorer le deuxième centenaire de la mort de Montesquieu*, 279–284. Bordeaux: Delmas.; and Alain Cotta. 1957. "Le développement economique dans la pensée de Montesquieu." *Revue d'histoire économique et social* 35 (4).
13. Hirschman notes that book 20 has been neglected, but gives it only a passing reference. See PAI, 71–73.
14. Some notable exceptions include Devletoglou, "Montesquieu and the Wealth of Nations"; Mark Hulliung. 1976. *Montesquieu and the Old Regime*. Berkeley: University of California Press; Catherine Larrère. 2001. "Montesquieu on Economics and Commerce." In Carrithers et al., *Montesquieu's Science of Politics*; Spector, Céline. 2004. *Montesquieu: Pouvoirs, richesses et sociétés*. Paris: PUF; Rahe, MLL; and Paul Cheney. 2010. *Revolutionary Commerce: Globalization and the French Monarchy*. CambridgeMA: Harvard University Press.

15. Devletoglou, "Montesquieu and the Wealth of Nations," 15. Two broad conclusions are made: either that Montesquieu had a coherent economic theory that was influential in the development of classical liberalism, or that his economic theory is merely a series of ad hoc economic policies that reflect unoriginal and common sense opinions of his own time.
16. VIII.17. Montesquieu uses this image twice elsewhere; once to describe a central difficulty with republics when they are at rest ("a republic must dread something... the more secure these states are, the more, as with tranquil waters, they are subject to corruption"); and a second time, in book 8 where he notes, suggestively, that all rivers "run together" into despotism.
17. Often missed in cursory accounts of Montesquieu's views on commerce are the tradeoffs. The price for curing destructive prejudices, Montesquieu notes, is the ruin of ancient moral and political virtue; above all, the Platonic emphasis on courage (XX.1). One of the penalties for progress in international trade and mutual economic interdependence is a corrosion of "hospitality" (which he equates suggestively with Aristotelian magnanimity, XX.2). But the most telling caveat is Montesquieu's remark about Holland, which is an example of a country that is "affected only by the spirit of commerce" (XX.2, emphasis added). Here, there is a "traffic in all human activities and all moral virtues; the smallest things, those required by humanity, are done or given for money" (XX.2). Jefferson knew Montesquieu and may be echoing this passage when he writes, "Money, not morality, is the principle commerce of civilized nations."
18. XIX.6.
19. See, for example, XX.21, where Montesquieu notes the decline of hospitality in civilized nations.
20. See XIX.4; "What the general spirit is."
21. XIX.4.
22. Ibid. Montesquieu uses the word "mores" eight times in this short paragraph.
23. Céline Spector, "Commerce," in Montesquieu Dictionary, http://dictionnaire-montesquieu.ens-lyon.fr/en/article/1378153189/en.
24. XIX.4. Sparta, for example, is described as *the* example of a nation wholly dominated by mores. Rome is another example, but its mores are diluted, so to speak, by the "maxims of government."
25. XIX.27.
26. XIX.27.
27. In this case, the climate has hardened the people (not a bad thing in itself). But the laws, Montesquieu argues, have also created a politically and socially servile population, focused only on survival and perpetuation. This combination of intense materialism with political servitude, Montesquieu suggests, will negate any of the beneficial effects that commerce might have, since every motive is directed at material gain and

survival, but no structural or political incentives are in place to pursue this material end through honest or decent means. As Montesquieu explains, the seller has no incentive to carry on an honest business, since there is no guarantee that he might keep what he earns. A consumer, on the other hand, is advised to carry his own scale because each merchant has three of his own: "a heavy one for buying, a light one for selling, and an accurate one for those who are on their guard."

28. XIX.20.
29. See Hulliung, *Montesquieu and the Old Regime*, 207, for a discussion of Montesquieu's skepticism.
30. The same qualification may be applied to the second claim, in Chapter 2, that commerce leads to peace. Hamilton, for example, famously rejects Montesquieu's claim as an empirical fraud: Has commerce hitherto done anything more than change the objects of war? Is not the love of wealth as domineering and enterprising a passion as that of power or glory? Have there not been as many wars founded upon commercial motives since that has become the prevailing system of nations, as were before occasioned by the cupidity of territory or domination? Has not the spirit of commerce, in many instances, administered new incentives to the appetite, both for the one and for the other? (*Federalist* No. 6). With space, we could show that Montesquieu was by no means ignorant of Hamilton's well-founded suspicions. Early on in book 1, he hints, for example, that the state of war is a result of the increasing number of motives for human beings to attack each other (I.2). We find out that commerce is in fact one of these motives, especially for conquest (XXI.8). And Montesquieu's concrete analysis of various trading states suggests there is nothing inviolable about this so-called law. There were, he notes, "great wars between Carthage and Marseilles concerning the fishery" (XXI.11). England and Holland, his two favorite trading states, went to war over the navigation acts (XX.8).
31. XX.4.
32. For helpful overviews of this distinction, with general and overlapping interpretations, see Rosow, "Commerce, Power and Justice"; Larrère, "Montesquieu on Economics and Commerce," Henry C. Clark. 2006. *Compass of Society: Commerce and Absolutism in Old-Regime France.* Lanham: Lexington, 117; Randal R. Hendrickson, 2007. "Montesquieu and the Transformation of Republicanism." PhD diss., Boston College 240; Rahe, MLL, 188–90; 228; Thomas L. Pangle. 2010. *The Theological Basis of Liberal Modernity in Montesquieu's "Spirit of the Laws."* Chicago: University of Chicago Press, 100. It is possible, although speculative on my part, that Montesquieu found this distinction originally in Cicero. Coyer refers directly to the phrase, which he finds in Cicero, "the commerce of economy." See Henry C. Clark. 2003. *Commerce, Culture, and Liberty: Readings on Capitalism before Adam Smith.* Indianapolis: Liberty Fund, 420. We know that Montesquieu had read Cicero closely, and

indeed, he refers to Cicero in the chapter in which this distinction is introduced (see XX.4).
33. In Pangle's summation, the commerce of luxury is roused by and reinforces "the desires aroused by vanity." See TTB, 100.
34. Larrère, "Montesquieu on Economics and Commerce," 347.
35. See, for example, Chapter 6, "Some effects of a great navigation."
36. Jean-Baptiste Say would later give a name to this type, in 1800. He calls him, for the first time, an "entrepreneur."
37. XX.4. Montesquieu notes a second reason why this type of person may exist only in republics. Traders who become "great" necessarily get mixed up with the "public business," but public business is "suspect" to the merchants in monarchies. This leads Montesquieu to conclude: "Therefore, great commercial enterprises are not for monarchies, but for the government of the many."
38. See VIII.16, "Qualities distinctive of a republic."
39. We will see that this distinction breaks down in the case of England.
40. Pangle, MPOL, 214 (see Hendrickson, "Montesquieu and the Transformation of Republicanism," 236, for an important qualification). In this chapter, I borrow extensively from Thomas Pangle and has written extensively on this question, and looks to book 1, in particular, as proof.
41. Pangle, MPOL, 205.
42. If Montesquieu seems cagey, or if he does not come out unequivocally in favor of commercial society, this is because Montesquieu knew that the subject matter—the commitment to commerce—was "at odds with traditional morality." Montesquieu's deeper position, from Pangle's reading, is unequivocal: "the commercial regime is the only one which allows man's natural humanity to fully assert itself."
43. Mannt, *City of Man*, 36–50; 86–99.
44. Ibid., 39; 45.
45. Ibid., 37.
46. Ibid., 40.
47. Ibid., 39.
48. I cannot agree with his conclusion, for reasons which will be made clear below.
49. Thomas Pangle recently notes his own divergence from Pierre Manent in TTB, 176. Montesquieu, according to Manent, embodies "*a forfeiture*" of reason and of nature as norm. See *City of Man*, 26; 39; 50–53; 68; 94; 107; 113; 115.
50. As Hendrickson has observed, this passage has a unique rhythm—a poetic style—that is mirrored almost precisely in book 21, Chapter 7, where Montesquieu speaks of Athens and its "projects for glory." See "Montesquieu and the Transformation of Republicanism," 227.
51. Ibid.
52. VII.15.

53. VII.15, fn. 37.
54. VIII.4.
55. Some commentators have noted that Marseilles is either a prototype for modern England (Carrithers et al., *Montesquieu's Science of Politics,* 348–349), or an awkward combination of republican virtue mixed with selfish commerce (Pangle, MPOL, 105–106). In either case, we can conclude that Marseilles is a problematic exemplar of a people who engage in economic commerce.
56. XX1.11; XX1.13. This is not to say that Marseilles is powerless. Caesar had noted its effect on the Gauls, whose warrior mores were "spoiled" by its proximity to this trading state (XX.1, fn. 2).
57. For a wonderful discussion of Montesquieu's understanding of liberty, especially, the less well-known version of "philosophic liberty," see Sharon R. Krause 2005. "Two Concepts of Liberty in Montesquieu." *Perspectives on Political Science* 34 (2): 88–96.
58. This exposes them to the same criticism leveled against the Dutch in book 20. Indeed, the lifestyle which is sketched of the people of Marseilles is directly related to the "vice" which Montesquieu will later pinpoint as the central flaw in the Dutch character (XX.1).
59. One may then ask: are the "pure" forms of the commercial republic are meant to be the *peak*, a "best regime" even, why must there be so few examples? This would imply, for one, that the whole world as Montesquieu knew it—including moderate monarchies—was corrupt and entirely beyond redemption. Second, what might be the significance of dropping Carthage and Florence from the original six? Why should these two commercial civilizations not be grouped with the hard core of the economic republics? The first question can be answered directly as follows: the pure commercial republic is a very rare phenomenon, and therefore so must be the "pure" commercial virtues mentioned in book 5. The second answer is perhaps less obvious. Might it be the case that by leaving Carthage and Florence out of Chapter 5, Montesquieu is quite consciously rejecting the premise of those critics who might argue that *all* commercial societies are founded on strict necessity, barrenness, and violence? Indeed, the original six tells a more flexible and inclusive story. Carthage and Florence are not grouped with Marseilles most likely because commerce, as a way of life, in these two major historical cases, seems to have involved a *choice*. More will be said on this point, but observe a second curiosity. In Chapter 5, there are only two commercial republics—out of the four remaining—that seem to have any relevance in the modern era. These are Venice and Holland. Tyre, on the one hand, had become a relic, even by Montesquieu's day (having been conquered by the Mameluks and absorbed into the Ottoman empire in 1291). Marseilles, similarly, had been ruined by a civil war, a point which Montesquieu openly discusses (he does not mention the devastating plague, the frequent sieges by the Holy Roman empire, the chaotic rebellions, and its ultimate incorporation into Provence).

60. Montesquieu is especially critical of Venice as a "model" because it is an immoderate aristocracy. See Rahe, MLL, 77. Compare David W. Carrithers. 1991. *Not So Virtuous Republics: Montesquieu, Venice, and the Theory of Aristocratic Republicanism*. Baltimore: Johns Hopkins University Press, 268 who initially gives a more flattering portrait of Venice, but eventually concludes, in agreement with Rahe, that Venice had become a "shorthand for tyranny." See also *PL* #130 where Montesquieu implies that the economy is its "only resource."
61. XI.21; a similar remark is made in XXII.10.
62. For a helpful statement on the differences between Pierre Manent's account here and Thomas Pangle, see Pangle, TTB, 176 fn.1. Pangle notes that the difference between their readings is based on a difference in their estimation of Montesquieu's rational conception of human nature. Pangle questions the "adequacy" of Montesquieu's account, while Manent thinks that Montesquieu's thought embodies a "forfeiture of reason and of nature as a norm, through an abandonment to 'faith' in the 'present epoch.'"
63. This fact may have helped to liberate the independent farmers from manorial obligations which kept them enslaved in fertile, aristocratic societies. As Bernstein has noted elsewhere, it was these ambitious land reclamation projects through the creation of dams, dikes, and drainage ditches which fueled industry, while also moderating Dutch politics.
64. This idea was adumbrated in book 18, and also by Usbek (*PL* #118), where it was argued that barrenness of soil, not fertility, is the most important spur of human industriousness, sobriety of mores, hearty defense, and hard work (compare XVIII.4).
65. XX.1 fn. 3; XI.5.
66. VIII.18.
67. XXVIII.1.
68. *PL* #118.
69. It is hard to say what Montesquieu means by the "spirit of liberty" here. The first reference to the "spirit of liberty" in the *Spirit of Laws* appears in book 6, Chapter 16. Here it is just a mood, an appetite for freedom, so to speak. But in book 11, Chapter 7, Montesquieu makes it clear that the "spirit of liberty" is psychologically quite complicated—it may in fact be an illusion: "The monarchies we know do not have liberty for their direct purpose as does the one we have just mentioned; they aim only for the glory of the citizens, the state, and the prince. But this glory results in a spirit of liberty that can, in these states, produce equally great things and can perhaps contribute as much to happiness as liberty itself" (XI.7). The "spirit of liberty" is also discussed in book 7, Chapter 9. There, it means something like sexual license or sexual freedom: "In monarchies women have so little restraint because, called to court by the distinction of ranks, they there take up the spirit of liberty that is almost the only one tolerated" (VII.9). The phrase appears one last time in book 13,

Chapter 14: "[In England] it is felt that the more moderate the government the more the spirit of liberty reigns" (XIII.14).
70. XX.6; *PL* #117.
71. See, for example, IX.1; IX.3; XI.5; XIII.12.
72. For example, XI.3
73. This is a somewhat misleading title, since the underlying purpose of the chapter is to explain why human beings might engage in economic commerce, a question Chapter 5 did not answer in a satisfactory way (indeed, Chapter 5 only raised the stakes of that question).
74. XX.6.
75. There is another reason lurking behind the wine example, which Montesquieu does not explore in any depth, although it could have been on his mind. In short, the whole idea of the international division of labor (see Lewinski, who criticizes Montesquieu on this point; Jan Lewinski. 1922. *The Founders of Political Economy*. London: Kind, 15).
76. This ambiguous pronoun can create considerable confusion: "they" refers to the *captains*, not the "investors" of the rigging, gear, and provisions, and so on.
77. Again, I refer to Boesche, "Fearing Monarchs," for an interesting attempt to defend this interpretation.
78. See XIII.2: "the effect of a wealth of a country is to fill all hearts with ambition"; cf. IV.6: "[Lycurgus] seemed to remove all its resources, arts, commerce, silver, walls: one had ambition there without the expectation of bettering oneself."
79. V.3.
80. XX.6. In any case, as Usbek notes in the *Persian Letters*, even gambling, which "disturbs our reason," is somehow ineradicable. It was impossible, he notes, for the holy Prophet to take away the "cause of our passions," which is why Islam had to resort to tempering those passions, by taking away and forbidding "as a special precsept" the "games of chance" (see *PL* #54).
81. Socrates hints, in the *Symposium*, that *eros* can be satisfied in other ways than by love—by "money-making, love of gymnastics, or philosophy," for example, 205d.
82. In presenting the other face of commerce, in Holland, Montesquieu does not suggest that we forget the origins of commercial civilization in "violence and harassment" (XX.5). And he does not suggest that economic commerce is more conducive to individual happiness than other ways of life (XIX.5). But humanity, for Montesquieu, is much more fully expressed in the energized commercial republic of Holland than it is in the admirable, stern, but desolate Marseilles. A nation of fugitives looking for security has been turned into a society of men eager to work together toward a common interest. In Chapter 6, Montesquieu merely expresses what later became known as the profit motive, in more beautiful terms—that is, as the pleasurable anticipation of turning up a "lucky number" on the whale hunt.

83. Interestingly, Montesquieu refrains from calling England a republic like Holland. And yet it is a remarkable kind of monarchy because it combines a "precarious" succession of monarchs with an "invulnerable throne."
84. Both Roger Caillois. 1949/1951. *Œuvres complètes*. Paris: Gallimard and Iain Stewart. 2002. "Montesquieu in England: His Notes on England, with Commentary and Translation." *Oxford University Comparative Law Forum* (6) who has recently translated the notes on England, repeat the word "liberté" although in the context, for parallel, the passage would make more immediate sense substituting the word "*égalité*" for liberty.
85. The most important criticism of Holland in Montesquieu's writings, however, touches on the scope of individual freedom. In the *Pensées*, Montesquieu locates Holland on a kind of spectrum between slavery and extreme individual liberty. Holland is superior to Venice because senators are politically free; in Venice, they are as well, but "non pas civillement" Montesquieu OC-I, 1432. On the other hand, Holland is inferior to England. In England, there is the greatest degree of individual freedom because the magistrates, in direct contrast to Venice, are "slaves" (esclaves), but the people remain free "comme citoyens." The critical issue here is not whether Holland has a great commercial empire. The standard is civil liberty. Further evidence that Montesquieu thought that this was the crucial dimension is found in book 12 of *The Spirit of Laws* when he discusses the possibility that "the constitution is free but the citizen is not" (XII.1).
86. For an overview of the literature see Cohler, SOL, xxxii.
87. VIII.13.
88. See Boesche, "Fearing Monarchs," 1754; cf. Stewart, "Montesquieu in England."
89. See D. Desserud. 1999. "Commerce and Political Participation in Montesquieu's Letter to Domville." *History of European Ideas* 25 (3): 135–151. for an extensive commentary on this letter.
90. It is important not to rest too much weight on these writings, especially the "Notes on England." Boesche notes that Montesquieu's grandson was a refugee in England during the French revolution and destroyed most them, for "fear that they would offend his English hosts." See "Fearing Monarchs," 754. Note, however, that Boesche's speculation (that the letters would "offend" his English hosts) might go both ways: Montesquieu's grandson may have also destroyed notes that would offend the authorities back home.
91. See, for example, IX.8; XI.13.
92. I.6, emphasis added.
93. See, for example, V.6; VIII.3.
94. Ibid.
95. XII.2–30; XIX.27.
96. *PL* #87.

3 Commerce, Honor, and Monarchy

1. Althusser likewise suggested that Montesquieu had little knowledge of political economy, and so could not comprehend the "totality of society" in *Politics and History*.
2. Groenewegen has made a compelling argument that his theory of trade was essentially made obsolete by the explosion of political economy shortly after his major publication. He concludes that the major reason why Montesquieu's economic writings are neglected today is because many of his arguments in book 20 simply faded away. Many of the issues that he raised here were solved—or deemed not to be puzzles—by around 1760, with the proliferation of scientific, systematic economic theory. In Groenewegen's words: "Many of the trade problems of the pre-1750 literature faded away. Notable examples are concern over the adequacy of the money supply and the balance of trade. Both were shown to be non-problems (at least in the long run)." See Peter Groenewegen. 2002. *Eighteenth Century Economics*, New York: Routledge, 63.
3. Henry C. Clark. 2006. *Compass of Society: Commerce and Absolutism in Old-Regime France*. Lanham: Lexington, 114.
4. For one reading of Montesquieu's role in the debate over the nobility's relationship to commerce, see Annelien de Dijn. 2008. *French Political Thought from Montesquieu to Tocqueville: Liberty in a Levelled Society?* Cambridge: Cambridge University Press. De Dijn rightly observes the political significance of Montesquieu's economic writings, but errs too far in the direction of Althusser's Marxist critique of Montesquieu in his *Politics and History*: specifically, that Montesquieu's aim was simply to "uphold the status quo" and "defend the monarchy from republican attacks."
5. I will not address this in full here. Certainly, there are moments where Montesquieu appears to have mercantilist sentiments. He seems to agree with the universally accepted mercantilist notion that the object of all trade and commerce should benefit the state, primarily, and not the individual, as for example when he writes that "the object of commerce is to export and import commodities in favor of the state" (XX.13). Montesquieu seems to agree with this mercantilist notion, in principle. In matters of specific trade policy, he unambiguously defends the English Navigation Acts, which drastically limited trade between the colonies and England's rivals (in Netherlands and France) (XX.12, fn. 10). Montesquieu displays some illiberal tendencies in domestic legal matters as well. Nowhere does he defend a right of property outright. More troubling still, for economic liberals, is his suggestion in Chapter 15 that economics is the one sphere in which it is perfectly legitimate to allow the state to trump individual liberties. "In agreements that derive from commerce," writes Montesquieu, "the law should make more of public convenience than of the liberty of the citizen" (XX.15).These isolated, conservative, vaguely mercantilist points are not hard to find, but it is easy to show that Montesquieu

did not agree with any of the core assumptions of mercantilist writers. First, Montesquieu clearly favors independent banks and private lending as superior alternatives to treasuries stuffed with gold and silver or public banks (at least, such as the one proposed by John Law, XX.10; XXII.4; XXII.19). Second, Montesquieu forcefully opposes the creation or protection of monopolies; especially the idea that trading companies should be granted exclusive privileges (XX.9). Finally, Montesquieu is profoundly critical of the mercantilist emphasis on building up exports through agriculture. Wealth comes from the industry of individuals, not from the surplus stock created by large populations of low-wage workers, whose job it is to build up exports and increase the influx of gold (XX.11). Any number of examples should be added for this list to be more complete. Government intervention is necessary, but only to prevent the *servitude* of the public to the trading companies and corporations, not to reinforce state power itself (XX.12). The farming of customs is highly inefficient, while over-regulation and arbitrary taxation is positively harmful to business (XX.13; XIII.19–20). Trade should go forward in times of war and the property of foreigners of enemy nations should be respected (XX.14). Debtor laws should be humane, but never so loose or uncertain as to decrease the confidence necessary for lending and borrowing (XX.16; XX.17).
6. de Dijn, *French Political Thought*, 32.
7. See Catherine Larrère. 2004. "Montesquieu's Paradoxical Economics." Paper presented at Gimon Conference on French Political Economy. <http://www-sul.stanford.edu/depts/hasrg/frnit/gimon_ papers.html>, and Catherine Larrère. 2005. "Montesquieu économiste? Une lecture paradoxale." SVEC 05.
8. Far from accepting the view that monarchies are incompatible with commerce, Montesquieu commerce has become so central to the survival of modern monarchies that Montesquieu is led to say that they absolutely cannot do without it (e.g., V.9). In his own time, there were some who argued that the French monarchy was more likely to guarantee the conditions of flourishing commerce than its competitors (see, e.g., Clark, *Compass of Society*, xi).
9. Less well understood are the advantages of monarchical government. Three were three of note. First, monarchies have a security advantage that Montesquieu links directly to the success of business and industry. By contrast to strict republics, where the "dread" of outside forces is necessary to stave off corruption and decadence (and not just the tax collector—the threat must be sufficiently large, say, a Persian invasion), monarchies are equally productive in times of war and in times of peace. To paraphrase Montesquieu, they need not fear a tranquil security environment (VIII.5). Second, monarchies have what we could call, for simplicity, a luxury advantage. In monarchies like France, there is a certain "joy in life." They "do frivolous things seriously and serious

things gaily," and this allows the people to possess "taste" (XIX.5–8), which Montesquieu argues is the very "source" of the nation's wealth (XIX.4). Unlike despotic governments, where materialism is "forced" and "depraved" because it arises out of destitution and oppression; or martial republics, where materialism is utterly rejected; or commercial republics, where the only object is commerce itself (XI.5), monarchies are capable of sustaining what might be called a "dignified consumerism," a tasteful commercialism. For some scholars, this is monarchy's great advantage. This is related to the third—and often neglected—advantage in monarchy. In Montesquieu's view, traditional monarchies often tend to produce better artisans and quality craftsmanship, which stimulates trade, encourages advance in industry, and further elevates the "taste" of the people. Commercial honor is the motive, as Usbek points out in the *Persian Letters*. It is when honor pervades all levels of society in a monarchy—even down to the professions—that craftsmen are more likely to take pride in their work: "even [among] the lowliest artisans there is not one who does not defend the excellence of his chosen craft." See *PL* #42.

10. They let their fingernails grow, "in order to indicate that they do not work."
11. Paul Rahe. 2009. *Montesquieu and the Logic of Liberty*. New Haven: Yale University Press, esp. 288–311.
12. Ibid. 190. While Rahe has demonstrated the extent to which commerce is a threat both to the nature (inequality) of the regime, and the love of honor which serves as monarchy's *principle* (191), this chapter addresses the question as to how exactly these chapters on trade fit into the larger argument.
13. I address the other major categories of the problem with the political economy of monarchy throughout. The other categories include, but are not limited to: difficulties issuing from uncontrolled luxury; domestic instability; a lack of private property and incentives for industry; and the specter of poverty, and massive social inequality. Of course, I must neglect a number of important arguments related to the positive case for liberty and modern republicanism: reform of the penal code, the case for an independent judiciary, the argument for separation of powers, and so on.
14. For a more complex analysis of Montesquieu's position, see Hont, Istvan. 2005. *Jealousy of Trade: International Competition and the Nation State in Historical Perspective*. Cambridge: Belknap Press.
15. XX.19.
16. Larrère, "MPE," and "Montesquieu économiste?"
17. Ibid.
18. Ibid.
19. See, for example, Montesquieu's direct attack on John Law's abuse of the banking establishment (e.g., XXII.10).

20. See Henry C. Clark. 2003. *Commerce, Culture, and Liberty: Readings on Capitalism before Adam Smith*. Indianapolis: Liberty Fund. Barbon, in Clark says this is a "common objection" that a public bank cannot be safe in a monarchy.
21. Samuel Bernard, quoted in Colin Jones. 2002. *The Great Nation: France from Louis XV to Napoleon 1715–99*. New York: Columbia University Press, 85.
22. XX.10.
23. See Jones, *The Great Nation*.
24. XX.14.
25. V.4; also V.10.
26. The contrast between France, hobbled by what I am calling "trade paradoxes," and the English and Dutch republics, becomes more stark. Impaired by the advantages of free trade, lacking cheap capital, deprived of access to the reduced risk made possible by trading companies (XX.4), monarchy increasingly became dependent on revenues from trade in luxury. As Montesquieu argued, the luxury trade depends on commissions, harsh and arbitrary taxes, and duties that hobble commerce. Such measures are necessary not only as a source of revenue for the court outside of the riches gained from plundering (XX.13). Of course, this just begs the question of the extent to which traditional monarchy must rely on plunder and foreign war, to supplement what it lacks through trade. They are "the only bridle on luxury itself."
27. See John Shovlin. 2000. "Toward a Reinterpretation of Revolutionary Antinobilism: The Political Economy of Honor in the Old Regime." *The Journal of Modern History* 72 (1): 35–66.
28. Larrère, Shovlin, and de Dijn adopt similar positions on this. For an excellent summary of the debate engendered by *La noblesse commerçante*, see J. Q. C. Mackrell. 1973. *The Attack on "Feudalism" in Eighteenth-Century France*. London: Routledge, 77–103.
29. Shovlin, TRRA, 37.
30. Gabriel François Coyer. 1756. *La noblesse commerçante*. Paris: Duchesne.
31. Philippe Auguste de Saint-Foix, Chevalier d'Arc. 1756. *La noblesse militaire, ou le patriote français*. Paris.
32. My reading puts Montesquieu closer to Helvetius, in *De l'esprit*. Helvetius thought that the public was a more efficient and reliable "source" of the dispensation of honor than the king's gaze. See Shovlin, TRRA, 41.
33. See de Dijn, *French Political Thought*, 33. For discussion of Chevalier d'Arc and Montesquieu's influence on him, see Ulrich Adam. *The Political Economy of Justi*. Bern: Peter Lang, 104. Adam provides the following summary, which demonstrates more fully what is at stake: "In contrast to Coyer, the Chevalier d'Arc was a follower of Montesquieu, fearing the leveling forces of markets. Like him, he believed that noble trade was likely to promote equality among the citizenry, which would finally destroy the monarchy and 'result either in republican government or

despotism.' D'Arc accepted that trade was necessary to sustain national power, but he refused to accept that the English model could be imitated in France. He rejected Coyer's negative assessment of French commerce as being swamped by both the Dutch and the English. D'Arc worried for France not in commerce, but in war."
34. Shovlin mistakenly argues that "The last great theorist of the view that the king should discern and reward honor was Montesquieu." See Shovlin, TRRA, 40.
35. There is some question as to whether this was falsely attributed to Helvetius. For some, it is an impossible project to try and reconcile the liberal commercial humanist with the reactionary aristocrat. A middle ground is staked out in Cheney, who believes that Montesquieu sought a "fusion" in trying to accommodate new forms of class and wealth. Paul Cheney. 2010. *Revolutionary Commerce: Globalization and the French Monarchy.* CambridgeMA: Harvard University Press, 64.
36. It may be a mistake, as Richter explains, to judge Montesquieu's project without reference to his own situation, which includes his class and economic interests. Melvin Richter. 1990. *Selected Political Writings.* Indianapolis: Hackett Publishing. 6.
37. Mathiez was one of the first to attempt to reinterpret Montesquieu along these lines—that is, as a reactionary landowning magistrate. Ford calls him a "rationalizer of reaction." See Franklin L. Ford. 1953. *Robe and Sword; the Regrouping of the French Aristocracy after Louis XIV.* Cambridge: Harvard University Press, 243; Mathiez, Albert. 1930. "La place de Montesquieu dans l'histoire des doctrines politiques du XVIIIe siècle." *Annales historiques de la Révolution française* 7: 97–112.
38. In Richter, *Selected Political Writings*, 10.
39. Louis Althusser. 2007. *Politics and History.* London : Verso, 106. Annelien de Dijn has an informative discussion in *French Political Thought*, 24–25, although the argument assumes his "aristocratic liberalism" from the start. De Dijn also underestimates Montesquieu's appreciation for the English constitution, and does not consider the possibility of a new constitutional form (i.e., a "republic hidden under the form of a monarchy").
40. Larrère's MPE. I use this article because it focuses much more on this problem than her other essays.
41. XX.9.
42. Melzer has argued that Rousseau thought the ancient régime was "irreversibly corrupt" by his own day. This argument above is being made in a similar vein, although I don't cite this as evidence that Montesquieu had exactly the same purposes as Rousseau. Arthur M. Melzer. 1983. "Rousseau's 'Mission' and the Intention of His Writings." *American Journal of Political Science* 27 (2): 294–320. Tocqueville notes, similar, that "The French nobility had not had contact with public administration for a long time except for one aspect... the political aspect had vanished; the monetary portion alone had remained and sometimes had considerably increased."

43. The most important social function of the nobility was to protect the nation, a service which requires courage, and therefore, insulation from the corrupting and "softening" effects of commerce and ordinary business.
44. A notable exception is Michael Sonenscher. 2007. *Before the Deluge: Public Debt, Inequality, and the Intellectual Origins of the French Revolution*. Princeton: Princeton University Press.
45. Felix "The Economy." See also William Doyle. 1984. "The Price of Offices in Pre-Revolutionary France." *The Historical Journal* 27 (4): 831–860.
46. Sonenscher, *Before the Deluge*.
47. Ibid. Also William Doyle. 1996. *Venality: The Sale of Offices in Eighteenth-Century France*. Oxford: Clarendon Press. They both agree it was "unusual." For Doyle, venality in the ancient regime had evolved from being a mild vice (a means to raise extra revenue by the sale of posts of public responsibility) to a principal cause of unrest, as evidenced by the fact that it was one of the first aspects of the old regime to be eliminated in the French Revolution.
48. Franklin L. Ford. 1953. *Robe and Sword; the Regrouping of the French Aristocracy after Louis XIV.* Cambridge: Harvard University Press, 107.
49. It increased during the 1730s and did not let off until the revolution. See Shovlin, TRRA, 48.
50. Doyle notes that by the eighteenth century there were 70,000 venal offices comprising the entire judiciary, most of the legal profession, officers in the army, and a wide range of other professions—from financiers handling the king's revenues down to auctioneers and even wigmakers. See Doyle, *Venality*.
51. XX.22. "When they do not get wealth, console themselves because they have acquired honor."
52. Shovlin, TRRA, 48.
53. Ibid.
54. See Ford, *Robe and Sword*, 120.
55. It was also an *insult* to noble pride. As Hulliung explains: "the rapid proliferation of the number of persons claiming nobility cheapened the meaning of nobility and insulted the old aristocracies of the Sword and Race by inviting wealthy parvenus to assume aristocratic pretension." Mark Hulliung. 1976. *Montesquieu and the Old Regime*. Berkeley: University of California Press.
56. J. H. Marchand, quoted in Shovlin, TRRA, 49.
57. See Ford, *Robe and Sword*. Montesquieu purchased an office of councilor in the Parliament of Guinne for his son, Jean-Baptiste Secondat, for a sum of 27,000 *livres* for three years. This example of the commercialization of public office is not politically relevant, however; for Ford, the most controversial aspect of venality was the link to hereditary office.
58. Ford, *Robe and Sword*, 106.

59. Ibid., 121.
60. Doyle, *Venality*, 253.
61. Ehrard, Jean. 2009. "Montesquieu and Us." In *Montesquieu and His Legacy*, ed. Rebecca Kingston. Albany: SUNY Press.
62. In a footnote, Montesquieu goes further and adds a warning: in order that France not become like Spain (and be ruined by laziness), it will *require* the selling of offices, or at least, some practice of this kind, which allows men to move up in society without having to rely on the handing out of offices from the king. V.19, fn. 66.
63. XX.22.
64. Kintzler Catherine. "Condorcet." http://dictionnaire-montesquieu.ens-lyon.fr/en/article/1377637319/en.
65. Quoted in Doyle, *Venality*, 258.
66. Ibid., 262.
67. This is noted by Gail Bossenga. 2001. "Society." In Doyle, *Old Regime France*.and Sonenscher, *Before the Deluge*.
68. *Pensées* #26.
69. V.19. A thing "badly needed" in monarchy.
70. In all governments, there have been complaints that people of merit attained honors less often than others. There are many reasons for this, and especially one that is quite natural: it is because there are many people who lack merit, and few who have it. Often, there is even great difficulty in distinguishing between them without being mistaken. That being the case, it is always better that rich people, who have much to lose and who, moreover, have been able to have a better education, assume public office.
71. According to Franklin Ford, this last topic is the crux of Montesquieu's defense, not, as Ford has argued, a personal interest in "solidifying his beloved *corps intermediaires*... Montesquieu's "ideology"...led him to pass over the abuses of the system. Montesquieu *opposed*.
72. See Shovlin, TRRA, 50.
73. Ibid., 51.
74. Among the ancient Persians, on the eighth day of the month named Chorem Ruz the kings would lay aside their pomp and eat with the plowmen. These institutions are remarkable for encouraging agriculture.
75. Shovlin, TRRA, 52.
76. Beccaria, who read Montesquieu, extended this argument in Italy. See Shovlin, TRRA, 53.
77. Ibid., 326.
78. Montesquieu found these stories in Father [Jean Baptiste] du Halde, *Description de l'Empire de la Chine*, vol. 2, 72.
79. David Hume, in a letter to Montesquieu, confirms this reading. The commercial justification, because here he provides *reasons* why social advancement through wealth inspires industry (an argument missing from book 5). These are three. First, he notes that venality increases

the individual's desire to become wealthy. Venality, it turns out, is the mechanism by which social mobility can be stoked by legislators and through policy. Where there is the selling of posts, there is a proliferation of "expectations," especially of moving up and out of one's own class (this is particularly powerful as a negative justification, if one has a particular desire to "quit one's given profession") (XX.22). Second, and added to this point, there is an increased *rivalry* among traders and moneymakers when the laws make allowance for professional advancement and social mobility. Third, there is a powerful motivation to choose, or to follow a profession in which one has natural talent or ability, since upward mobility depends crucially on choosing a profession in which one has a reasonable chance to excel (XX.22).

80. Cited in John Lough. 1970. *The "Encyclopedie" in Eighteenth-Century England and Other Studies.* New Castle: Oriel Press, 357.

4 The Maligned Merchant and the New History of Commerce

1. XX.22.
2. Tocqueville distinguishes between general members of the middle class, and those at the "heart" of the bourgeois, people of wealth and birth who lived comfortably without the need to work for money. See Alexis de Tocqueville. 2008. *The Ancien Régime and the French Revolution.* Trans. Gerald Bevan, ed. Hugh Brogan. London: Penguin.
3. Gaile Bossenga. 2001. "Society." In *Old Regime France: 1648–1788*, ed. William Doyle. Oxford: Oxford University Press, 49. See also Tocqueville, *Ancien Régime,* who distinguishes further between shopkeepers of a low background, and wholesalers.
4. I emphasize a different purpose in book 21 than previous scholarship. Spector has argued that the primary ambition of book 21 of *The Spirit of Law* is to establish in history the dissociation of the spirit of conquest and the spirit of commerce by disqualifying the Roman model: "their genius, their glory, their military education, the force of their government, kept them out of trade." Spector sees book 21 as a continuation of Montesquieu's considerations: the Romans did not make use of trade in order to increase their power: their money was the result of pillage, and a system of fiscal collection leading to the ruin of the conquered peoples as well as to the most pitiless demands."
5. See Michael Sonenscher. 2007. *Before the Deluge: Public Debt, Inequality, and the Intellectual Origins of the French Revolution.* Princeton: Princeton University Press.
6. Quoted in Paul Cheney. 2003. "A False Dawn for Enlightenment Cosmopolitanism? Franco-America Trade during the American War of Independence." *William and Mary Quarterly* 63 (3): 463–488.

7. It is hard to agree with the conclusion that "Montesquieu frankly regarded commerce as a petty undertaking, not worthy of a great people." In Roger Boesche. 1990. "Fearing Monarchs and Merchants: Montesquieu's Two Theories of Despotism." *The Western Political Quarterly* 43 (4): 741, 755.
8. Montesquieu was personal friends with Melon, and he had no difficulty endorsing the "fashion-driven" concept of trade on which it was based. Michael Sonenscher, *Before the Deluge.*
9. Istvan Hont. 2005. *Jealousy of Trade: International Competition and the Nation State in Historical Perspective.* Cambridge: Belknap Press.
10. See also Catherine Larrère. 1992. *Histoire de la Pensée économique.* Paris: Éditions du Centre National de la Recherche Scientifique; Simone Meyssonnier. 1989. *La balance et l'horloge: la genèse de la pensée libérale en France au 18.e siècle.* Montreuil: Les éditions de la Passion.
11. Both Montesquieu and Melon saw the history of commerce as an opportunity for applying economic reasoning to influence contemporary debates on the logic of modern war. This is the view of Montesquieu scholar Paul Rahe. Montesquieu did not set out merely to establish his reputation as a rising philosophical historian who could write scholarly works on a noble theme. As Rahe correctly notes, the problem with such a view is not only that Montesquieu does not view himself as an antiquarian historian. The larger problem is that commerce was not generally considered a noble theme. See Paul Rahe 2009. *Montesquieu and the Logic of Liberty.* New Haven: Yale University Press, 19; compare 252, fn 61. He only flirts with antiquarianism, Montesquieu writes in book 28. But, he always comes back to his own country and his own times (XXVIII.45).
12. This was largely a study of the colonial Dutch trading companies, and while it was written with a broad view, the work did not address the political implications of commerce in any meaningful sense. According to Paul Cheney, Huet's history of commerce was mostly antiquarian; a work of "erudition" rather than "philosophy"; it was "neither synthetic nor polemical but instead factual and even antiquarian in its approach." Paul Cheney. 2010. *Revolutionary Commerce: Globalization and the French Monarchy.* Cambridge, MA: Harvard University Press, 29.
13. Quoted in Thomas E. Kaiser. 1991. "Money, Despotism, and Public Opinion in Early Eighteenth-Century France: John Law and the Debate on Royal Credit." *The Journal of Modern History* 63 (1), 27.
14. XXI.3.
15. Ibid.
16. Proceeding with equanimity, in the fourth and fifth chapters, Montesquieu offers his reader two competing approaches. In Chapter 4, Montesquieu focuses almost exclusively on the climatic or environmental determinants of changes in world trade patterns, arguing, for example, that the "principal difference" between ancient and modern commerce arises out

of simple economic needs which "make people have a great need for each other's commodities" (XXI.4). Shifting demand for liquor, for example, has produced dramatic reversals in both the patterns of—and the *volume* of—exchange.

17. For a discussion of Defoe's description of Credit as an elusive female, see J. G. A. Pocock. 1975. *The Machiavellian Moment: Florentine Political Thought and the Atlantic Republican Tradition*. Princeton: Princeton University Press, 470.
18. For more, see Mark Goldie and Robert Wokler. 2006. *The Cambridge History of Eighteenth-Century Political Thought*. Cambridge: Cambridge University Press, 780. Trenchard, along with Thomas Gordon, became an influential voice in defending individual liberty and constitutionalism both in England (in the 1720s) and also, later in the American colonies.
19. Henry C. Clark. 2003. *Commerce, Culture, and Liberty: Readings on Capitalism before Adam Smith*. Indianapolis: Liberty Fund.
20. Perhaps the most revealing omission in Montesquieu's updated (1748) portrait of commerce has to do with his skepticism about the effects of commerce on intellectual life.
21. XX1.6.
22. XX1.6.
23. *Pensées* #122, 115.
24. *Pensées* #108.
25. Whose fictional Salente is suitable "only to the small Greek city." See Spector, "Fénelon." In Montesquieu Dictionary. http://dictionnaire -montesquieu.ens-lyon.fr/en/article/1376474508/en.
26. XXI.6.
27. XXI.8.
28. *Pensées* #35–36.
29. Pierre Briant and Amélie Kuhrt. 2010. *Alexander the Great and His Empire: A Short Introduction*. Princeton: Princeton University Press.
30. Ibid., 5.
31. Ibid., 7. Montesquieu's economic history did not provide the royalist, Sainte-Croix, much evidence to support his counter-claim against the tide of historians who, by his time, were following Montesquieu's lead in emphasizing Alexander the civilizer and a legislator. Briant shows that even if this emphasis was wrong, it was nonetheless true that this understanding prevailed: a conqueror could "only be ranked among the heroes of history if the war that he conducts spreads civilization."
32. This difference is actually reflected in the ongoing interpretative debates about Alexander's significance. For Larrère, Alexander's significance is that of the "image of modernity found in the midst of ancient ages." See Catherine Larrère. 2001. "Montesquieu on Economics and Commerce." In *Montesquieu's Science of Politics: Essays on the Spirit of Laws*, ed. Carrithers et al. Lanham: Rowman & Littlefield. Some take Alexander literally and believe him to be Montesquieu's model for benign or beneficial

conquest and empire—or even as the original model for the creation of the Universal and Homogenous State, for example Robert Howse. 2006. "Montesquieu on Commerce, Conquest, War, and Peace." *Brooklyn Journal of International Law* 31 (3): 693–708. See also Leo Strauss, Alexandre Kojève, Victor Gourevitch, and Michael S. Roth. 2000. *On Tyranny: Including the Strauss-Kojève Correspondence*. Chicago: University of Chicago Press, 135, 170. Others take him to be a conjuring of a more lasting version of the Alexandrian dream of a commercial union between East and West: Thomas L. Pangle. 2010. *The Theological Basis of Liberal Modernity in Montesquieu's "Spirit of the Laws."* Chicago: University of Chicago Press, 124. See also Volpilhac-Auger, "Alexander the Great." Montesquieu Dictionary, http://dictionnaire-montesquieu.ens-lyon.fr/fr/article/1376392530/en.
33. Catherine Volpilhac-Auger. 2002. "Montesquieu et l'impérialisme grec: Alexandre ou l'art de la conquête." In *Montesquieu and the Spirit of Modernity,* eds. David W. Carrithers and Patrick Coleman. Oxford: Voltaire Foundation. Contrast with Rahe, MLL, and Orwin, Clifford. 2009. "Montesquieu's humanité and Rousseau's pitié." In Kingston, *Montesquieu and His Legacy,* who do not view Alexander as reinforcing the Plutarchian image of Alexander as one "sent by the gods to be the conciliator and arbitrator of the universe." Alexander, viewed through the prism of economic history is made famous in book 21 not only for his military genius, but for his roads, bridges, canals, and other civil works.
34. Although Montesquieu does not believe that Alexander set out to unite East and West through commerce, the result was that he opened up the world for exploration and trade (XXI.8).
35. For a thorough discussion, see Cheney, *Revolutionary Commerce*, 56.
36. Commerce no longer had to rely on the strict seasonal rhythms of Mother Nature for long distance trade (XXI.9). Connecting history with technology through psychology. Technology is a powerful historical force not only because it makes our lives easier, or because it provides access to functional knowledge of how the world works. For Montesquieu, technology gives mankind a confidence that he lacks in his original condition. In contrast to Hobbes, mankind is not bellicose, but timid (I.2); thus the supreme importance of science, which provides a dose of courage that human beings naturally lack. Practical science produces the impression, as we have seen, that man is no longer determined or constrained by natural cycles and supernatural forces.
37. XXI.10.
38. XXI.11.
39. XXI.14.
40. XXI.10; 14.
41. X.13; 14.
42. XXI.8.
43. XXI.11–12.

44. XXI.12.
45. XXI.14.
46. Montesquieu's library contained two editions of the *Discourses*, in Latin and in French. He also had in his possession three copies of *The Prince*, and *The Art of War* and the *Florentine Histories*.
47. Compare *Discourses* I.6.
48. X.14.
49. X.14.
50. *Considerations*, ch. II.
51. Ibid., 40.
52. *Considerations*, ch. X.
53. *Considerations*, ch. IV.
54. *Considerations*, ch. VI.
55. *Considerations*, ch. VIII.
56. Ibid.
57. Ibid.
58. The "two causes" of Rome's ruin are explained in Chapter 9.
59. XXI.13.
60. XXI.14.
61. XXI.14.
62. XXI.15.
63. XXI.16.
64. XXI.16.
65. XXI.15.
66. XXI.20.
67. XXI.21.
68. See Bacon, "Of Usury" in *The Essays*. London: Penguin
69. For an exhaustive analysis of the "legend" in which Jews, expelled from France during the middle ages, invented bills of exchange, see Francesca Trivellato. 2012. "Credit, Honor, and the Early Modern French legend of the Jewish Invention of the Bills of Exchange." *Journal of Modern History* 84 (2): 289–334.
70. Howse, for example, emphasizes the storing of wealth as an intangible form so that commerce can elude violence. See Howse, "Montesquieu on Commerce."
71. Ibid.
72. Pangle, TTB, 93.
73. So Montesquieu's difference with Machiavelli can be understood best, argues Rahe, in light of the moderation that commercial activity provides to men who, though their passions "inspire them with the thought of being rogues" have an "interest in not being so" (XXI.20). Commercial activity becomes a moderate and humane substitute for Machiavelli's "extreme measures."
74. Commerce and international business creates unfavorable conditions for war. The solution to economic Machiavellianism thus blends "realist"

and "liberal" theories (the cure can be thought of as "using liberal theory as a realist critique of military power"). Similarly, Rahe notes that because state power now depends on money and trade, Machiavelli's famous dictum is reversed. Rahe, MLL, 24.
75. XXI.20.
76. XXI.5.
77. Joyce Oldham Appleby. 1978. *Economic Thought and Ideology in Seventeenth Century England*. Princeton: Princeton University Press, 25–26. See also Robert Weisberg. 1986. "Commercial Morality and the Merchant Character, and the History of the Voidable Preference." *Stanford Law Review* 39 (1): 3–138.
78. Weisberg, "Commercial Morality," 16.
79. Thomas Mun for example, in Appleby, *Economic Thought*, 37–41.
80. Larrère, in "Montesquieu on Ecomonics and Commerce," has noted that Montesquieu is more "discreet" in his criticism of lending money at interest in book 22.
81. See David A. Bell. 2001. "Culture and Religion." In Doyle, *Old Regime France*, 80.

5 Commerce and the Rhetoric of Toleration

1. It is used *not* to describe great moral or political acts on behalf of a prince that knows how to enter into evil, but rather, the petty, grasping, and ultimately self-defeating, confiscation of monies and property by princes who do not know what is truly in their own interest. See Peter Gay. 1996. *The Enlightenment: The Science of Freedom*. New York: W. W. Norton., who correctly identifies Montesquieu's separation. For Hume, see "Of Civil Liberty"; "Of the Study of History." From David Hume. 1742. *Essays, Moral, Political and Literary*. Rousseau, Social Contract III.6. See also, Diderot's article in the *Encyclopedie*. How to refute Machiavellianism? He quotes a philosopher, "Sire, I should think the first lesson Machiavelli taught his disciple was to refute his work."
2. See Peter Gay, *The Enlightenment*, 286.
3. XXI.20.
4. XXIV.3.
5. VIII.17.
6. Published, finally, in a highly condensed chapter at the end of book 21.
7. "...industry of the nation, the number of its inhabitants, the cultivation of its lands."
8. II.4; see also: *LP* #58, 60, 117, 121.
9. 2001. "Montesquieu on Economics and Commerce." In *Montesquieu's Science of Politics: Essays on the Spirit of Laws,* ed. Carrithers et al. Lanham: Rowman & Littlefield.
10. Ibid.

11. See Thomas E. Kaiser. 1991. "Money, Despotism, and Public Opinion in Early Eighteenth-Century France: John Law and the Debate on Royal Credit." *The Journal of Modern History* 63 (1).
12. Ibid.
13. Ibid., 19.
14. As Thomas Pangle has argued in MPOL, 24, book 22 is "with only minor exceptions…an endorsement of laissez-faire economics *avant la letter*" and, therefore, does not require investigating too closely.
15. XXII.14.
16. XX.19.
17. XXVI.9.
18. XX.20. If the condemnation of usury occurs alongside weak or nonexisting property rights (where "most men have nothing that is secure"), usury becomes almost impossible to control: "almost no relation between the present possession of a sum and the expectation of having it back after lending it; therefore, usury increases in proportion to the peril of insolvency.
19. XXII.20.
20. XXII.22.
21. XXI.20.
22. See J. A. Schumpeter. 1954. *History of Economic Analysis*. New York: Oxford University Press, 60.
23. XXIII.1.
24. For a balanced attempt at sorting out Montesquieu's religious views, see Roger B. Oake. 1953. "Montesquieu's Religious Ideas." *Journal of the History of Ideas* 14 (4): 548. Oake does not agree (as do the scholars below) with Faguet's judgment that "Montesquieu's mind was as little religious as possible." For a review of the French literature, see Rebecca Kingston. 2001. "Montesquieu on Religion and on the Question of Toleration." In Carrithers et al., *Montesquieu's Science of Politics,* 399 fn.4. Lacordaire is one of the very few who see Montesquieu as a religious thinker (he notes, in 1861, that the *Spirit of Laws* was *"la plus belle apologie du christianisme au XVIIIe siècle"*). Robert Shackleton1961. *Montesquieu: A Critical Biography*. London: Oxford University Press, also views Montesquieu as a practicing Catholic but "with deist convictions." Andrew Lynch highlights the subversive side of Montesquieu's writing on religion, which, he concludes, is good only for social utility. See Andrew Lynch. 1977. "Montesquieu and the Ecclesiastical Critics of l'Esprit des lois." *Journal of the History of Ideas* 38 (3): 487–500. Sanford Kessler examines Montesquieu's *Persian Letters* and finds an interesting depth to his analysis and critique of biblical religion. Kessler concludes that Montesquieu was attempting to provide a "new theology" based in the principles of natural religion. See Sanford Kessler. 1983. "Religion and Liberalism in the *Persian Letters.*" *Polity* 15 (3): 383–386. Judith Shklar follows Kessler and Lynch in regarding Montesquieu as largely an anti-religious thinker; see Judith Shklar.

1987. *Montesquieu*. Oxford: Oxford University Press., 84. Peter Gay puts Montesquieu's views in context, and argues that he is "exceptional" among the *philosophes* for assigning Christianity to a privileged position among religions, "largely for its historical role." Still, Gay's Montesquieu is part of the majority view: religion had lost all its vitality, and remained a "harmful survival" even in the eighteenth century. See Gay, *The Enlightenment*, 373 fn. 2. Rebecca Kingston compares Montesquieu's views on natural law to the modern school of natural law; "Montesquieu on Religion," 376–380, and though she attempts to portray Montesquieu as more friendly to religion than is generally conceded, she concludes, again in line with other scholars, that Montesquieu considered religion as a "cultural artifact whose truths and doctrines are largely fashioned by humans themselves." Diana Schaub, in OBB, gives what may be the most astute and challenging interpretation of Montesquieu's views on toleration in the literature, more of which is highlighted in this essay. Robert Bartlett, OPFR, gives an equally compelling analysis but emphasizes Montesquieu's antipathy toward religion and compares him, unrealistically, in my view, with Bayle (see Diana J. Schaub. 1999. "Of Believers and Barbarians in Montesquieu's Enlightened Toleration." In *Early Modern Skepticism and the Origins of Toleration,* ed. Alan Levine, 236–239. Lanham: Lexington, for a different reading of Montesquieu's attitude toward Bayle). For Bartlett, the two are nearly identical: they both have a "staggering ambition" to overcome the Bible as a political authority, for example. The main difference between Bayle and Montesquieu, according to Bartlett, is their judgment on the "political utility" of Christianity. "I suggest that Montesquieu and 'this great man'...do not have fundamentally different ends in mind and that they disagree only over the best strategy to attain that end: Both philosophers envisage a day when, to the very great benefit of politics, the concern for religion in general and Christianity in particular would fall into desuetude." See Bartlett, Robert C. 2001. "On the Politics of Faith and Reason: The Project of Enlightenment in Pierre Bayle and Montesquieu." *The Journal of Politics* 63 (1): 14–17; 24–25.

25. For example, Kingston, "Montesquieu on Religion and on the Question of Toleration."
26. See Bartlett, OPFR, 16–17. Or is it neither? Is Montesquieu's goal to *transform* and perform a kind of transmutation of monotheistic religion? See Schaub, OBB.
27. For Bartlett, as for many others, the key to Montesquieu's views on religion are found in book One (compare, for e.g., Lowenthal, *Montesquieu*; Shackleton, *Montesquieu*; Pangle, TTB). This is where we find the "theoretical foundation" of Montesquieu's anti-theological project in Part Five. Montesquieu's anti-religious radicalism. This section in book 25 is more than just a clue of Montesquieu's irreligion. It is "the audacious peak of Montesquieu's political philosophy." See Bartlett, OPFR, 18.

28. Montesquieu's utilitarian analysis of religion is only the *beginning*, argues Bartlett, of an attack that goes beyond merely reducing religion to its good or bad political effects. Montesquieu's utilitarianism "culminates," argues Bartlett, in an attempt to destroy religion. See Bartlett, OPFR, 18; compare Pangle, MPOL.
29. The obvious major exception is Pangle, TTB. See also Bartlett, OPFR, emphasis added.
30. Diana J. Schaub. 1995. *Erotic Liberalism: Women and Revolution in Montesquieu's Persian Letters*. Lanham: Rowman & Littlefield.
31. Ibid., 225–239.
32. Ibid., 233.
33. XXIV.1.
34. XXIII.2; XXIII.5; XXII.7.
35. If Montesquieu were only concerned with money—and the ways in which religion depresses the GDP—he could have omitted book 23, and proceeded directly to Part 5 of the *Spirit of Laws*. Instead, he turns to discuss the ways in which it impoverishes human sexuality.
36. XXIII.1.
37. A cursory overview of the topics reminds us just how powerfully religion affects the ways human beings think about sex and procreation. Montesquieu will discuss marriages (XXIII.2), the condition of children (XXIII.3), the family (XXIII.4), the various orders of legitimate wives (XXIII.5), the problem of bastards (XXIII.6), the role of fathers in consenting to their daughter's marriage (XXIII.7), the different attitudes of girls and boys to settling down and creating a home (XXIII.9–10). In his treatment of each of these subjects, religious laws are always hovering over the discussion. Religion, Montesquieu shows, haunts every aspect of our love lives. It reaches very deeply into our marriages, into our conceptions of family, and the way we believe it is best to raise our children. The simple point being made here, to repeat, is that Montesquieu does *not* believe that the essential tension is between religion and *commerce*. For an exhaustive analysis of this topic, see Diana Schaub's *Erotic Liberalism*. See especially, Chapter four, "The Politics of Fecundity" for a helpful explanation of the importance of series of letters on population in the *Persian Letters*, which are critical for understanding Montesquieu's remarks on population here in book 23.
38. XXIII.11–18.
39. The key idea here is that religion too often distorts the natural needs and bonds of love and family. Too little attention is given to what Montesquieu calls the "circumstances" of the family (XXIII.16). Circumstances vary: from the moderateness or harshness of government (XXIII.11); to the fertility rate and birth differential between girls and boys (XXIII.12); to the proximity of a people to seaports; to the *diets* of the people (the amount of ingestion of the "oily parts of fish") (XXIII.13); to the quality of the

pastureland (or coal mines) (XXIII.14); to the level of industrialization and sophistication of the arts (XXIII.15).
40. It should not be ignored that Montesquieu believes that "public continence" plays an important role in maintaining healthy growth rates, and more importantly, healthy families where children are cared for and not corrupted by the profligacy of their parents (XXIII.2). But this is not the driving theme of the chapter, or of Montesquieu's analysis of religion as a whole.
41. For example, XXIII.21; 25.
42. See *Considerations* XXII–XXIII, and *PL* #109.
43. For nuance, see Pangle, TTB, 158, fn 26.
44. Carol Blum. 2002. "Montesquieu, the Sex Ratio and 'Natural Polygamy.'" In Carrithers and Coleman, *Montesquieu and the Spirit of Modernity*, xi; 3; 77; 192.
45. Montesquieu considers feudal Europe as a stage of regrowth (XXIII.24), mainly because of the incentives provided by the "infinity of small sovereignties." Montesquieu cites Pufendorf and gives an estimate of the population in France in 1550 (XXIII.24). He speculates, however, in Chapter 26, that Europe is continually declining and that "laws are needed to favor the propagation of the human species" (XXIII.26). Montesquieu's empirical assessment of population is not unproblematic, but it should be put in perspective. First, his aim, in short, is to contrast "Europe today" with yesterday's Greeks. Second, his observation has less to do with demographic speculation, and more to do with a general observation about the difference between classical republicanism and Christian monarchies: the Greeks were tormented by having too many citizens; modern Christian monarchies are tormented by having too few (XXIII.26).
46. Montesquieu's anti-clericalism should not be understated here. He is highly critical of the "excessive advantages of the clergy over the laity," which he compares to the worst kind of despotism (XXIII.28).
47. *PL* #109.
48. See XII.10 and XII.22. See also *Pensées* #373, 583, 626, and 651.
49. XXIII.28.
50. XXIV.1; XXV.9.
51. XXIV.1.
52. See *OC-II, 112*.
53. A caveat: I do not argue that the *only* purpose of these two books is to make religion more compatible with commerce. I do argue, however, that this is the most important difficulty to understand, in Part 5. To understand this relationship in a Montesquieuean spirit is to think of it as a productive, rather than destructive tension.
54. Such an approach could be found, for example, in the tradition of natural law, as reinterpreted in the late seventeeth century by Grotius

and Pufendorf. In France, the idea had been discussed by philosophers ranging from Vico to Voltaire.
55. For an example of contemporary approaches to this field, see Rachel McCleary and Robert Barro. 2006. "Religion and Economy." *Journal of Economic Perspectives* Spring. For a great survey, see Iannaccone, Laurence R. 1998. "Introduction to the Economics of Religion." *Stanford Journal of Economic Literature* 36 (3).
56. McCleary and Barro, "Religion and Economy."
57. These examples are drawn from the first 15 chapters, XXIV.1–14.
58. For a discussion of Bayle, see Ernst Cassirer. 1951. *The Philosophy of the Enlightenment*. Ed. Fritz C. A. Koelln and James P. Pettegrove. Princeton: Princeton University Press, 167. Cassirer notes that Bayle's *Dictionary* was a kind of weapons storage area for freethinkers; the "real arsenal" of all Enlightenment philosophy.
59. For a helpful background, with a slightly different emphasis, see: Robert Shackleton. 1988. "Les mots 'despote' et 'despotime.'" In *Essays on Montesquieu and on the Enlightenment*, ed. David Gilson and Martin Smith, 287–294. Oxford: Voltaire Foundation.
60. XXIV.3.
61. *Pensées* #1230.
62. "In order to preserve its liberty, it would borrow from its subjects, and its subjects, who would see that its credit would be lost if it were conquered, would have a further motive to make efforts to defend its liberty." See XIX.27.
63. But Montesquieu had already foreshadowed a true Christian patriotism is unnecessary in the context of a modern commercial world. To put this more directly still, the example of commercial England proves that longer worry about Bayle's disturbing hypothetical. English Christianity, having made its peace with commerce, is, to its great fortune, backed up and supported by English commercialism. In Montesquieu's portrait of England, Christian patriotism had begun to merge with commercial patriotism. Hence, there is no need for Montesquieu to write a long tract defending a pure Christian patriotism in book 24, for he had already shown, in book 19, that Bayle's attack on the weakness of Christianity had been rendered moot by the transformation of orthodox Christianity by commerce.
64. *PL* #104.
65. XX.1.
66. Or to put it more accurately, a sophisticated matching of an unlikely couple.
67. XXIV.10, emphasis added.
68. XXIV.10.
69. XXIV.11.
70. XXIV.14.
71. Religions that have only a "kind of hell," but no positive notion of heavenly reward or salvation tend to have loose or dubious morals and are

often created merely to justify accidental things that the society considers bad, such as gathering oysters or wearing clothing of linen and not of silk (XXIV.14). Religions that only have a place of reward, or that provide a road to salvation that does nothing to provoke any degree of fear of punishment are also dangerous. Montesquieu uses Hinduism to make his point. Hindus believe that the "waters of the Ganges have a sanctifying virtue" and that those who die on its banks will be "exempt from the penalties of the other life and... to live in a region of delights." In Montesquieu's irreverent wording, "What does it matter if one lives virtuously, or not? One will have oneself thrown into the Ganges."
72. It should be noted here that this implies a providential God, although Montesquieu does not come close to demanding that a good religion must have one god, or that this god cares about human affairs.
73. XXIV.19.
74. *PL* #135.
75. Ibid.
76. Montesquieu's meaning can be illustrated by drawing a distinction between the idea of a pure, sense-less soul, on one extreme; and an embodied, sensual soul on the other (with all of its sexual, reproductive, appetitive desires, feelings, and organs intact). This hyper-sexualized, sensual soul, is the view Montesquieu rejects. Such an existence, he argues, is too "easily grasped" by our minds. Being easily grasped, it is easily exploited. But more importantly, this opinion is dangerous because it promises to fulfil our unfulfilled desires—to satisfy every unsatisfied, subjective, and personal pleasure. Here, Montesquieu suggests, are the roots of the most violent fanaticism (as he says in a footnote, "thus, the disciples of Foë kill themselves by the thousands").
77. In Usbek's words, "With all religions, it's a delicate matter to portray the pleasures in store for those who have lived virtuously," *PL* #120.
78. XXIV.19–21. On this score, Christianity has done a remarkably good job. There are actually three "dogmas" about the immortality of the soul that Montesquieu considers. The first is that of pure immortality; the second is "simple change of abode"; and the third is metempsychosis (the system of the Indians). As to this third possibility, Montesquieu places it between the first two in terms of its desirability. On the one hand, it increases the "horror of spilling blood." But "wives burn themselves when their husbands die; only innocent people suffer violent death there."
79. See XXIV.19.
80. XXIV.16. Chapter 16 provides a clear and important example of how religion can promote not only peaceful co-preservation, but also protect industry and promote economic productivity. When a state is "agitated by civil wars," for example, religious authorities have often, throughout history, stepped in to help establish "times of peace or truce" so that the people can "do the things, such as harvesting and similar work, without which the state could not continue to exist."

81. XXIV.24.
82. XXIV.22.
83. XXIV.24.
84. I.2; 2.
85. XXV.1.
86. This is the title of Chapter 11, XXV.11.
87. Part of the reason for this is that we feel pride in choosing a non-corporeal God that does not have bodily functions, as Montesquieu explains. But imagine the opposite combination: an "idolatrous" god that eats, sleeps, breathes, and performs bodily functions, *but* that does not care, or share, that "natural penchant for things that [we feel]." This, in Montesquieu's view, is the *least* potent source of attachment to religion: we should lose respect for the God itself, who has our needs, and therefore is not removed from "the humiliation" of our condition.
88. XXV.2.
89. Ibid.
90. Ibid.
91. Ibid.
92. That this is Montesquieu's goal is not apparent until XXV.13.
93. Return to the days of Genghis Khan (whom Montesquieu, humorously, treats as infinitely Enlightened compared to the Muslims of Buchara) in which god could be worshipped "everywhere (XXV.3), one can at least push (and look forward to) a day when religion attaches people not through state-sanctioned control of land and wealth, but through God and community. A realistic remedy is something like the Jews' "portable tabernacle." A religion that gives no permanent "asylum" to crooks and criminals will lead not merely to less "attachment," but less attachment of the wrong sort.
94. XIX.5.
95. XIX.12.
96. XIX.14.
97. XIX.14.
98. XXV.6.
99. XXV.7.
100. Mixed in with the economic argument is a quiet, understated, plea for scriptural literacy: the idea of a "pontificate" should always be checked by the careful recording of religious laws in "sacred books" that can be put "in everyone's hands" (XXV.8; cf. XII.29).
101. See also Rebecca Kingston. "Montesquieu on Religion and on the Question of Toleration," 375–408.
102. See *PL* #83.
103. XXV.9–10.
104. This "closed door" policy also has its problems, as other scholars have noticed. See Schaub, OBB.
105. XIX.27; XXV.12. In Bartlett's phrase, society must cultivate an "effective indifference" or a "certain benign zealotry. See Bartlett, OPFR.

106. XXV.12. Moreover, Montesquieu reminds us throughout the *Spirit of Laws* that the achievement of toleration in England followed other developments: notably, the disillusionment of the Puritan attempt at rule; the bloody civil wars; the experience of freedom; and the liberation of the spirit of commerce and industry. Nowhere in the *Spirit of Laws* does Montesquieu suggest that the liberal triumph of religious toleration can be secured by reason, by philosophy, or by rational argument alone. In the short term, the best argument for toleration is the *experience* of it, and this, the philosopher cannot provide, except indirectly. This explains why Montesquieu returns, in Chapter 12, to remind his reader of the vital importance of the "penal laws," a topic which has not been directly addressed since book 12. Disestablishment matters little, or nothing, if the criminal laws are immoderate or if they confuse crimes of religion with crimes of tranquility, for example (XII.4). For a fuller discussion of Montesquieu's views on toleration as it relates to the liberal tradition, see Steven Kautz. 1997. *Liberalism and Community*. Ithaca: Cornell University Press, 624–628.
107. Berns, "Thomas Hobbes," 416.
108. Montesquieu accepts Hobbes' basic premise that fear (or more accurately, the "marks of mutual fear") does drive men into society (I.2). But this is a transitory passion. The fear of being attacked or killed dissolves, on the one hand, when one realizes that one's "enemy" is equally fearful; and it is tempered, on the other hand, by the surge of other "sociable" passions, or animal pleasures, like the "charm that the two sexes inspire in each other" and by the pleasure men and women receive from interacting and sharing the bond of knowledge (I.2).
109. If the sovereign power competes against the fear of God, both sources of authority (religious and political) may lose out, while the soul, Montesquieu says, "becomes atrocious." It should be no surprise that Montesquieu thinks it impossible—on this basis—to form a tolerant society.
110. Kingston notes that Montesquieu did not follow Locke. But while allowing for state intervention in ways to regulate religious practice, Montesquieu does place limits on what the state can do. For example, he does not allow for the imposition of civil penalties for crimes specific to religious doctrines, such as heresy. Also, nowhere does he suggest, as Locke had, that whole sects or groups, such as atheists, ought not to be tolerated in principle given the content of their beliefs. Finally, he notes that the state, while able to police incoming sects, must tolerate them once they have been established in the country (XXV.10). See Kingston, "Montesquieu on Religion and on the Question of Toleration."
111. David A. Bell, 2001. "Culture and Religion." In *Old Regime France: 1648–1788,* ed. William Doyle, 98. Oxford: Oxford University Press.
112. XXV.13.
113. XXV.13.

114. For a different, but not incompatible, interpretation of the importance of this passage, see Pangle, TTB, 104–105.
115. It is double-edged because it is an appeal to compassion grounded in a very pointed charge of hypocrisy.
116. XXV.13; 6–8.
117. XXV.13; 8. This appeal mirrors, in some ways, Locke's first argument for toleration in his Letter Concerning Toleration (i.e., that toleration is itself the chief characteristic mark of "the True Church"), see Nathan Tarcov. 1999. "John Locke and the Foundations of Toleration." In *Early Modern Skepticism and the Origins of Toleration,* ed. Alan Levine, 182. Lanham: Lexington.
118. XXV.13; 9.
119. Schaub calls this a "sophisticated appeal to the vanity of Christian believers." See OBB, 229.
120. The inquisitors not of how God will judge them in the afterlife, but how "someone in the future" will judge them. In future ages, persecutors will be cited as *proof* that religion was, or is, "barbaric," "ignorant" and crude. This, he says, will "stigmatize your century." The enemies of religion will be able to use this and to "bring hatred on all your contemporaries." See XXV.13; 15.

6 The Problem of Property in *The Spirit of the Laws*

1. It has been pointed out, of course, that there are numerous "Enlightenments," although here for space I will avoid the terminological debates. As others have pointed out, the Enlightenment as it increasingly becomes "everything" becomes increasingly nothing.
2. See, for example, Jonathan Israel. 2002. *Radical Enlightenment: Philosophy and the Making of Modernity 1650–1750.* Oxford: Oxford University Press, 11–13.
3. See Rebecca Kingston2001. "Montesquieu on Religion and on the Question of Toleration." In *Montesquieu's Science of Politics: Essays on the Spirit of Laws,* eds. Carrithers et al., Lanham: Rowman & Littlefield. Montesquieu's theory of toleration could not support separation of church and state. Montesquieu was bound to the reality of the Catholic church, its dominance in society, and its political ties to the monarchy.
4. One exception is Mark H. Waddicor. 1970. *Montesquieu and the Philosophy of Natural Law.* The Hague: Nijhoff, 162–167. "Property...for Montesquieu was a natural right; it was one aspect of the right to liberty." I note my disagreements with Waddicor below.
5. In this I follow Michael Zuckert. 2004. "Natural Rights and Modern Constitutionalism." *Northwestern Journal of International Human Rights* 2 (Spring): 1–25. Zuckert contests Lowenthal's view that Montesquieu was not a natural rights thinker, pointing to book X as the place in which Montesquieu's commitment to natural rights "becomes decisive."

While this article owes much to Zuckert's basic insight, I am focused less on Montesquieu's theoretical discussion of property. I also diverge from Zuckert's analysis in a second respect. While I agree that Montesquieu's modification of Locke's teaching does not require a fundamental change of Lockean principles, I believe Montesquieu's modification to be a major, not a minor, rhetorical modification.
6. For an exception, see Waddicor, *Montesquieu and the Philosophy of Natural Law*. See also Jean Bart. "Property, Succession." http://dictionnaire-montesquieu.ens-lyon.fr/en/article/1367163276/en.
7. XXVI.15.
8. XXVI.8–9.
9. XXVI.16.
10. In Waddicor, *Montesquieu and the Philosophy of Natural Law*, 164.
11. Michael Sonenscher. 2007. *Before the Deluge: Public Debt, Inequality, and the Intellectual Origins of the French Revolution*. Princeton: Princeton University Press.
12. Jean-Pierre Gross. 1993. "Progressive Taxation and Social Justice in Eighteenth-Century France." *Past and Present* 140 (1): 79–126.
13. Ibid., 90–91.
14. Carrithers, 2001. "Democratic and Aristocratic Republics." In Carrithers et al., *Montesquieu's Science of Politics*.
15. V.1.
16. *Pensées* #1208.
17. One should read IV.6 in conjunction with VIII.1; this companion chapter shows why the institutions of Lycurgus failed.
18. *Pensées* #1378.
19. For more on this fascinating book, see John Christian Laursen and Cyrus Masroori. 2006. *The History of the Sevarambians: A Utopian Novel*. Albany, NY: University of New York Press., esp. vii–xxii.
20. This is a mistake, although perhaps a minor one, given her article in the Montesquieu Dictionary, "Plato."
21. IV.6.
22. Laursen and Masroori characterize it, in fact, as a combination of the two.
23. Immanuel Kant. 1991. *Political Writings*. Cambridge: Cambridge University Press, 188. Kant said it was full of "brilliant ideas" "that have never been tried in practice."
24. David Hume. 1987. "Of Polygamy and Divorces." In *Essays, Moral, Political, and Literary*, ed. Eugene F. Miller. Indianapolis: Liberty Fund.
25. It tells the story of a group of unfortunates "shipwrecked" on *Terra Australis* (the "southern continent"). The novel then describes the construction of an "ideal city" (which takes the name "Sevarinde"). And while the novel is presented as a "true work" by the narrator, it is clearly not supposed to be interpreted as such—as a real possibility. On the contrary, Verais's work is hilariously fanciful, presenting as it does a perfect society where property has been abolished, poverty eradicated. Men dance with naked virgins in the hills, cavort with talking animals, and travel by unicorn.
26. IV.6.

27. IV.6; see also IV.7.
28. IV.6.
29. Ibid. Mr. Penn, says Montesquieu, is an *honnete homme* whose purpose is *not* to form a people whose chief quality is military courage, or "bravery." Rather, his purpose is to form a religious people with "an integrity as natural as bravery was among the Spartans."
30. IV.6.
31. See Nannerl O. Keohane. 1980. *Philosophy and the State in France: The Renaissance to the Enlightenment*. Princeton: Princeton University Press, 384; 395.
32. VI.1.
33. VI.2.
34. Ibid.
35. Tom Bethell. 1998. *The Noblest Triumph: Property and Prosperity through the Ages*. New York: St. Martin's Press, 19.
36. See, for example, Honore, A. M. 1961. "Ownership." In *Oxford Essays in Jurisprudence*. Oxford: Oxford University Press.
37. Bethell, *The Noblest Triumph*, 19.
38. Honore, "Ownership."
39. XXXI.9; XXX.17; VI.15; XXVI.18; XXX.7; XI.18.
40. XII.15; XXVI.6; XXVI.9.
41. On the additional question of the difference between English and French feudal law, as it relates to translation, see Cohler. Montesquieu pointed out, for example, that in England the Magna Carta forbid confiscation even in times of war; and that it prohibited the seizing the lands or the income of a debtor when his movable or personal goods are sufficient for the payment.
42. XXX.14.
43. XXIII.28–29.
44. XXXI.7.
45. Ibid.
46. When offices became hereditary, he noted, they were abused greatly. XXXI.28–29.
47. On the "judicial profit" or *Freda* see XXX.20.
48. XXX.13.
49. XXX.18.
50. When representatives asked Charlemagne to be exempt from going to war, the Church "lost public regard."
51. XXX.11.
52. XXX.17.
53. XXX.12; XXX.22.
54. XXX.1–3.
55. Church property was not secure, and a great deal of property was turned over during the Norman disturbances (XXXI.10). But the wealth of the Church was partially restored through the establishment of tithes

(which became universal after commoners were exploited by being told that devils were eating their corn for not paying them (XXX.12). The establishment of the tithe was acceptable to the Church, as a new "kind of good," the main advantage to the clergy "was that later usurpations would be more easily recognizable, as they were given exclusively to the church."

56. XXX.15.
57. Donald Kelley and Bonnie Smith. "What Was Property? Legal Dimensions of the Social Question in France (1789–1848)." *Proceedings of the American Philosophical Society* (128) 3: 204.
58. Ibid.
59. Ibid.
60. Ibid.
61. The idea that one might have a right to property in one's self was a concept that had been well-established at least as far back as the thirteenth century. Zuckert notes that a "self-ownership" understanding of property had developed slowly over time, reaching its zenith in the writings of John Locke. See Zuckert, "Natural Rights and Modern Constitutionalism." For a more detailed discussion of the history of the development of the theme, see John Tierney. 2011. "Do You Have Free Will? Yes, It's the Only Choice." *New York Times*. http://www.nytimes.com/2011/03/22/science/22tier.html?_r=1&scp=1&sq=Do%20you%20have%20free%20will?&st=cse, 83–89.
62. This is not the consensus view. Consult Paul Rahe. 2012. "Montesquieu's Natural Rights Constitutionalism." *Social Philosophy & Policy* 29 (2): 51–81.
63. See Waddicor, *Montesquieu and the Philosophy of Natural Law*, 118.
64. Ibid., 119. See also Lester Crocker. 1952. "The Discussion of Suicide in the Eighteenth Century." *Journal of the History of Ideas* 13 (1): 47–72. In the eighteenth century, debate on the question of suicide was heavily contested, as it was seen as a"crucial test" of man's freedom, or in one scholar's words "his dependence on a superior force.
65. Is suicide a form of murder? Usbek admits that the act of suicide contradicts the religious prohibition against the taking of life. Yet he rejects the notion that it constitutes a moral "harm" and therefore murder. "Is there any less order or purpose in the universe," he asks, "after the soul of the suicide is separated from the body?" *PL* #74.
66. One may object either to Usbek's materialist rationale, or to the assumption that Usbek represents Montesquieu's own view. Consider, however, the famous ending of the *Persian Letters*, which appears to further justify Usbek's tough stance—at least insofar as the reader sympathizes with the fate of Roxane, whose suicide concludes the novel. Indeed, it is not hard to understand why so many readers have viewed Roxane's death as a positive reaffirmation of her freedom. Rosso, for example, has argued that Roxane, through her suicide "*pose un acte d'indépendance à ses propres yeux*

et aux yeux d'autrui." See Jeannette Geffriaud Rosso. 1977. *Montesquieu et la féminité.* Pise: Libreria Goliardica, 334. Roxane's suicide note is in fact the final letter in the novel. Roxane writes, in the final letter, "No: I may have lived in servitude, but I have always been free: I have rewritten your laws to conform to those of nature, and my spirit has always remained independent" *PL* #150. Through Roxane's suicide, Montesquieu ultimately affirmed the idea of selfhood and autonomy that he would later defend in more concrete ways in his *De l'esprit des lois.* A right to self-disposal, however controversial, was considered by Montesquieu a necessary consequence of the Lockean belief that the individual truly has "a property in his own person. For an interesting analysis of Locke's views on suicide, which do not appear at first to line up with Montesquieu's defense of the act, see George Windstrup. 1980. "Locke on Suicide." *Political Theory* 2: 175–176. Windstrup sees the suicide taboo as giving two "rhetorical advantages": it provides a nonutilitarian argument against the taking of human life; and it lends support to the Lockean justification of the right to revolution.

67. Waddicor, *Montesquieu and the Philosophy of Natural Law,* 120.
68. XIV.12, fn.23. According to a French law of 1670, suicide was regarded as a civil crime as well as a religious offence. See Margaret Mauldon and Andrew Khan, eds. 2008. *Persian Letters.* Oxford: Oxford University Press, xx. Mauldon is correct in noting that "When Usbek defends suicide in *PL* #74 as a legitimate choice—a position that was regarded as heretical by the church and therefore as a provocation on Montesquieu's part—it is without any foresight into the outcome of his own affairs.
69. Dedieu provides a historical survey of Montesquieu's attitude, claiming that Montesquieu opposed slavery on moral and sentimental grounds in his early career; on moral and utilitarian grounds in the middle; and finally he condemned it completely on the grounds that it was selfish. (Joseph Dedieu. 1913. *Montesquieu.* Paris: Alcan.) See, by contrast, Waddicor, *Montesquieu and the Philosophy of Natural Law,* 149–162, who provides an analytical presentation. See also Jean Jean Ehrard. 2008. *Lumières et esclavage.* Brussels: André Versaille; and Russell Parsons Jameson. 1971. *Montesquieu et l'esclavage: étude sur les origines de l'opinion antiesclavagiste en France au XVIIIe siècle.* New York: B. Franklin. Also, Jean Goldzink. "Negro." <http://dictionnaire-montesquieu.ens-lyon.fr/en/article/1377621295/en/> as well as Diana J. Schaub. 2005. "Montesquieu on Slavery." *Perspectives on Political Science* 34 (Spring): 70–78 and F. T. H. Fletcher. 1933. "Montesquieu's Influence on Anti-Slavery Opinion in England." *Journal of Negro History* XVIII: 414–426. A comprehensive account of the literature on this topic is found in Jameson, *Montesquieu et l'esclavage.*
70. Goldzink, "Negro."
71. His clear influence on pro-slavery opinion in England in Europe removes all doubt as to Montesquieu's intentions. See, Fletcher, "Montesquieu's Influence."

72. XV; XVI; XVII.
73. Schaub, "Montesquieu on Slavery," 75.
74. Goldzink, "Negro."
75. Goldzink counts these as six, although the number is not essential.
76. Ibid. "Placed first, the economic argument hits the bull's eye but yields clearly in number to the plea in favor of the equality of the human race, it being understood that all the arguments against slavery in general, of a moral, religious, and political order obviously apply to Africans."
77. See V.2 and *PL* #72.
78. XV.1; XV.16.
79. XV.8.
80. Compare XV.1 and XV.18.
81. XV.7.
82. Slavery is wholly incompatible with the nature of democracy, which presupposes basic equality (XV.1). Slavery is irreconcilable with monarchy, where it is "sovereignly important neither to beat down nor to debase human nature." Despotism, then, is the only important exception; it is "very easy to sell oneself" there not because the person is *not* an owner of his own body or labor, but because civil liberty is effectively "annihilated" by pre-exiting conditions of political slavery (XV.6).
83. Politics book I, Chapter 1 (1254a17–1255a2).
84. XV.7.
85. See Schaub's expansion on this point, in relation to Montesquieu: "Montesquieu on Slavery," 74.
86. XV.1. If there is an argument for a "slave by nature" it must, at a minimum, demonstrate some utility to both master and slave.
87. See Fletcher, "Montesquieu's Influence."
88. Where possible, they should follow the natural law (Preface).In each case above, protect property narrowly construed, but to enforce more broadly the natural laws in book 1 related to sociability (I.2).
89. In Sparta, fathers not only enjoyed the rights to their own child: "each father had the right to correct the child of another" XVI.7; XII.29.
90. XXI.19.
91. CXXIX; *Pensées* #174.
92. I.3; repeated in VI.20.
93. I.3.
94. V.7. In classical antiquity, for example, paternalism was "of great use" because these states lacked a unifying "coercive force." Laws were created to "endeavor to supply this defect by some means or other; and this is done by paternal authority."
95. XXIII.22.
96. V.7. monarchies require distinctions, not only between "types of property" but between people (VI.1). Paternalism maintains those distinctions, thus preserving the "nature" of monarchical inequality.
97. VI.1.
98. Following Grotius, Locke, and Pufendorf.

99. V.7.
100. V.7.
101. In despotic states, children are also condemned to punishment for the offenses of their parents (XVI.20). This justified exposing the young, especially girls, the deformed, or the "monstrous" (but not until after "they had been shown to five of the closest relatives"), who are bought and sold "like property" (XII.29).
102. In book 1, Montesquieu notes that paternal power "proves nothing" beyond a limited set of parental considerations. Even the families not burdened by customs of patrilineal property, rule passed to the most responsible heir.
103. In some way, this section is a continuation of the "proto-feminism" which critics have often seen as a major theme of the *Persian Letters*. It is true that many writers in the 1970s castigated Montesquieu for misogyny and patriarchalism (e.g., Robert F. O'Reilly 1973. "Montesquieu: Anti-Feminist." *Studies on Voltaire and the Eighteenth Century* 102: 143–156; Rosso, *Montesquieu et la féminité*; M. J Pollock. 1979. "Montesquieu on the Patriarchal Family: A Discussion and Critique." *Nottingham French Studies* 18: 9–21.). But, as Schaub, OBB, has pointed out, there was a shift in the 1980s toward viewing Montesquieu (albeit in varying degrees) as "sympathetic to the cause of women's liberation." See also Sheila Mason. 2008. "Montesquieu, Europe, and the Imperatives of Commerce." *Journal for Eighteenth-Century Studies* 17 (1): 65–72; Mary L. Shanley and Peter G. Stillman. 1982. "The Harem Sequence in Montesquieu's Persian Letters: A Critique of Political and Familial Despotism." In *The Family in Political Thought,* ed. Jean Elshtain, 66–79. Amherst: University of Massachusetts Press; Tenenbaum, Susan. 1982. "Woman through the Prism of Political Thought." *Polity* 15 (Fall): 67–79; Pauline Kra. 1984. "Montesquieu and Women." In *French Women and the Age of Enlightenment,* ed. Samia I. Spencer, 272–284. Bloomington: Indiana University Press; and Katherine M. Rogers. 1986. "Subversion of Patriarchy in Les *Lettres Persanes."* *Philological Quarterly* 65 (1): 61–78. These interpretations pick up on a much earlier view of Montesquieu as "a pioneer feminist." See Roger Oake. 1941. "Montesquieu and Hume." *Modern Language Quarterly* 2 (1): 25-41.
104. Example, VIII.5, XV.3.
105. See XVI.1; see also XVI.9; "A link between domestic government and politics."
106. See *Pensées* #1726.
107. VII.9. and XVI.2.
108. VII.
109. VII.17.
110. XVI.2.
111. See Waddicor, *Montesquieu and the Philosophy of Natural Law,* 113. This latter mistake was worse because polyandry was a "monstrous disorder, which was never permitted in any case."

112. In theory, one might entertain the possibility that a husband could treat his wives equally, "in all or most respects." But even so, there remains the problem of natural jealousy, which, Montesquieu says, inspires "intrigue," suspicion, and eventually, mistrust and discord within the family. Polygamy leads to sexual jealousy, and sexual jealousy leads to the "enclosure" and separation of the women from each other until "each one becomes almost a particular family within the family" (XVI.10).
113. In what sense can this family be considered their own? Montesquieu argues that such conditions are demeaning, reducing women to the status of dependents (the wives of polygamous marriages "are given their clothing as it would be given to children") XVI.14. Ultimately, Montesquieu rejected polygamy because it diminished the capacity for true self-government. To minimize female autonomy in sexual relations made it impossible for "domestic government" to ever truly be theirs (XVI.14).
114. Compare XVI; XXIII; XXVI.
115. Compare XVI.16.
116. Blum's brilliant analysis is undermined somewhat by her insistence that Montesquieu favored divorce merely for "populationist" reasons.
117. "A husband is the master of the house; he has a thousand ways to hold his wives to their duty or to return them to it, and it seems that, in his hands, repudiation is only a new abuse of power."
118. This hearkens back to "an ancient patriarchal privilege" while divorce carries a "protomodern, egalitarian connotation."
119. The question of indissolubility is put aside, providing Montesquieu greater freedom to explore the advantages of ancient practice Montesquieu to praise the ancient practice of repudiation while avoiding a head-on confrontation with the Catholic church over the theology of the sacrament of marriage This was seen in Carol Blum's words, "as protecting women from arbitrary expulsion" see Carol Blum. 2002. "Montesquieu, the Sex Ratio and 'Natural Polygamy.'" In Carrithers and Coleman, *Montesquieu and the Spirit of Modernity*, 65.
120. Repeated from XVI.15–16.
121. XXVI.7.
122. XXVI.9.
123. The "fundamental principle of divorce," he says, in a surprising affirmation of the underlying logic of the Romans, is to allow the "dissolution of one marriage only *in the expectation* of another" (emphasis added).
124. XXVI.13. Relative to goods, to reciprocal advantages, to all that is relative to the new family, the one from which it has come, and the one that will be born"—that is, to property—all this "concerns the civil laws."
125. See, for example, Jens Beckert. 2010. *Are We Still Modern? Inheritance Law and the Broken Promise of the Enlightenment*. Köln: Max Planck Institut für Gesellschaftsforschung. Beckert provides a useful historical overview. As Beckert has pointed out, the danger of reform in this area was indeed something of an "open secret." Radical changes on this dimension of

family and property law was seen by many writers as the first necessary step toward the creation and eventual realization of new liberal orders in Europe.
126. Tocqueville later summed up the significance of the topic memorably: "the legislator had once regulated the law of inheritance, he may rest from his labor" *Democracy in America*, Vol. I. 48.
127. See, for example, Annelien de Dijn's helpful discussion in *French Political Thought from Montesquieu to Tocqueville: Liberty in a Levelled Society?* Cambridge: Cambridge University Press, 64.
128. XXVI.16.
129. XXXI.27.
130. II.4.
131. See, for example, XXVI.6.
132. XII.6.
133. XXVI.6.
134. Ibid.
135. When a man leaves children, Montesquieu writes, the "Salic Law wants the males to inherit the Salic land in preference to the daughters."
136. They did not own the *land* surrounding their house. "The Germans had no patrimony other than the house and a bit of land within the enclosure around the house." The Germanic tribes, in other words, did not enjoy "stable ownership"—that is, property rights (the land around their house became "public" after only a year).
137. "[This law] was found harsh, that the daughters and their children could not have a share."
138. The prejudice in favor of male inheritance was strengthened in Rome after the Punic Wars, with the introduction of the Voconian law (XVII).
139. Daughters of poor families not enrolled in the census were allowed to inherit, as this did not undermine republican equality.
140. Cox, Iris. 2001. "Montesquieu and the History of Laws." In Carrithers et al, Lanham: Rowman and Littlefield, 411.
141. Ibid., 411.
142. Ibid., 412.
143. XXX.1.
144. XXX.2.
145. XXX.19.
146. XXX.4.
147. Feudal domains grew from the spoils of war (XXX.4). The barbarian Franks did not "establish" servitude or "serfdom," however. During this time, fiefs were revocable. But this did not mean that the king "owned" the disposition of the fiefs. This would mean that the king would have had "the only property" in all of the kingdom, giving him a power "as arbitrary as that of the sultan of Turkey" (XXX.5).
148. XXX.5; XXX.10.

149. XXX.5.
150. XXX.5.
151. XXVI.16.
152. XXX.9.
153. XXX.10.
154. XXX.9.
155. XXX.10.
156. XXX.10.
157. XXX.11.
158. XXX.11. An "infinity of lands" then became subject to mortmain, a subject Montesquieu had tackled in book 25 (XXV.5), arguing that it had led to a series of "endless acquisitions" that increased the wealth of the clergy. Landowners gave these lands to the churches, believing that by *their* servitude they "participated in the saintliness of the churches" (XXX.11).
159. XXX.12–13.
160. XXX.14–15.
161. XXX.15.
162. Originally, these lands were revocable; at first these were granted only for a year, it became more common for lands to be given for life but titles or "goods of the fisc" and "honors" or "fiefs" (XXX.16). Freemen (who had neither benefices nor fiefs but were not subject to serfdom) possessed "allodial lands." The *cause* of this shift was not pure legal arrogation. In return for security of property, there was military service (XXX.17) but also the "double service" of judging one's peers in the lord's court (XXX.18).
163. XXX.19.
164. In addition to the settlement for wrongs and injuries, the guilty party had to pay an additional fee, a certain "right," in exchange protection (XXX.20). The size of the *fredum* was proportional to the size of the protection.
165. XXX.20.
166. XXX.21.
167. XXX.10.
168. See XXX.23–24.
169. XXX.7.
170. By contrast, Montesquieu views the ancient nobility as providing an historical anchor, emphasizing its political function as a defense against the royal monopoly of justice.
171. See XXX.25.
172. XXXI.31–2.
173. XXXI.7.
174. XXXI.10.
175. XXXI.12.
176. XXXI.16.

177. *Pensées* 1392.
178. The peak of liberty was achieved under Charlemagne, whose tenure held in balance agains the forces of fragmentation and autocracy. This depended on the genius of Charlemagne (XXXI.18) to recreate a moment of "the best kind of government" conceived until that time (XI.8).
179. Jean Ehrard. "Charlemagne." <http://dictionnaire-montesquieu.ens-lyon.fr/en/article/1377615820/en.>
180. XXXI.18.
181. XXXI.22.
182. XXXI.29.
183. XXX.30.
184. XXX.32.
185. XXX.32.
186. XXX.33.
187. See XXX.34.
188. XXX.34.
189. XXVI.23.
190. XXVI.23. See Bart, "Property, Succession," for evidence that the capitals were added by the printer.

Conclusion

1. Carcassonee and Mathiez: Carcassone is an example of the former, Mathiez, an example of the latter; see Franklin L. Ford 1953. *Robe and Sword; the Regrouping of the French Aristocracy after Louis XIV.* Cambridge: Harvard University Press.
2. See Annelien de Dijn. 2014. "Was Montesquieu a Liberal Republican?" *The Review of Politics* 76 (1): 21–41.
3. Thomas L. Pangle. 1989. *Montesquieu's Philosophy of Liberalism: A Commentary on the Spirit of the Laws.* Chicago: University of Chicago Press.
4. *PL* #102.
5. First, Rhedi worries that military technology ("bombs" and gunpowder) will undermine the traditional reliance on virtue and make European life "inhumane." The realities of technological warfare, he says, will someday "deprive all the peoples of Europe of their freedom." Rhedi worries, furthermore, that the "men of science" will "eventually discover some secret which would offer a faster way to kill people, destroy races, and wipe out entire nations" (*PL* #102). With science and technology and the rapid spread of knowledge through commerce, come new and dangerous forms of biotechnology. Rhedi describes chemistry as a "fourth plague" that will ruin men's health and destroy them. Even the compass—which Montesquieu celebrates as a "hero" in book 21 of *The Spirit of the Laws*—has done more harm than good.

In Rhedi's opinion, the compass will bring just as many "diseases [as wealth]." Indeed, trade and exploration has been "very harmful" to the countries discovered. Because of men like Alexander, old cultures and civilizations will be either destroyed or "reduced to such harsh servitude that the accounts alone will make [religious men] tremble."

6. Usbek is clearly sympathetic. He admits, moreover, that commerce brings ugly social consequences: "In Paris for one man to lead an epicurean life, it is necessary for a hundred others to work unremittingly" (*PL* #103). Earlier, he had complained that "the greatest man in Paris is the one with the best horses to draw his carriage" (*PL* #86). Echoing Montesquieu's critique of Holland in the *Spirit of Laws*, Usbek argues that everything in commercial society runs on "favor" and honors are almost never awarded for real virtue. Providence, he says, does not ensure that wealth is given to "good people" in a commercial society. When one "closely examines the sort of people who have the most wealth, by dint of despising the wealthy, one comes to have a scorn for wealth" (*PL* #95).
7. The fact that many ancient empires—including the Persian Empire—were ruined by "indolence" is far "from being a conclusive example." Most importantly, it is not true, argues Usbek, that commerce and the arts make men "effeminate." In a well-regulated country, where men take a pleasure in such activities, artists, and commercial men, will have to work particularly hard to "avoid the disgrace of penury."
8. XI.6.
9. XI.5.
10. Michael Sonenscher. 2007. *Before the Deluge: Public Debt, Inequality, and the Intellectual Origins of the French Revolution*. Princeton: Princeton University Press.
11. There are at least four references; see numbers 423, 874, 943: "Un gouvernement libre peut être comparé à un grand filet dans lequel les poissons se promènent et ne se croient pas pris."
12. No. 943.
13. Montesquieu, OC-II 1798; emphasis added.

BIBLIOGRAPHY

Adam, Ulrich. 2009. "Justi and the Post-Montesquieu French Debate on Commercial Nobility in 1756." In *The Beginnings of Political Economy: Johann Heinrich Gottlob von Justi,* ed. Jurgen G. Backhaus, 75–98. New York: Springer.
———. 2006. *The Political Economy of Justi.* Bern: Peter Lang.
Allen, William B. 2009. *The Personal and the Political: Three Fables by Montesquieu.* Lanham: University Press of America.
———. 2004. "That All Tragedy Is Local: Book 18 of Spirit of the Laws." *Interpretation: A Journal of Political Philosophy* 31 (2): 193–216.
———. 2000. *The Federalist Papers: A Commentary.* New York: Lang.
———. 1975. "Review of *Montesquieu's Philosophy of Liberalism: A Commentary on the Spirit of the Laws* by Thomas Pangle." *Journal of the History of Philosophy* 13 (2): 256–259.
Althusser, Louis. 2007. *Politics and History.* London: Verso.
Appleby, Joyce Oldham. 1978. *Economic Thought and Ideology in Seventeenth Century England.* Princeton: Princeton University Press.
Bacon, Francis and John Pitcher. 1985. *Francis Bacon: The Essays.* London: Penguin.
Barrière, Pierre Ferdinand. 1951. *L'Académie de Bordeaux. Centre de culture internationale au XVIIIe siècle (1712–1792).* Bordeaux: PUF.
Bartlett, Robert C. 2001. "On the Politics of Faith and Reason: The Project of Enlightenment in Pierre Bayle and Montesquieu." *The Journal of Politics* 63 (1): 1–28.
Beckert, Jens. 2010. *Are We Still Modern? Inheritance Law and the Broken Promise of the Enlightenment.* Köln: Max Planck Institut für Gesellschaftsforschung.
Bell, David A. 2001. "Culture and Religion." In Doyle, *Old Regime France.*
Berg, Maxine and Elizabeth Eger. 2003. *Luxury in the Eighteenth Century: Debates, Desires and Delectable Goods.* New York: Palgrave.
Berns, Laurence. 1987. "Thomas Hobbes." In *History of Political Philosophy,* eds. Leo Strauss and Joseph Cropsey. Chicago: University of Chicago Press.
Berlin, Isaiah and Henry Hardy. 1980. *Against the Current: Essays in the History of Ideas.* New York: Viking Press.
Bernstein, William J. 2008. *A Splendid Exchange: How Trade Shaped the World.* New York: Atlantic Monthly Press.

Bernstein, William J. 2004. *The Birth of Plenty : How the Prosperity of the Modern World Was Created.* New York: McGraw–Hill.
Bethell, Tom. 1998. *The Noblest Triumph: Property and Prosperity through the Ages.* New York: St. Martin's Press.
Blancheton, B. 2005. "Les faux bilans de la Banque de France dans les années 1920." In *L'enterprise, le chiffre et le droit,* eds. J. G. Degos and S. Trébucq. Bordeaux: Université Montesquieu.
Blanqui, Jérôme-Adolphe. 1968. *History of Political Economy in Europe.* Trans. Emily J. Leonard. New York: Augustus M. Kelley.
Blum, Carol. 2002. *Strength in Numbers: Population, Reproduction, and Power in Eighteenth-Century France.* Baltimore: Johns Hopkins University Press.
———. 2002. "Montesquieu, the Sex Ratio and 'Natural Polygamy.'" In Carrithers and Coleman, *Montesquieu and the Spirit of Modernity.*
Boesche, Roger. 1990. "Fearing Monarchs and Merchants: Montesquieu's Two Theories of Despotism." *The Western Political Quarterly* 43 (4): 741.
Bonar, James. 1966. *Philosophy and Political Economy in Some of Their Historical Relations.* New York: A. M. Kelley.
Bossenga, Gaile. 2001. "Society." In Doyle, *Old Regime France.*
Briant, Pierre and Amélie Kuhrt. 2010. *Alexander the Great and His Empire: A Short Introduction.* Princeton: Princeton University Press.
Cadilhon, François. 1996. *Montesquieu ou l'ingrate réalité du quotidien bordelaise.* Mont-de-Marsan: Éditions interuniversitaires.
Carcassonne, Elie. 1927. *Montesquieu et le problème de la Constitution française au XVIIIe siècle.* Paris: PUF.
Carrese, Paul. 2006. "The Machiavellian Spirit of Montesquieu's Liberal Republic." In *Machiavelli's Liberal Republican Legacy,* ed. Paul A. Rahe, 121–142. Cambridge UK: Cambridge University Press.
Carrithers, David W. 2002. "Montesquieu and the Spirit of French Finance: An Analysis of His *Mémoire sur les dettes de l'état* (1715)." In Carrithers and Coleman, *Montesquieu and the Spirit of Modernity.*
———. 2001. "Democratic and Aristocratic Republics." In Carrithers et al., *Montesquieu's Science of Politics..*
———. 1991. *Not So Virtuous Republics: Montesquieu, Venice, and the Theory of Aristocratic Republicanism.* Baltimore: Johns Hopkins University Press.
———. 1986. "Montesquieu's Philosophy of History." *Journal of the History of Ideas* 47 (1): 61–80.
Carrithers, David W. and Patrick Coleman, eds. 2002. *Montesquieu and the Spirit of Modernity.* Oxford: Voltaire Foundation.
Carrithers, David W., Michael A. Mosher, and Paul A. Rahe, eds. 2001. *Montesquieu's Science of Politics: Essays on the Spirit of Laws.* Lanham: Rowman & Littlefield.
Cassirer, Ernst. 1951. *The Philosophy of the Enlightenment.* Ed. Fritz C. A. Koelln and James P. Pettegrove. Princeton: Princeton University Press.
Cheney, Paul. 2010. *Revolutionary Commerce: Globalization and the French Monarchy.* Cambridge, MA: Harvard University Press.

———. 2008. "Constitution and Economy in David Hume's Enlightenment." In *David Hume's Political Economy*, eds. Carl Wennerlind and Margaret Schabas, 223–242. London: Routledge.

———. 2003. "A False Dawn for Enlightenment Cosmopolitanism? Franco-America Trade during the American War of Independence." *William and Mary Quarterly* 63 (3): 463–488.

Clark, Henry C. 2006. *Compass of Society: Commerce and Absolutism in Old-Regime France*. Lanham: Lexington.

———. 2003. *Commerce, Culture, and Liberty: Readings on Capitalism before Adam Smith*. Indianapolis: Liberty Fund.

Cotta, Alain. 1957. "Le développement economique dans la pensée de Montesquieu." *Revue d'histoire économique et social* 35 (4) : 370–415.

Courtney, Cecil P. 2009. "Review of *Three Women, A Novel*, by the Abbé de la Tour." *Eighteenth Century Fiction* 21 (3): 481–483.

———. 2001. "Montesquieu and Natural Law." In Carrithers et al., *Montesquieu's Science of Politics*.

———. 1963. *Montesquieu and Burke*. Oxford: Blackwell.

Cox, Iris. 2001. "Montesquieu and the History of Laws." In *Montesquieu's Science of Politics: Essays on the Spirit of Laws*, ed, Carrithers et al., 409–457. Lanham: Rowman & Littlefield.

———. 1983. *Montesquieu and the History of French Laws*. Oxford: Voltaire Foundation.

Crocker, Lester. 1952. "The Discussion of Suicide in the Eighteenth Century." *Journal of the History of Ideas* 13 (1): 47–72.

Desgraves, Louis, ed. 1991. *Pensées, Le Spicilège*. Paris: Robert Laffont.

———. 1985. *Montesquieu*. Paris: Mazarine.

Desserud, D. 1999. "Commerce and Political Participation in Montesquieu's Letter to Domville." *History of European Ideas* 25 (3): 135–151.

Devletoglou, Nicos E. 1969. "The Economic Philosophy of Montesquieu." *Kyklos: Internationale Zeitschrift* 22 (3): 530–541.

———. 1963. "Montesquieu and the Wealth of Nations." *Canadian Journal of Economics and Political Science* 29 (1): 1–25.

Dijn, Annelien de. 2014. "Was Montesquieu a Liberal Republican?" *The Review of Politics* 76 (1): 21–41.

———. 2011. "On Political Liberty: Montesquieu's Missing Manuscript." *Political Theory* 39 (2): 181–204.

———. 2008. *French Political Thought from Montesquieu to Tocqueville: Liberty in a Levelled Society?* Cambridge, UK: Cambridge University Press.

Doyle, Michael. 2004. "Liberal Internationalism: Peace, War and Democracy." *Nobelprize.org*. <http://www.nobelprize.org/nobel_prizes/themes/peace/doyle/index.html>

Doyle, William. 2001. *Old Regime France: 1648–1788*. Oxford: Oxford University Press.

———. 1996. *Venality: The Sale of Offices in Eighteenth-Century France*. Oxford: Clarendon Press.

Doyle, William. 1984. "The Price of Offices in Pre-Revolutionary France." *The Historical Journal* 27 (4): 831–860.
Ehrard, Jean. 2009. "Montesquieu and Us." In Kingston, *Montesquieu and His Legacy*.
———. 2008. *Lumières et esclavage*. Brussels: André Versaille.
Faccarello, Gilbert. 1998. *Studies in the History of French Political Economy: From Bodin to Walras*. London: Routledge.
Felix, Joel. 2001. "The Economy." In Doyle, *Old Regime France*.
Fletcher, F. T. H. 1933. "Montesquieu's Influence on Anti-Slavery Opinion in England." *Journal of Negro History* XVIII: 414–426.
Fontaine, Phillippe. 1996. "The French Economists and Politics, 1750–1850: The Science and Art of Political Economy." *The Canadian Journal of Economics* 29 (2): 379–393.
Ford, Franklin L. 1953. *Robe and Sword; the Regrouping of the French Aristocracy after Louis XIV*. Cambridge, MA: Harvard University Press.
Garrigou-Lagrange, André. 1956. "Montesquieu et les Economists." In *Actes du congrès Montesquieu: réuni à Bordeaux du 23 au 26 mai 1955 pour commémorer le deuxième centenaire de la mort de Montesquieu*, 279–284. Bordeaux: Delmas.
Gartzke, Erik. 2007. "The Capitalist Peace." *American Journal of Political Science* 51 (1): 167–194.
Gay, Peter. 1996. *The Enlightenment: The Science of Freedom*. New York: W. W. Norton.
Goldie, Mark and Robert Wokler. 2006. *The Cambridge History of Eighteenth-Century Political Thought*. Cambridge, UK: Cambridge University Press.
Goyard-Fabre, Simone. 1980. *Montesquieu: Adversaire de Hobbes*. Paris: Minard.
Groenewegen, Peter. 2008. "Political Economy." In *The New Palgrave Dictionary of Economics, Second Edition*. <http://www.dictionaryofeconomics.com/article?id=pde2008_P000114>
———. 2002. *Eighteenth Century Economics*. New York: Routledge.
Grospelier, Joelle. 2005. "What Could Have Prompted Keynes to Call Montesquieu 'The Real Equivalent of Adam Smith, the Greatest of French Economists?'" *Student Economic Review* 19: 3–15. <http://www.tcd.ie/Economics/SER/pasti.php?y=05>.
Gross, Jean-Pierre. 1993. "Progressive Taxation and Social Justice in Eighteenth-Century France." *Past and Present* 140 (1): 79–126.
Helvetius, Claude Adrien. 1973. *De l'esprit*. Vervier: Editions Gerard.
Hendrickson, Randal R. 2014. "Ordinary Passions and Philosophic Morality: On the Uniqueness of Montesquieu's Commercial Republic." *Perspectives on Political Science* 43 (1): 1–11.
———. 2013. "Montesquieu's (Anti-) Machiavellianism: Ordinary Acquisitiveness and Its Obstacles in the Spirit of Laws." *The Journal of Politics* 75 (2): 385–396.
———. 2007. "Montesquieu and the Transformation of Republicanism." PhD diss., Boston College.

Hirschman, Albert O. 1977. *The Passions and the Interests: Political Arguments for Capitalism before Its Triumph*. Princeton: Princeton University Press.

Honore, A. M. 1961. "Ownership." In *Oxford Essays in Jurisprudence*. Oxford: Oxford University Press.

Hont, Istvan. 2005. *Jealousy of Trade: International Competition and the Nation State in Historical Perspective*. Cambridge, MA: Belknap Press.

Howse, Robert, 2006. "Montesquieu on Commerce, Conquest, War, and Peace." *Brooklyn Journal of International Law* 31 (3): 693–708.

Hulliung, Mark. 1976. *Montesquieu and the Old Regime*. Berkeley: University of California Press.

Hume, David. 1987. "Of Polygamy and Divorces." In *Essays, Moral, Political, and Literary*, ed. Eugene F. Miller. Indianapolis: Liberty Fund.

———. 1754. *Political Discourses*. London: Kincaid & Donaldson.

Hume, David and J. Y. T. Greig. 1969. *The Letters of David Hume*. Oxford: Clarendon Press.

Hunt, E. K. and Mark Lautzenheiser. 2011. *History of Economic Thought: A Critical Perspective*. New York: M. E. Sharpe.

Iannaccone, Laurence R. 1998. "Introduction to the Economics of Religion." *Stanford Journal of Economic Literature* 36 (3): 1464–1496.

Israel, Jonathan. 2002. *Radical Enlightenment: Philosophy and the Making of Modernity 1650– 1750*. Oxford: Oxford University Press.

Jameson, Russell Parsons. 1971. *Montesquieu et l'esclavage: étude sur les origines de l'opinion antiesclavagiste en France au XVIIIe siècle*. New York: B. Franklin.

Jones, Colin. 2002. *The Great Nation: France from Louis XV to Napoleon 1715–99*. New York: Columbia University Press.

Jones, James F. 1978. "Montesquieu and Jefferson Revisited: Aspects of a Legacy." *The French Review* 51 (4): 577–585.

Kaiser, Thomas E. 1991. "Money, Despotism, and Public Opinion in Early Eighteenth-Century France: John Law and the Debate on Royal Credit." *The Journal of Modern History* 63 (1): 1–28.

———. 1989. "The Abbé Dubos and the Historical Defence of Monarchy in Early Eighteenth-Century France." *Studies on Voltaire and the Eighteenth Century* 267: 77–102.

Kant, Immanuel. 1991. *Political Writings*. Cambridge, UK: Cambridge University Press.

Kautz, Steven. 1997. *Liberalism and Community*. Ithaca: Cornell University Press.

———. 1993. "Liberalism and the Idea of Toleration." *American Journal of Political Science* 37 (2): 610–632.

Kelley, Donald and Bonnie Smith. "What Was Property? Legal Dimensions of the Social Question in France (1789–1848)." *Proceedings of the American Philosophical Society* (128) 3: 200–230.

Kellow, Geoffrey. 2011. "Strength and Riches: Nicolas Barbon's New Politics of Commerce." *Erasmus Journal for Philosophy and Economics* 4 (1): 1–22.

Keohane, Nannerl O. 1980. *Philosophy and the State in France: The Renaissance to the Enlightenment*. Princeton: Princeton University Press.

Kessler, Sanford. 1983. "Religion and Liberalism in the *Persian Letters*." *Polity* 15 (3): 380–396.

Kingston, Rebecca. 2009. *Montesquieu and His Legacy*. Albany: SUNY Press.

———. 2001. "Montesquieu on Religion and on the Question of Toleration." In Carrithers et al., *Montesquieu's Science of Politics*.

———. 1996. *Montesquieu and the Parlement of Bordeaux*. Geneva: Droz.

Kra, Pauline. 1984. "Montesquieu and Women." In *French Women and the Age of Enlightenment*, ed. Samia I. Spencer, 272–284. Bloomington: Indiana University Press.

———. 1970. *Religion in Montesquieu's Lettres Persanes*: Geneva: Institut et musée Voltaire Les Délices.

Krause, Sharon R. 2010. "Beyond Capitalism?" *Political Theory* 38 (6): 884–890.

———. 2005. "Two Concepts of Liberty in Montesquieu." *Perspectives on Political Science* 34 (2): 88–96.

———. 2003. "History and the Human Soul in Montesquieu." *History of Political Thought* 24 (2): 235–261.

———. 2002. *Liberalism with Honor*. Cambridge, MA: Harvard University Press.

———. 2001. "Despotism in the *Spirit of Laws*." In Carrithers et al., *Montesquieu's Science of Politics*.

Kries, Douglas. 1997. "The Displacement of Christian Historiography." In *Piety and Humanity: Essays on Religion and Early Modern Political Philosophy*, ed. Douglas Kries, 233–258. Lanham: Rowman & Littlefield.

Larrère, Catherine. 2009. "Montesquieu and Liberalism: The Question of Pluralism." In Kingston, *Montesquieu and His Legacy*.

———. 2005. *Montesquieu, oeuvre ouverte 1748–1755 actes du colloque de Bordeaux, 6–8 décembre 2001, Bordeaux, bibliothèque municipale*. Napoli: Liguori.

———. 2004. "Montesquieu's Paradoxical Economics." Paper presented at Gimon Conference on French Political Economy. <http://www-sul.stanford.edu/depts/hasrg/frnit/gimon_ papers.html>

———. 2002. "L'histoire du commerce dans *L'Esprit des lois*." In *Le Temps de Montesquieu*, ed. Michel Porret and Catherine Volpilhac-Auger, 319–336. Geneva: Droz.

———. 2002. "Impôts directs, impôts indirects: économie, politique, droit." *Archives De Philosophie Du Droit*. 117–130.

———. 2001. "Montesquieu on Economics and Commerce." In Carrithers et al., *Montesquieu's Science of Politics*.

———. 1999. "Montesquieu: commerce de luxe et commerce d'économie." *In Actes du colloque international de Bordeaux pour le 250e anniversaire de "L'Esprit des lois,"* ed. Louis Desgraves, 467–484. Bordeaux: Bibliothèque Municipal.

———. 1995. "Montesquieu et l'idée de fédération." *L'Europe de Montesquieu* 2: 137–152.

———. 1992. *Histoire de la Pensée économique*. Paris: Éditions du Centre National de la Recherche Scientifique.

Laursen, John Christian and Cyrus Masroori. 2006. *The History of the Sevarambians: A Utopian Novel*. Albany, NY: University of New York Press.
Lewinski, Jan. 1922. *The Founders of Political Economy*. London: Kind.
Locke, John and Peter Laslett. 1988. *Locke: Two Treatises of Government*. Cambridge, UK: Cambridge University Press.
Lough, John. 1970. *The "Encyclopedie" in Eighteenth-Century England and Other Studies*. New Castle: Oriel Press.
Lowenthal, David. 1963. "Montesquieu." In *History of Political Philosophy*, ed. Leo Strauss and Joseph Cropsey, 470–90. Chicago: Rand McNally.
Lutz, Donald S. 1984. "The Relative Influence of European Writers on Late Eighteenth-Century American Political Thought." *The American Political Science Review* 78 (1): 189–197.
Lynch, Andrew J. 1977. "Montesquieu and the Ecclesiastical Critics of l'Esprit des lois." *Journal of the History of Ideas* 38 (3): 487–500.
Mackrell, J. Q. C. 1973. *The Attack on "Feudalism" in Eighteenth-Century France*. London: Routledge.
Manent, Pierre. 1998. *The City of Man*. Princeton: Princeton University Press.
Manicas, Peter T. 1981. "Montesquieu and the Eighteenth-Century Vision of the State." *History of Political Thought* 2 (2): 313–347.
Mansfield, Harvey. 1995. "Self-Interest Rightly Understood." *Political Theory* 23 (1): 48–66.
———. 1993. *Taming the Prince: The Ambivalence of Modern Executive Power*. Baltimore: Johns Hopkins University Press.
Mason, Sheila. 2008. "Montesquieu, Europe, and the Imperatives of Commerce." *Journal for Eighteenth-Century Studies* 17 (1): 65–72.
———. 1978. "Montesquieu and the Old Regime." *Philosophical Books* 19 (1): 11.
Manin, Bernard. 2001. "Montesquieu, la république et le commerce." *Archives européennes de sociologie* 42: 573–602.
Mathiez, Albert. 1930. "La place de Montesquieu dans l'histoire des doctrines politiques du XVIIIe siècle." *Annales historiques de la Révolution française* 7: 97–112.
Mauldon, Margaret and Andrew Khan, eds. 2008. *Persian Letters*. Oxford: Oxford University Press.
Maza, Sarah. 1997. "Luxury, Morality, and Social Change: Why There Was No Middle-Class Consciousness in Prerevolutionary France." *The Journal of Modern History* 69 (2): 199–229.
Melzer, Arthur M. 1983. "Rousseau's 'Mission' and the Intention of His Writings." *American Journal of Political Science* 27 (2): 294–320.
Meyssonnier, Simone. 1989. *La balance et l'horloge: la genèse de la pensée libérale en France au 18.e siècle*. Montreuil: Les éditions de la Passion.
McCleary, Rachel and Robert Barro. 2006. "Religion and Economy." *Journal of Economic Perspectives* Spring.
Montesquieu, C. L. S. 2008. *Persian Letters*. Trans. Margaret Mauldon. Oxford: Oxford University Press.

Montesquieu, C. L. S. 1990. *Selected Political Writings*. Ed. Melvin Richter. Indianapolis: Hackett Publishing.
———. 1989. *The Spirit of the Laws*. Eds. Anne M. Cohler, Basia C. Miller, and Harold S. Stone. Cambridge, UK: Cambridge University Press.
———. 1965. *Considerations on the Causes of the Greatness of the Romans and Their Decline*. Trans. David Lowenthal. New York: Free Press.
———. 1949/1951. *Œuvres complètes*. Ed. Roger Caillois. Paris: Gallimard.
———. 1914. *The Spirit of Laws*. Trans. Thomas Nugent. London: G. Bell.
Morilhat, Claude. 1996. *Montesquieu: politique et richesses*, Paris: PUF.
Muller, Jerry Z. 2002. *The Mind and the Market: Capitalism in Modern European Thought*. New York: Alfred A. Knopf.
Murphy, Antoin E. 1997. *John Law: Economic Theorist and Policy-Maker*. Oxford: Clarendon Press.
O'Reilly, Robert F. 1973. "Montesquieu: Anti-Feminist." *Studies on Voltaire and the Eighteenth Century* 102: 143–156.
Oake, Roger B. 1953. "Montesquieu's Religious Ideas." *Journal of the History of Ideas* 14 (4): 548–560.
———. 1941. "Montesquieu and Hume." *Modern Language Quarterly* 2 (1): 25–41.
Orwin, Clifford. 2009. "Montesquieu's humanité and Rousseau's pitié." In Kingston, *Montesquieu and His Legacy*.
Pangle, Thomas L. 2010. *The Theological Basis of Liberal Modernity in Montesquieu's "Spirit of the Laws."* Chicago: University of Chicago Press.
———. 1989. *Montesquieu's Philosophy of Liberalism: A Commentary on the Spirit of the Laws*. Chicago: University of Chicago Press.
Pii, Eluggero. 1998. "I libri sull commercio nell'Esprit des lois." In *Leggere L'Esprit des lois, Stato, societa e storia nel pensiero di Montesquieu*, ed. Domenico Felice, 165–200. Napoli: Liguori.
Pocock, J. G. A. 1985. *Virtue, Commerce, and History: Essays on Political Thought and History, Chiefly in the Eighteenth Century*. Cambridge, UK: Cambridge University Press.
———. 1975. *The Machiavellian Moment: Florentine Political Thought and the Atlantic Republican Tradition*. Princeton: Princeton University Press.
Pollock, M. J. 1979. "Montesquieu on the Patriarchal Family: A Discussion and Critique." *Nottingham French Studies* 18: 9–21.
Rahe, Paul. 2012. "Montesquieu's Natural Rights Constitutionalism." *Social Philosophy & Policy* 29 (2): 51–81.
———. 2011. "Montesquieu's anti-Machiavellian Machiavellianism." *History of European Ideas* 37 (2): 128–136.
———. 2009. *Montesquieu and the Logic of Liberty*. New Haven: Yale University Press.
———. 2005. "The Book That Never Was: Montesquieu's Considerations on the Romans in Historical Context." *History of Political Thought* 26: 43–89.
Richter, Melvin. 1977. *The Political Theory of Montesquieu*. Cambridge, UK: Cambridge University Press.
Rogers, Katherine M. 1986. "Subversion of Patriarchy in Les *Lettres Persanes*." *Philological Quarterly* 65 (1): 61–78.

Rosow, Stephen J. 1984. "Commerce, Power and Justice: Montesquieu on International Politics." *Review of Politics* 46 (3): 346–366.
Rosso, Jeannette Geffriaud. 1977. *Montesquieu et la féminité*. Pise: Libreria Goliardica.
Samuel, Ana J. 2009. "The Design of Montesquieu's *Spirit of the Laws*: The Triumph of Freedom over Determinism." *American Political Science Review* 103 (2): 305–321.
Schaub, Diana J. 2010. "Women, Christianity, and the Modern in Montesquieu's *Considerations on the Romans*." In *The Pious Sex: Essays on Women and Religion in the History of Political Thought*, ed. Andrea Radasanu. Lanham: Lexington.
———. 2009. "Montesquieu's Education of the Sentiments in the *Temple of Gnidus*." In *The Arts of Rule: Essays in Honor of Harvey C. Mansfield*, ed. Sharon R. Krause and Mary A. McGrail, 125–146. Lanham: Lexington.
———. 2005. "Montesquieu on Slavery." *Perspectives on Political Science* 34 (Spring): 70–78.
———. 2002. "The Regime and Montesquieu's Principles of Education." In Carrithers and Coleman, *Montesquieu and the Spirit of Modernity*.
———. 1999. "Of Believers and Barbarians in Montesquieu's Enlightened Toleration." In *Early Modern Skepticism and the Origins of Toleration*, ed. Alan Levine, 225–249. Lanham: Lexington.
———. 1995. *Erotic Liberalism: Women and Revolution in Montesquieu's Persian Letters*. Lanham: Rowman & Littlefield.
Schumpeter, J. A. 1954. *History of Economic Analysis*. New York: Oxford University Press.
Shackleton, Robert. 1988. "Les mots 'despote' et 'despotime.'" In *Essays on Montesquieu and on the Enlightenment*, ed. David Gilson and Martin Smith, 109–116. Oxford: Voltaire Foundation.
———. 1964. "Montesquieu and Machiavelli: A Reappraisal." *Comparative Literature Studies* 1 (1): 1–13.
———. 1961. *Montesquieu: A Critical Biography*. London: Oxford University Press.
Shanley, Mary L. and Peter G. Stillman. 1982. "The Harem Sequence in Montesquieu's Persian Letters: A Critique of Political and Familial Despotism." In *The Family in Political Thought*, ed. Jean Elshtain, 66–79. Amherst: University of Massachusetts Press.
Shklar, Judith N. 1990. "Montesquieu and the New Republicanism." In *Machiavelli and Republicanism*, ed. Gisela Bock et al., 265–280. Cambridge, UK: Cambridge University Press.
———. 1987. *Montesquieu*. Oxford: Oxford University Press.
———. 1984. *Ordinary Vices*. Cambridge, MA: Belknap Press.
———. 1981. "Jean D'Alembert and the Rehabilitation of History." *Journal of the History of Ideas* 42 (4): 643–664.
Shovlin, John. 2006. *The Political Economy of Virtue: Luxury, Patriotism, and the Origins of the French Revolution*. Ithaca: Cornell University Press.
———. 2000. "Toward a Reinterpretation of Revolutionary Antinobilism: The Political Economy of Honor in the Old Regime." *The Journal of Modern History* 72 (1): 35–66.

Skousen, Mark. 2009. *The Making of Modern Economics: The Lives and Ideas of the Great Thinkers.* New York: M. E. Sharpe.
Sonenscher, Michael. 2007. *Before the Deluge: Public Debt, Inequality, and the Intellectual Origins of the French Revolution.* Princeton: Princeton University Press.
Sorel, Albert. 1888. *Montesquieu.* Trans. Melville B. Anderson and Edward P. Anderson. Chicago: A. C. McClurg & Company.
Spector, Céline. 2004. *Montesquieu: Pouvoirs, richesses et sociétés.* Paris: PUF.
———. 1999. *Le pouvoir.* Paris: GF Flammarion.
Stapelbroek, Koen. 2005. "The Devaluation Controversy in Eighteenth-Century Italy." *History of Economic Ideas* 13 (2): 79–110.
Strauss, Leo, Alexandre Kojève, Victor Gourevitch, and Michael S. Roth. 2000. *On Tyranny: Including the Strauss-Kojève Correspondence.* Chicago: University of Chicago Press.
Stewart, Iain. 2002. "Montesquieu in England: His Notes on England, with Commentary and Translation." *Oxford University Comparative Law Forum.* http://ouclf.iuscomp.org/articles/montesquieu.shtml.
Tarcov, Nathan. 1999. "John Locke and the Foundations of Toleration." In *Early Modern Skepticism and the Origins of Toleration,* ed. Alan Levine, 179–197. Lanham: Lexington.
Tenenbaum, Susan. 1982. "Woman through the Prism of Political Thought." *Polity* 15 (Fall): 67–79.
Tierney, John. 2011. "Do You Have Free Will? Yes, It's the Only Choice." *New York Times.* <http://www.nytimes.com/2011/03/22/science/22tier.html?_r=1&scp=1&sq=Do%20you%20have%20free%20will?&st=cse>
Tocqueville, Alexis de. 2008. *The Ancien Régime and the French Revolution.* Trans. Gerald Bevan, ed. Hugh Brogan. London: Penguin.
Tocqueville, Alexis de, ed. Phillips Bradley, Henry Reeve, and Francis Bowen. 1980. *Democracy in America.* New York: Alfred A. Knopf.
Tracy, Destutt de, ed. Jeremy Jennings. 2011. *Treatise on Political Economy by Antoine Louis Claude Destutt de Tracy.* Indianapolis: Liberty Fund.
Trenchard, John. 2003. "Cato's Letters (1721)." In Clark, *Commerce, Culture, and Liberty.*
Trivellato, Francesca. 2012. "Credit, Honor, and the Early Modern French Legend of the Jewish Invention of the Bills of Exchange." *Journal of Modern History* 84 (2): 289–334.
Vile, John R. 2005. *The Constitutional Convention of 1787: A Comprehensive Encyclopedia of America's Founding.* Santa Barbara: ABC-CLIO.
Volpilhac-Auger, Catherine. 2002. "Montesquieu et l'impérialisme grec: Alexandre ou l'art de la conquête." In Carrithers and Coleman, *Montesquieu and the Spirit of Modernity.*
Voltaire, ed. Sheila Mason. 2009. *Commentaire sur L'Esprit des lois.* Oxford: Voltaire Foundation.
Waddicor, Mark H. 1970. *Montesquieu and the Philosophy of Natural Law.* The Hague: Nijhoff.
Weisberg, Robert. 1986. "Commercial Morality and the Merchant Character, and the History of the Voidable Preference." *Stanford Law Review* 39 (1): 3–138.

Windstrup, George. 1980. "Locke on Suicide." *Political Theory* 2: 169–182.
Wright, Johnson Kent. 2006. "A Rhetoric of Aristocratic Reaction? Nobility in *De l'esprit de lois.*" In *The French Nobility at the End of the Old Regime*, ed. Jay Smith, 227–251. University Park, PA: Pennsylvania State University Press.
Zuckert, Michael. 2004. "Natural Rights and Modern Constitutionalism." *Northwestern Journal of International Human Rights* 2 (Spring): 1–25.

A Montesquieu Dictionary

The following entries are from the online *Dictionnaire Montesquieu*, a project directed by Catherine Volpilhac-Auger. The articles written in French have been translated into English by Philip Stewart.

Bart, Jean. "Property, Succession." http://dictionnaire-montesquieu.ens-lyon.fr/en/article/1367163276/en.
Bertrand, Binoche. "Despotism." http://dictionnaire-montesquieu.ens-lyon.fr/en/article/1367168359/en.
Cadilhon, François. "Biography of Montesquieu." http://dictionnaire-montesquieu.ens-lyon.fr/en/article/1376476261/en
Ehrard, Jean. "Charlemagne." http://dictionnaire-montesquieu.ens-lyon.fr/en/article/1377615820/en.
Goldzink, Jean. "Negro." http://dictionnaire-montesquieu.ens-lyon.fr/en/article/1377621295/en/.
Kingston Rebecca. "Toleration." http://dictionnaire-montesquieu.ens-lyon.fr/en/article/1377637092/en.
Kintzler Catherine. "Condorcet." http://dictionnaire-montesquieu.ens-lyon.fr/en/article/1377637319/en.
Minuti, Rolando. "Spicilège." http://dictionnaire-montesquieu.ens-lyon.fr/en/article/1377668580/en.
Spector Céline. "Commerce." http://dictionnaire-montesquieu.ens-lyon.fr/en/article/1378153189/en.
———. "Fénelon." http://dictionnaire-montesquieu.ens-lyon.fr/en/article/1376474508/en.
———. "Plato." http://dictionnaire-montesquieu.ens-lyon.fr/en/article/1376474965/en.
Volpilhac-Auger, Catherine. "Alexander the Great."

Thomas Jefferson

The following references are from the papers of Thomas Jefferson.

"Thomas Jefferson to Destutt de Tracy, 28 November 1813," Founders Online, National Archives (http://founders.archives.gov/documents/Jefferson/03-07-02-0001). Source: *The Papers of Thomas Jefferson*, Retirement Series, vol. 7, *28 November 1813 to 30 September 1814*, ed. J. Jefferson Looney. Princeton: Princeton University Press, 2010, pp. 3–5.

"Thomas Jefferson to Destutt de Tracy, 26 January 1811," Founders Online, National Archives (http://founders.archives.gov/documents/Jefferson/03-03-02-0258). Source: *The Papers of Thomas Jefferson*, Retirement Series, vol. 3, *12 August 1810 to 17 June 1811*, ed. J. Jefferson Looney. Princeton: Princeton University Press, 2006, pp. 334–339.

"From Thomas Jefferson to Thomas Mann Randolph, Jr., 30 May 1790," Founders Online, National Archives (http://founders.archives.gov/documents/Jefferson/01-16-02-0264 [last update: 2015–03–20]). Source: *The Papers of Thomas Jefferson*, vol. 16, *30 November 1789 to 4 July 1790*, ed. Julian P. Boyd. Princeton: Princeton University Press, 1961, pp. 448–450.

Jefferson, Thomas. 1810. "Translation of Destutt de Tracy's Commentary on Book 2 of Montesquieu's Esprit des Lois" Founders Online, National Archives (http://founders.archives.gov/documents/Jefferson/03-03-02-0001-0004). Source: *The Papers of Thomas Jefferson*, Retirement Series, vol. 3, *12 August 1810 to 17 June 1811*, ed. J. Jefferson Looney. Princeton: Princeton University Press, 2006, pp. 11–15.

INDEX

Adventures of Telemachus (Fénelon), 78
afterlife, and the soul, 104–6
Alexander the Great, 79–80
Althusser, Louis, 63–4
ambition, 40
anti-commercialism
   pernicious effects of, 76
   in Rome, 81–3
Aquinas. *See* Aquinas, Thomas
Aquinas, Thomas, 84, 125
Arabic countries
   inheritance law in, 136
   Roman commerce with, 83
Aristotle, 90, 127–8
Aron, Raymond, 3
arrogance, 39, 57, 70
"Atlantis" (Plato), 117
Augustine of Hippo, 135
avarice (*avaritia*), 85, 93

Bacon, Francis, 89
banks, 59–60
Bartlett, Robert, 94
Bayle, Pierre, 30, 61, 100–2, 109
Bentham, Jeremy, 34
Berlin, Isaiah, 3
Bernard, Samuel, 59
bills of exchange. *See* letters (bills) of exchange
Binoche, Bertrand, 3
Blackstone, William, 120
Blum, Carol, 131
Bodin, Jean, 138
Bolingbroke, Henry St. John, 29, 30

Boulainvilliers, Comte de, 34, 66, 140–2
bourgeoisie, 73–4
bureaucracy, 20, 121

Caesar, 136
Calas, Jean, 111
Capet, Hugh, 144
capitalism
   emergence of, 2–3, 11
   liberal, 148
   modern, 113, 149
Catholic church, 105, 108
   cultural influence of, 87
   and divorce, 131–2
   economic power base of, 98
   on marriage, 133
   property rights of, 122–3
Cato's Letters, 31, 76, 77
celibacy, 97
censorship, 26, 29, 30
Charlemagne, 143, 144
Charles the Bald, 144
children and family, 93, 132
China
   materialism in, 38
   royal inheritance in, 135–6
Christianity
   compatibility with commerce, 102–5
   doctrine of, 93–4
   ideals of, 112
   and modern government, 99
   and patriotism, 101

Christianity—*Continued*
 see also Catholic church; Church of
  England; Protestantism
Church of England, 98
civil law
 evolution of, 142–3
 French, 121, 124, 134, 138, 145
 German, 141
 in Japan, 103
 Montesquieu's views on, 9, 13–14,
  87, 92–4, 98, 103, 114, 121,
  125, 128, 133, 138–40
 pre-Christian, 97
 and primogeniture, 145
 Roman, 138
Clark, Henry C., 55
Cobden, Richard, 35
Colbert, Jean-Baptiste, 19, 60
*Commentaire sur l'esprit des lois de
 Montesquieu* (Tracy), 10
Commentaries on the Laws of England
 (Blackstone), 120
commerce
 attempt at making honorable,
  55, 91
 benefits resulting from, 33–4, 73–6
 causes of, 12, 38–41
 and civilization, 34
 defense of, 33
 destruction and subsequent revival
  of, 84–7
 economy of, 47
 of economy, 39–41, 49, 77–8
 effects of, 35–8
 English formula of, 44–54, 59
 history of, 13, 15, 77, 80–7
 in Holland, 46–50, 60
 as honorable profession, 55
 and human nature, 41–3
 and international relations, 33–4
 and liberty, 76
 of luxury, 39–40
 in Marseilles, 44–50
 as a "mean" profession, 93
 moral objections to, 85, 90
 nature of, 12

 and pacification, 37
 philosophy of, 29–30
 political economy as, 7
 as political phenomenon, 24
 prohibition of nobility from, 59,
  61–71
 promise of, 33–5
 and religion, 23, 37, 93
 spirit of, 44
 in *Spirit of the Laws*, 1–2, 12–15,
  32, 35
 as Trojan Horse, 57
 in Venice, 148
 and virtue, 93
 virtues of, 48
commercialization, 25
communal property, 115–18
communalism, 115–18, 148
communism, 118
compass, 79, 80–1
Compass of Society (Clark), 55
Condorcet, Nicolas de (Marquis de),
 69, 74, 115
*Considérations dur les richesses de
 l'Espagne* (Montesquieu), 90
*Considerations on the Causes of the
 Greatness of the Romans and
 Their Decline* (Montesquieu),
 15, 30, 82
Conti, Antonio, 27
corporate privilege, 56
Coste, Pierre, 30
courtiers. *See* nobility
Courtney, Cecil, 27, 31
Coyer, Abbé, 61
The Craftsman, 30, 31
creative destruction, 78
credit. *See* public credit
criminal justice reform, 111
criminal law, 119–20
customs, hereditary, 143

d'Alembert, Jean le Rond, 4, 70
d'Arc, Chevalier, 62, 63
Das Kapital (Marx), 11
De la politique (Montesquieu), 14

INDEX

debt, public, 15–18, 92
delayed gratification, 40
depopulation, 97–8
Desmaretz, Nicolas, 59
despotism, 3–4, 22, 24, 91, 92, 108, 148
Diderot, Denis, 70
Discourses (Machiavelli), 82
divorce law, 131–3
domestic servitude, 128–31
Domville, 52
doux commerce, 25, 34
Doyle, William, 67
Dubos, Abbé, 140, 142
Dutch trade, 46–8
Dutch whale hunting, 60

economic growth, 25
economic history, 74–7
economic literacy, 75
economic rights, 141
economics
  modern, 5, 6
  Montesquieu's writings on, 3, 8, 12, 13, 18, 25, 27
  relationship with politics, 2, 7, 22, 27, 74, 78, 91
  religion and, 13, 94–5
  of toleration, 105–6
  see also political economy
economy of commerce, in Holland, 47
Edict of Nantes, 8
efficiency, 56
Engels, Friedrich, 7
England
  commerce in, 44–54, 59
  liberty in, 47, 51, 52, 59
  Montesquieu's travels to, 29–32
  sanctions on commerce in, 90
  as superior model, 26, 30
Enlightenment thought, 100, 110–11, 113, 148
equality and inequality
  in ancient Greece, 115–16
  economic, 41

  in England, 51–2
  female, 130
  legal, 27–8
  in monarchies, 134
  natural, 126, 129–30
  in republics, 56, 115–17
Essai politique sur le commerce (Melon), 9, 24, 28
Essay concerning Human Understanding (Locke), 30
Eugene of Savoy (prince), 27
exchange rates, 92

Fable of the Bees (Mandeville), 8
family law, 124, 128–31, 136–7
family life
  and children, 93, 132
  love and sex, 93
  marriage, 132
  see also divorce
Federalist Papers (Madison/Hamilton), 9–10
Fénelon, François, 66
Feudal Age, 2
feudal law, 1, 8, 138–9, 141
feudalism
  abhorrence of commerce in, 98
  depopulation and, 98
  and property, 119, 123–4, 138–42
  restoration of, 62, 64
  and the sale of hereditary posts, 69
  and the system of heredity, 135, 138–42, 145
First Treatise (Locke), 30
Ford, Franklin, 67
France
  civil law in, 121, 124, 134, 138, 145
  public debt in, 15–18
free ports, 59–60
free trade, 12, 35, 55–8, 86
free will, 42
freemen, 141

General Theory of Employment, Interest and Money (Keynes), 11
Germany, inheritance law in, 136–41

global trade, 77
Gournay, Vincent, 56
government
  popular, 40
  role of, 8
  see also feudalism; monarchy/ies; republicanism
Great Famine, 8
Groenewegen, Peter, 6
Grotius, Hugo, 129
Gulliver's Travels (Swift), 117

Hamilton, Alexander, 9–10
Henry VIII (England), 98–9
Hirschman, Albert, 2–3, 5, 34
Histoire du commerce et de la navigation des anciens (Huet), 74–5
history, economic, 74–7
History of Economic Analysis (Schumpeter), 6–7
"History of the Sevarambians: A Utopian Novel" (Montesquieu and Denis Verais), 116–17
Hobbes, 5, 148
  on religious tolerance, 109–10
Holland, 46–8, 60
Homer, 78
honor
  connection to property, 135
  connection to wealth, 12, 69
  desire for, 61
  self-interest, 56
  tradition of, 55
  see also venality
Hont, István, 75
Howse, Robert, 85
Huet, Paul, 74
human nature
  commerce and, 41–3
  and polygamy, 130
humanism, ancient vs. modern, 5–6
Hume, David, 8, 23, 89, 117
Hungary, Montesquieu's travels to, 27

idealism, 77
Idéologues, 10

idleness, 20, 70, 149
idolatry, 15, 100
Iliad (Homer), 78
"In Defense" (Montesquieu), 15
independence, 45, 47, 99, 131, 138
India, Roman commerce with, 83
industry, 68
inequality. See equality and inequality
inheritance law(s), 124, 135, 137
  evolution of, 138–41
  see also primogeniture
innovation, 9, 18, 78
Inquiries into Principles of Political Economy (Steuart), 115
Inquisition, 111–12
interest, on loans, 28, 84, 92
Islam (Mohammedanism), 99, 100, 103

Jansenist theology, 105
jealousy of trade, 58
Jefferson, Thomas, 10–11
Jesuit theology, 105, 118
Jews
  commerce and, 84–5
  and the Inquisition, 111
Jones, Colin, 15
Justinian, 121, 137

Kant, Immanuel, 34, 117
Kelley, Donald, 123
Keohane, Nannerl O., 118
Keynes, John Maynard, 11

La cité de l'homme (Manent), 42
Larrère, Catherine, 5–6, 39, 64
Law, John, 20–6, 28, 59, 91, 92
law(s)
  criminal law, 119–20
  divorce law, 131–3
  family law, 124, 128–31, 136–7
  feudal law, 1, 8, 138–9, 141
  inheritance law(s), 124, 135, 137–41
  natural law, 99, 106, 114, 125, 126, 128, 133, 135
  property laws, 92, 120, 123, 129, 140

relating to the use of money, 91–2
Roman law, 121
Salic laws, 136–7
of succession, 133–7, 139
Voconian laws, 137
see also civil law
Law of the Twelve Tables, 137
Laws (Plato), 108
laziness, 70
lechery (*luxuria*), 85
L'Essai politique sur le Commerce (Melon), 75
letters (bills) of exchange, 13, 78, 80, 84, 85, 89, 90
Lettres philosophiques (Voltaire), 30
liberalism
  classical, 147
  economic, 5, 61
  in Montesquieu's thought, 1, 3, 5
liberalization, economic, 36
liberty
  and commerce, 14, 32, 76
  in England, 31–2, 51, 52, 59
  feudal, 61
  in Holland, 47
  Montesquieu's view of, 4, 6, 151
  political, 64
  and religion, 32, 95
  sexual, 56–7
life, value of, 96
literacy, economic, 75
Locke, John, 3, 5, 30, 42, 49, 123, 125, 129, 148
Louis XIV, 121
Louis the Pious, 144
love and sex, 93
Lycurgus, 115–16, 117, 148

Machiavelli, Niccolò, 31, 81, 82, 90
Machiavellianism, 13, 86, 89
Madison, James, 9
Mandeville, Bernard, 8
Manent, Pierre, 3, 35, 42–3
Manin, Bernard, 3
marriage, 132. *See also* divorce
Marseilles, 43, 44–6, 47, 49, 50

Marx, Karl, 7, 11
materialism, Chinese, 38
Mathiez, Albert, 63
Melon, Jean-François, 9, 24, 28, 74, 75
Mémoire sur les dettes de l'etat (Memoir on state debts; Montesquieu), 17, 18, 24
mercantilism, 8, 24, 60, 148
merchant(s)
  as "hero," 71
  maligned, 73, 93
  upward mobility of, 65–6
merchant class, 85–6
metaphysics
  Christian, 105
  encouraging idleness, 70
Mississippi Company, 21
modernity, 36, 79, 113, 148, 151
modernization, 25, 94
monarchy
  and the connection of wealth and honor, 12
  criticism of, 58–9, 63
  defense of, 1, 14, 56
  economic advantage of, 56
  and economic growth, 25
  and royal succession, 134, 137–8, 144–5
  see also nobility
money
  laws relating to the use of, 91–2
  meaning and nature of, 91–2
  value of, 96
moneylending, moral legitimacy of, 84, 92–3
monopolies, 60
Montesquieu
  on Alexander the Great, 80
  commercial interests of, 25
  conflicting interpretations of, 61–4
  early writings and the context of Regency finance, 15–18
  as economist, 3, 5, 6–7
  education and early career, 15–16
  influences on, 24–5, 30–1

224   INDEX

Montesquieu—*Continued*
  interpreted by political science, 3
  letters from, 29, 52
  on moral and ethical issues, 8
  as political economist, 12
  and the revolutionary movement, 2–3
  skepticism of religion, 94–5, 106
  as sociologist, 7, 55
  views on women, 131–3
  voyage and travels, 27
  see also Montesquieu's political economy; Montesquieu's writings; *The Spirit of the Laws* (Montesquieu)
Montesquieu and the Logic of Liberty (Rahe), 57, 147
Montesquieu's Philosophy of Liberalism: A Commentary on The Spirit of the Laws (Pangle), 4–5, 42, 147
Montesquieu's political economy
  and the commerce of economy, 53
  critical of France, 18, 24
  and the "English formula," 35
  and *eros*, 96–7
  evolution of, 14, 24, 26, 32
  foundations of, 12, 114
  and human nature, 41
  and inheritance laws, 133, 143
  liberal interpretation of, 53
  major themes of, 15
  and mercantilism, 24
  in the *Persian Letters*, 18–24
  and politics, 41
  religion in, 37, 89, 93–4, 99, 103
  rhetorical complexity of, 87
  study of, 1, 2, 6–12, 54, 56–7, 62, 66, 113–14, 148, 150–1
  in various kinds of commerce, 39
moral philosophy, 8
morality
  commercial, 34, 40, 47, 64, 77–9, 83
  politics conflicting with, 14
  pure, 107
  religious, 102, 112

  republican, 68
  see also mores
More, Thomas, 117
mores
  corruption of, 29
  Greek, 116–17
  influence of commerce on, 33–8, 42, 52, 53, 75, 102, 108
  paternalism and, 129
  and religion, 99
  sexual, 57
  see also morality

natural law, 99, 106, 114, 125, 126, 128, 133, 135
natural right, 114, 124, 126–8, 133, 135, 147
navigation, 80–1
new science, 150. *See also* political economy
Nicole, Pierre, 61
nobility
  commercial, 61
  prohibition of, 59, 61–71, 91
  and the sale of offices, 12, 65–7
  see also monarchy
Noblesse commerçante (Coyer), 61
Noblesse militaire (d'Arc), 62
Notes sur l'Angleterre (Montesquieu), 29, 31, 51, 52
Numidia, inheritance law in, 136

Oceana (Harrington), 117
Odyssey (Homer), 78
"On state debt" (Montesquieu), 18, 23
Orientalism, 38
ownership, 7, 70, 115, 120, 136. *See also* property rights; self-ownership

Pangle, Thomas, 3, 4–5, 34, 42, 85, 147, 148
Parallel Lives (Plutarch), 115
Parlement of Paris, 138
paternalism, 128–9

patriotism, Christian, 10
peace, commerce contributing to, 33–4
Penn, William, 118, 148
Pensées (Montesquieu), 23, 69
Persian Letters (Montesquieu)
  on the afterlife, 103–4
  allusion to Holland in, 47, 50–1
  on Christianity and commerce, 102
  on commerce, 12, 148–9
  History of the Troglodytes, 25
  Montesquieu's writing of, 8, 15, 18
  political economy in, 18–21
  on suicide, 125
  on virtue, 12, 28
Philippe duc Orléans, 16–17
philosophy, vs. religion, 102
Phoenician traders, 77–8
physiocrats, 148
Plato, 68, 78, 80, 108, 145, 116, 117
Plutarch, 115, 115
political economy
  ancient, 11, 118
  Dutch, 48, 52
  English, 13, 26, 87
  eros in, 96
  feudal, 98
  French, 18, 69
  of honor, 80
  liberal, 52, 151
  of Lycurgus, 5, 115
  in Marseilles, 52
  and monarchy, 25
  and the *Persian Letters*, 18–21
  religion and, 37, 94, 99, 105, 106
  Roman, 82
  in Spain, 91
  Venetian, 27
  see also Montesquieu's political economy
Politics (Aristotle), 116
politics, and religion, 113
Politics and History: Montesquieu, Rousseau, Marx (Althusser), 63
polygamy, 130–1
population
  decline of, 97–8
  growth of, 97–8
  and the perpetuation of the human species, 93, 96, 132
poverty, 58
primogeniture, 27–8, 133–5
  argument against, 135–45
  see also inheritance law(s)
property
  absolute, 143
  and the Church, 143
  and communalism, 115–18
  as convention, 114–15
  and civil law, 13–14
  and criminal law, 118–24
  and divorce law, 131–3
  and domestic servitude, 128–31
  and family law, 128–31
  and the government, 119
  issues of, 98, 113–14
  and primogeniture, 133–45
  private, 118, 123
  as qualified self-ownership, 124–8
  and self-ownership, 133
property laws, 92, 120, 123, 129, 140
property rights, 95, 118–22, 141, 142, 145. *See also* ownership
Protestantism, 99, 105
Public Banks and Trading Companies, 23
public credit, 8, 12, 16, 21, 24, 59, 60, 91
public debt, 15–18, 92
public good(s), 61
  for the needy, 93, 98
Pufendorf, Samuel von, 129

Quesnay, François, 150

Rahe, Paul, 57, 85, 147
Reflections on Universal Monarchy in Europe (*Réflexions sur la monarchie universelle*, Montesquieu), 30, 90

religion
  and the afterlife, 104–6
  and citizenship, 101–4
  and commerce, 13, 23, 32, 37
  comparisons of, 103
  and economics, 13, 94, 95
  in England, 51, 101
  function of, 106–8, 110
  and the Inquisition, 111–12
  and the interests of the soul, 93–5
  and liberty, 32, 95
  and philosophy, 94–5, 102–3
  and political economy, 37, 94, 99, 105, 106
  and politics, 113
  vs. "real needs," 95–8
  social utility of, 99–100
  as sociology, 99, 106
religious reform, 97–9, 107
religious tolerance, 105–6, 108–11
remonstrance, limits of, 110
Republic (Plato), 116, 117
republicanism, 3, 5, 11, 32, 99
rights
  civil, 133
  of the clergy, 144
  of dominion, 142
  economic, 141
  of national defense, 101
  natural, 126, 147
  of the nobility, 67, 142
  of persons, 142
  political, 141
  property, 95, 118–22, 141, 142, 145
  religious, 133
  social, 122
  of women, 95
Robertson, William, 79, 80
Robespierre, Maximilien, 115
Roman law, 121
Rome
  anti-commercialism in, 81–3
  decline of, 83
  greatness of, 52
  inheritance laws in, 137–40
  military prowess of, 82
  Montesquieu's travels to, 28
  significance of, 81–2
  suppression of commerce in, 82
  trading habits of, 83
Rosow, Stephen J., 85
Rousseau, Jean-Jacques, 11, 34, 89, 115
royal inheritance, 134. *See also* inheritance law(s); monarchy

Sainte-Croix, Baron de, 79–80
Saint-Foix, Philippe Auguste de. *See* d'Arc, Chevalier
Saint-Pierre, Abbé de, 34, 115
Saint-Simon, 66, 68
Salic laws, 136–7
Scholastics, 84, 90
"Schoolmen," 84, 90
Schumpeter, Joseph, 6–7, 55, 78
Second Treatise (Locke), 30, 42
secularization, 13, 94, 108
self-ownership, 120, 124–5, 130–3
  and the divorce law, 131–3, 135
servitude
  domestic, 128–31
  political, 128–30
  see also slavery
sex and love, 93
sexual freedom, 56–7
sexuality, 96–7
Shinto mythology, 103
Shklar, Judith, 3, 11
Shovlin, John, 69
Six books of the Commonwealth (Bodin), 138
slavery, 4, 126–8, 133
  of women, 130
  see also servitude
Smith, Adam, 5, 7, 8, 11, 34
Smith, Bonnie, 123–4
social mobility, 12, 40, 67
Sonenscher, Michael, 25–6
soul, and the afterlife, 104–6
Spain
  commerce in, 90–3
  political economy in, 91

INDEX

Sparta, 11, 36, 118
Spector, Céline, 3–4, 6, 36, 116, 117
Spinoza, Bernard (Baruch), 5, 148
The Spirit of the Laws (Montesquieu)
  Book I
    on human nature, 42
  Book II
    on the English system of trade, 59
  Book IV
    on communal property, 117
    on the Dutch trade, 47
    on Lycurgus' political economy, 115
  Book V
    on the ban of nobility in commerce, 59, 64
    on Lycurgus' political economy, 115
    on Marseilles, 49
    on the spirit of commerce, 44
    on venality, 67–8
    on the virtues of commerce, 48
  Book VI
    on criminal law, 120
  Book VII
    on Marseilles, 44–5
  Book VIII
    on the Dutch trade, 47
  Book X
    on Alexander the Great, 80
    on the Dutch trade, 47
  Book XI
    on the English economic system, 30
    on Marseilles, 44–6
    on Venice, 46
  Book XIV
    on laziness and arrogance, 70
    on metaphysics encouraging idleness, 70
    Montesquieu's more cautious tone in, 62
  Book XVI
    on civil vs. religious rights, 133
    on divorce, 131–2
    on domestic servitude, 128–30
    on laws removing the spirit of ownership, 70
    on polygamy, 130–1
  Book XVII
    on political servitude, 128–30
  Book XVIII
    on inheritance laws, 137
    on Salic laws, 136
  Book XIX
    on commerce and pacification, 37
    on the English economic system, 30
    on English liberty, 52
    on the English trade, 47
    on sexual freedom, 57
  Book XX
    analysis of free trade, 35
    on the ban of nobility in commerce, 59, 62–6, 91
    on the causes of commerce, 38–41
    on the commerce of economy, 49
    on commerce and mores, 102
    on commerce and religion, 23
    on commerce as Trojan Horse, 57
    defense of commerce, 33
    as defense of monarchy, 56
    on the Dutch trade, 48
    and the effects of commerce, 35–8
    on the English trade, 52–4
    on the jealousy of trade, 58
    on Marseilles, 47, 49
    on nobility and the sale of honor, 12
    political overtones in, 56
    on sexual freedom, 57
    similarities to Book XXI, 63
    on the tradition of honor, 55
    on trade, 55

The Spirit of the Laws—Continued
   on vanity, 57
   on venality, 67–8
   Book XXI
      on Alexander the Great, 80
      on commerce as an honorable profession, 55
      on commerce in medieval Europe, 77, 84–7
      on commerce in the ancient world, 77, 80–3
      history of commerce, 13
      on Machiavellianism, 89
      on the merits of commerce, 73–6
      similarities to Book XX, 63
      on Spain, 90–1
   Book XXII
      on credit and exchange rates, 92
      on John Law's financial system, 92
      on laws relating to the use of money, 91–2
      on Machiavellianism, 89
      on the nature of money, 92
      on the prejudice against lending at interest, 92–3
      on property laws, 92
      on public credit, 91
      on the relationship between exchange and despotism, 92
      on the value of life, 96
      on the value of money, 96
   Book XXIII
      on children and family, 93, 132
      on feudal political economy, 98
      on the mutual sharing of burdens, 93
      on the perpetuation of the human species, 93, 96, 132
      on provision of public goods for the needy, 93, 98
      on religion and liberty, 95
      on the religious objections to trade, 93
      on religious reform, 97–9
      on sex and love, 93
      on sexuality, 96–7
      on the value and dignity of work, 93
   Book XXIV
      on the afterlife, 104
      on Christian doctrine, 93–4
      on Christian patriotism, 101
      on religion and economy, 95
      on religion, 100–6
      on religion and politics, 113
   Book XXV
      on Christian ideals, 112
      on Machiavellianism, 89
      on religion, 106–8, 110
      on religious tolerance, 109
      on slavery, 126–8
   Book XXVI
      on marriage, 132
      on order of succession, 145
      on private property, 123
      on property, 114, 135
   Book XXVII
      inheritance laws, 133, 137
      on property and private succession, 135
   Book XXVIII
      on the Dutch, 47
   Book XXX
      on economic vs. political rights, 141
      on primogeniture, 133
      on property rights, 142
   Book XXXI
      on feudal government, 135
      on hereditary customs, 143
      on the monarchy, 144–5
      on primogeniture, 145
      on property and the Church, 143
state banks, 17
Steuart, James, 115
Stoicism, 102–3
succession
   laws of, 133–7, 139
   order of, 138, 145

suicide, 124–5
superstition, 37
Swift, Jonathan, 117

Tacitus, 136, 141
Taoism, 103
taxation, 8, 17–18, 19, 27, 28, 30, 125, 140
temples, building of, 107–8
Tocqueville, Alexis de, 64, 73
toleration, religious, 108–10
Tracy, Destutt de, 10
trade. *See* commerce
"Trade and Naval Power the Offspring of Civil Liberty Only, and Cannot Subsist without It" (Trenchard), 76
trading companies, 59, 60
Traité des devoirs (Montesquieu), 129
A Treatise on Political Economy (de Tracy), 10
Treize livres des Parlements de France (de La Roche-Flavin), 138
Trenchard, John, 76
trust, 40–1
  public, 58
Turkey, criminal law in, 119
Tyre, 46

usury. *See* moneylending
Utopia (More), 117
utopian societies, 116–17
utopianism, 115–18

vanity, 8, 19, 40, 57, 112
vassalage, 141

Vauban, Sébastien Le Prestre de, 8
venality, 12, 66–70
Venice
  ban on mercantile nobility in, 64
  commerce in, 46, 148
  political economy in, 27
Vienna, Montesquieu's travels to, 27
virtue
  civic, 5
  and commerce, 5–6, 12, 28, 38, 74, 77, 93
  in monarchies, 56, 67
  of Phoenician traders, 77–8, 81
  in republics, 37, 43, 68, 101, 115–16
  of Romans, 82
  and wealth, 6, 25–6, 66, 68
Visigoths, 84
Voconian laws, 137
Voltaire, 4, 7, 9, 24, 26, 30, 69, 80, 89, 111

Waddicor, Mark H., 125
Walpole, Horace, 29
war finance, 8, 9, 15
wealth
  connection to honor, 12
  movable, 85–6
  vs. virtue, 6, 25–6, 66, 68
women
  and inheritance law, 135
  Montesquieu's views of, 131–3
  rights of, 95
  and slavery, 130
work, value and dignity of, 93

Zeno, 102